MIXERMAN

STUDIO FIELD MANUAL

MUSICIAN'S SURVIVAL GUIDE to a KILLER RECORD

MIXERMAN
PUBLISHES

Published in 2018 by Mixerman Publishes
Asheville, NC
mixerman@mixermanpublishes.com

Cover by James Croisdale

Library of Congress Cataloging-in-Publication Data is available upon request.

ISBN-13: 978-0692194393
ISBN-10: 0692194398

ATTENTION: This is an Amazon Print On Demand product. In the unusual event that this copy does not print properly, or if you find the binding is falling apart, or if there are any other issues, please contact Amazon for a replacement. Tell them that your book did not print properly. If that doesn't work (it will), email me: mixerman@mixermanpublishes.com

Acknowledgements

Special Thanks to:

Tanya Rodriguez

John Dooher

Faith & Eugene Sarafin

Tony DeStefano

William Wittman

Robert Campion

Roland Cozzolino

Jamie Schultz

Stupid Games

Amanda Vallejo

Adam Strange

Bob Brown

John Kay

Michael Selverne

Ken Bogdanowicz

Randy Fuchs & Tanya Hamilton

Roman Perschon

Steven Slate

Max Sarafin

The Contents

i

The
Intro

This Survival Guide is not intended to make you a better recordist. It's designed to get you thinking about your Art and the creation of it from a musical place—regardless of genre—and to turn technical decisions into practical ones.

Given the title, it should be no surprise that I wrote this guide specifically for musicians. Every explanation and recommendation that I make is based on the realities of the recording musician today. Some of you are relatively new to the process. Others of you have recorded for years, but may be frustrated with the incremental improvements in your records.

This is not the book to learn how to plug in an interface or how to choose a DAW. This is a Survival Guide, it's not a From-The-Ground-Up Guide. If you don't know what converters are, or what a mic preamp is, or a compressor, or the difference between a real mic and a USB mic, then this book will be a little advanced for you. If, on the other hand, you want to know how to make all of those tools work for you rather than against you—that I can help you with.

Very few of us operate purely as a musician these days. You're probably also an Artist, a producer, a recordist and a mixer. Those creative positions were formerly held by a team of people who were ideally experts at their respective jobs. These days, it's more likely that one person is doing them all.

You.

Which is a little problematic, because there's an inherent tension that occurs between the recordist, who is tasked with an accurate capture, and the producer, who is more concerned with performance. This sometimes results in making a take before the recordist is ready (which really annoys the recordist I have to say).

Personally, I'd rather have a less than ideal capture of my Artist when she's itching to perform, than to have her shut down because my recordist spent too much time dicking around with tone. If there's a usable signal coming through the monitors, and an inspired singer standing in front of the mic, I'm hitting record, regardless of protests from my recordist. I'm not going to allow technical bullshit to prevent me from capturing the performance of a lifetime. Even if there's a sonic technical issue, if it's a great performance, we're good. Sound Schmound.

Unfortunately, if you're both the performer and the recordist and there's no producer to crack the whip, it can be difficult to extract yourself from the engineering mindset, mostly because you want your record to sound good, and if you don't focus on the sound, you could very well ruin your record. In reality it's an uninspired performance that will ruin your record, and the best way I know to achieve an uninspired performance is to focus on sound.

So does that mean you should just haphazardly throw up a mic, plug it into the nearest preamp and hope for the best? Of course not. But there are strategies that you can implement. In the case of a vocal, you could do some advance work, so that the mic and the preamp are ready to go the moment you're inspired.

It's critical that you learn good habits in your quest to make a Killer Record. Oh, and not just one Killer Record, but many. As such, the intent of this book is to provide you with a blueprint—a method, as it were—to bring you along the path of success. Which all starts with the acceptance that if you want a prosperous and successful record career, the music is where you should focus your attention.

This requires discipline. Not in doing the work. Most of you love recording and if you could do it all day and night you would. No, I'm talking about the discipline to make musical decisions rather than sonic ones. That will take some practice. Hey, you're a musician. You should be used to practice by now.

You don't need to know anything about how anything works from a technical perspective where it comes to making a Killer Record. Seriously, for many years I couldn't tell you how any of this shit works beyond the basics myself. I literally learned how to record by rote, and picked up everything else along the way. Here we are five gold records, one platinum, and a multi-platinum record later, so clearly, all that you need to know is how things work from a practical perspective. And if you'd like to dive deeper into the technical aspects of recording, then by all means jump on the Internet and do some research.

It's not like it's difficult to find obviously reputable sources who can accurately explain how recording tools work. I just typed "how does ratio work on a compressor," into my search engine, and on the first page there are several legitimate articles, and a few questionable ones. All of the well-known sources offer an accurate technical explanation of how ratio works. None of them really offers a practical explanation of how to choose your ratio.

Despite the ubiquitous nature of information on how to get started recording, somehow that doesn't stop people from going on to a professional recording forum and asking what an interface does (bless their hearts). Fortunately, there are many people with far more patience than I who will gladly dispense that sort of information to you. They're called Gear Pimps. Seriously, why would you ask strangers on the Internet advice on gear when a Gear Pimp will go out of her way to give you the best consultation she can based on your needs and workflow? Because she wants to sell you something? Good! She wants to sell you lots of somethings, and it makes no sense for her to sell you the wrong thing. If you're asking about the best converter under $1000, then you clearly want to buy something. Go talk to the person who wants to sell you something.

Sheesh.

The mantra of this book is you have what you have and what you have is going to change. In fact, I did not mention any audio gear brands or models in the body of this book, nor did I need to. In other words, if all you have is a DAW, an interface, and a mic, that's probably enough to get you started. But you have to face some reality here. You will be severely limited in what you can do.

There's nothing wrong with limitations. We deal with them on a daily basis. Music has limitations. Our creativity manifests in how we operate within those limitations. And when you get really good, you learn how to expand your limitations into assets.

I peruse the various recording forums on the Internet a fair bit, and the mythology that is passed around in regards to recording and mixing is rather remarkable. Oftentimes, those who would be educators don't know much of anything themselves and have never been involved in a record of note. Believe me, a record of note is not a prerequisite for explaining basic signal flow. It is, however, an absolute requirement when it comes to understanding how to make a record of note.

Further problematic, where Internet recording questions are concerned, the situation at hand is rarely considered. For the last 20 years, I've advised young mixers to put a compressor on their main stereo outputs (often called the 2-bus). I'm downright adamant about it. But if you ask me if a musician making her own record should put a compressor on the 2-bus? Probably not. It took me several days of internal debate to finally come to that conclusion.

That's why I decided I had to write this book. It was clear that musicians are getting answers that don't take into account their reality. Of course, some people don't seem able to properly set up a question either. And social media all but trains us to post open-ended statements posing as inquiries designed to provoke a reaction. That's rarely a good way to get information.

Hey fellow recording enthusiasts! Longtime lurker, first time poster. Should I mix with headphones?

Absolutely not.

300 posts later we find out the original poster is a hobbyist who gets complaints from neighbors when she uses her monitors, and is in danger of being evicted, which will be a real problem since her credit rating is down around 500 and no one else will rent to her.

Should I mix with headphones?

Um. Yes?

Of course, who is answering the question might influence the response.

Should I mix with headphones?

Absolutely not! Says the major label mix engineer.

Absolutely! Says the home recordist whose wife is fast asleep in the bed behind her.

As you might imagine, I spend quite a bit of time thinking about recording, mixing, and producing. Things have changed dramatically in the past few years. There is no doubt in my mind there are more musicians producing their own records than ever before in history. DAWs are powerful tools that generally don't cost very much, and often come stocked with massive libraries and impressive manipulation tools. As such, there is a definitive need for practical information based on the current realities.

When it comes to record-making, there are no rules, and we're going to use that fact to our advantage. But as I pointed out, there are indeed limitations, and you need to understand and accept those limitations in order to operate within them. If you go into your record with a vision that can't be achieved given the circumstances, then you're going to be disappointed with the results.

In order to set you up for success, the first thing that we must address is your thinking. So long as your expectations align with reality, you'll have a good shot at making a record you'll adore. That is to say, a Killer Record.

Mindset

You've probably noticed the cover of this book is modeled off a US Army Field Manual. Much like a Field Manual, this document is meant to provide you an enormous amount of practical and useful information in a relatively compact package. Unlike a Field Manual, it's intended to be somewhat entertaining. At the very least engaging.

I can assure you, dryly explaining signal flow and gain staging is neither entertaining nor engaging, and you're not going to get a whole lot of that kind of nonsense from me. Sure, I'll address both of those wholly technical considerations, but let us not forget that the goal here is to make a Killer Record. Not a technically perfect recording, whatever the hell that is.

Now, I recognize that it's quite possible you don't want to make a Killer Record at all and don't understand why anyone would. Perhaps what you want is a Phat record. Worry not. I can help you with that too! Or maybe you want your record to be wicked. Or awesome. Dope, stellar, righteous, super, super-duper, bomb, epic, kick-ass, unmotherfuckingdeniable. It doesn't really matter what word you choose, these terms all describe the same thing. A record that moves you.

Clearly, some of those descriptors will resonate with you more than others. After all, we identify with certain expressions based on our culture, our location, even our friendships. When you think about it, it's no different with music. Some music resonates with us. Some doesn't. And although the manner in which we describe our favorite records can vary greatly, we do have one thing in common. We're musicians. And as such, we record music.

Let me repeat that. We record *music*.

Yet for some inexplicable reason, most musicians I know, and I assume most that I don't, seek to improve their engineering skills. If you spend any time at all on audio forums, the trend is obvious. Musicians everywhere mistakenly believe they should think like recordists. Perhaps because that's how you improve your recordings.

It's not really. In fact, the headspace of a recordist is literally the last place you want to be in when you're recording music. Strange, I know.

As someone who has operated as a professional recordist at the highest level (the $1000 per day kind), when you're recording someone amazing, when you're recording someone who understands how to project confidence and perform with artistry, you literally need only to set a mic in front of that amazingness and make sure that you're in record when it matters. Yet, when you're capturing something particularly atrocious, you'll have to muster every bit of your experience and creativity in order to deliver what we can ostensibly refer to as a halfway decent recording.

Right. So, as a recordist or an engineer, if you merely avoid fucking a record up you're a genius. But if you bring it miles ahead of where it was, you'll be judged as wholly mediocre.

Which begs the obvious question: Why would anyone want to be a recordist? Because going from the thankless job of musician to an even more thankless job, with no chance of fame or the corresponding perks is somehow forward movement? Nearly every recordist I know is either a frustrated musician or a roadie who wanted more out of life. This is what you want to strive for as a musician? To be a recordist?

Look, I'm not saying there's no merit to being a recordist, or even an engineer for that matter. But the main purpose of the gig, done properly, is to keep technology out of the way of the performers. The recordist concentrates on all the technical bullshit, so that the rest of us can concentrate on the music. Yet, like every other job in this industry, it has been elevated in importance beyond reason, despite the complete erosion of the position. These days, you're far more likely to record yourself than to hire a recordist to do the job.

Anyone and everyone who has ever spent any part of their career as a designated recordist can tell you without equivocation, that the quality of a recording is based purely on the artistry before them. If the artistry is great, the recording will be great.

Notice I used the word artistry and not musicianship. Whether someone is a great musician or not is somewhat irrelevant. U2's The Edge was no virtuoso back in the early eighties when they put out *Boy*. But he sure understood how to convert his limitations into strengths. That's what artistry is. Understanding how to use the resources around and within you in order to make a statement that moves people. Art can be technically ugly and artistically beautiful at the same time. In other words, you don't have to be a great musician to make a Killer Record. You just need artistry.

It makes far more sense for a musician to think like an Artist than to think like a recordist. As such, your artistry is your musicianship. And whereas recordists focus on how the music *sounds*, Artists and producers focus on how the music makes them *feel*. After all, that's how Music Fan judges our work, by how it makes her feel. So, if the listener feels the music, why then would we ever concentrate on the sound? Because if the music makes you feel a certain way, then there's a good chance it'll make the listener feel that way too.

The thing we have to keep in mind is music is inexorably attached to sound. Yes, you can have sound without music. But you can't have music without sound. Therefore, if you get the music right, if you arrange the parts such that they work together in balance and push the listener forward through the track, it's going to sound good too.

I operated for many years as both producer and recordist. As such, I began to realize that anytime I was antsy about the sound during a take, it was actually a performance issue. The take didn't sound good because the music wasn't being performed well, and no amount of knob twiddling or fader riding could fix that.

Surely, when you first open up a haphazardly placed mic it can sound horrible. There is a process after all and we're going to go through all of that. But once you've pulled your tones and you're happy with them, barring some weird electrical anomaly or perhaps a bumped mic, what could possibly cause the sound to change other than the performance?

Oh, I know. *The drummer played way harder once he was making a take.*

For anyone with a little seasoning, that's predictable.

Hitting the skins harder will certainly change the timbre of the drum, which will produce less overall tone. The drums will also be louder, which means the mic preamps are hit with more signal, same with the compressors. And yeah, one possible solution to the problem is to notch down the mic pres, which will also address the over-compression. But not only is that the least simple solution, it's a technical evaluation that only serves to ignore the more likely possibilities.

For starters, if the drummer is hitting the drums harder than usual during a take, her performance can stiffen. This will often manifest as sonic degradation, even when you inherently understand it as a performance issue. If the drummer is doing anything outside of her normal practices, the performance very well could suffer. Notching down the mic pres isn't going to fix that.

There's no doubt that you need to understand how to get a mic into a mic preamp into an EQ and a compressor. You also need to understand the basics of how all those operate. And you can use these tools to mangle and to manipulate your tones to some degree. But if the initial rundown of the track sounds better than the early takes, this is a performance issue far more often than not. A bad performance can, and will, cause the sound to fall apart.

Still don't believe me? If I bring super cellist Yo-Yo Ma into a world class studio, and place a good mic in front of him, he will sound amazing. If I immediately bring in Ma-Ma Yo—a first year cellist of questionable talent—and ask her to play the same song, with the same cello, in the same place, it will most assuredly disappoint.

What changed? The player and therefore the performance.

Logically speaking, if a poor performance can cause the sound to crumble, then to address the performance is to address the sound. Admittedly, when you're in the act of setting up a cheaply built microphone that's distorting both at the capsule and the preamp, it becomes a little difficult to keep the focus on the music. That's what mantras are for. Repeat after me:

May all of my recording decisions be musical ones, and all of my technical decisions practical ones.

Say that three times. That should fix it!

Ahem.

Okay, so unfortunately, a mantra alone isn't going to do it. You'll also need to understand some recording things in order to keep the technical process out of your way. At least now, going forward, you no longer need to feel pressure to become a great engineer. Really, you just need to learn how not to fuck things up. The best way to accomplish that? Keep it simple.

Keep It Simple, Stupid

It never ceases to amaze me how many people wish to complicate recording. Take acoustic guitar. For whatever reason, this seems to be the instrument that musicians and would-be recordists are most interested in overcomplicating. Before you know it, there's two microphones on that guitar in the hopes of capturing every nuance of a secondary strumming guitar part—one mic on the bridge to get that lovely honkiness, and another on the 7th fret (or some-odd nonsense) to pick up the brilliance. Which may seem like a solid strategy, until you consider that the player shifts as she plays. That's problematic.

Mics in close proximity to a relatively small instrument, such as an acoustic guitar, don't have enough distance (and thereby time) to produce a proper stereo image. To make matters worse, the guitar sits in your lap and, therefore, isn't stationary. Which means those two mics will interact audibly and negatively any time the player shifts her body or her guitar. Once combined as a mono signal, there will be obvious frequency cancellation and comb filtering. And if those two mics are panned out to the sides for stereo? Not only will the image shift and frequencies cancel, the sound will swirl uncomfortably around your head due to what we call phase coherency issues.

That may all sound like gibberish at the moment, but once you understand what phase coherency issues sound like and how they occur, you will likely seek to avoid them.

You complicate matters significantly when you place multiple mics in close proximity to a relatively small and shifting source. And sometimes that's necessary such as in the case of an acoustic guitar/vocal capture. But overall, we want to simplify matters. Not complicate them. A *faux* stereo acoustic guitar on your production not only complicates matters, it offers no real advantage. So, why on earth do people do it?

One reason is that young recordists can't fathom an asymmetrical image. The horror! Sorry, but to seek symmetry in your sonic image at all times is a ridiculous distraction, one that completely ignores 50 years of precedence in stereo record production. Aggressive hard panning is commonplace in music, as is an asymmetrical image. These are not things to fear.

Rather than to attempt to capture an acoustic guitar employing a two-mic technique that I don't recommend to the most seasoned of recordists, you would be far better off to consider precisely what you want that part to accomplish in your arrangement aside from symmetry.

Is the acoustic guitar part meant to provide the driving rhythm for the track? Is the part meant to fill in the low-mid frequencies? Is the part offering countermelodies? Musical call and response interjections? And what of the player? Do you have the right player for the part? Even if it's you? Would another player make that part pop more appropriately for the production?

You can spend your time recording in fancy ways if you like, but it's your musical decisions that affect your record most significantly. Seemingly sophisticated recording techniques are nothing but a distraction.

It's an acoustic guitar. If you record it with one mic, it will still sound like an acoustic guitar, and no music fan on earth is going to question the decision to record an acoustic guitar mono. All that matters is how that acoustic guitar works within the production. And if it's the featured instrument? I would just point out that a vocal is a featured instrument in most musical productions. How often do you hear a stereo vocal? I'll answer that. Almost never. If you want a stereo image on your featured instrument, either record the room stereo and balance it with your close mic or introduce a stereo reverb to your mono capture. In the case of vocals and guitars, the stereo image is best derived from the space around it, not the instrument itself.

There was a ton of information packed into all of that, and if you're relatively new to recording, some of it may have been difficult to follow. By the time you finish this book, not only will it all make perfect sense to you, you'll know what all of it sounds like too. How? You're going to open your DAW and we're going to try some things so that you can hear what happens for yourself. That's how. At the moment, we have a bit more to discuss.

Intent

I can't tell you how often I'm handed a track to mix in which a grand piano was recorded in stereo despite its role as a secondary part meant to offer texture within the production. That kind of piano part is often best presented as a lo-fi, dark, over-compressed mono piano. The crazy thing is the recordist will admit outright that she was uncomfortable with the idea of recording the part mono because, well, her job is to capture good sound.

Everything in recording is relative, and, as such, it's not good sound if it's the wrong sound. A hard rock kik drum that would make the most ardent metal-head smile will likely sound whack and out of place on a hip-hop production. Where judging sound is concerned, context matters. And yes, we can easily break that stereo piano recording down to mono and mangle the part after the fact with minimal repercussions. But wouldn't it have made more sense to record the part in the manner it was intended rather than adhering to someone else's idea of what a good piano recording is?

I can certainly understand how a professional recordist might be uncomfortable sticking a relatively inexpensive dynamic microphone in the sound hole of a $50,000 grand piano. It only takes one or two clients to berate you for sloughing off the piano capture before you decide it's best to record everything as if it's a featured instrument. That's how you cover your ass as a recordist. That's not how you make a Killer Record.

Fortunately, you're not a recordist at all. You're a musician making a record and you only have to answer to yourself. You aren't judged on your ability to pull an amazing tone, nor should you care about what anyone thinks of your tones. All that really matters is the song and the arrangement and the performances. As someone who has produced, recorded, and mixed hundreds of records over the course of 30 years, I'm here to tell you, recording becomes downright efficient when you build your parts with intent throughout the process.

Still, there will be many of you who can't fathom the idea of recording a mono piano, because, well, you might regret the decision.

What if I decide later that I want a big beautiful piano on the last chorus? Shouldn't I protect against that possibility?

How do you protect against the possibility of a mistake when you perform live?

I mean, when you perform live you don't have the luxury of a safety net. You go out there, some of you nearly every night, some on the weekends, and you perform in front of people. Strangers even! Do you worry about making mistakes? Does concern over mistakes help matters?

To operate with intent requires that you trust yourself. When you approach your record based on preconceived notions of process rather than the purposeful intent of your production, you approach your record based on fear. This is when self-doubt creeps in, and you begin to second-guess your earlier decisions. The worst is when you begin to second-guess your second-guessing.

When you build your arrangement with intent, whether through the preproduction process or the overdub process, then every decision that you make is based on the decisions that came before. By the time you get to the end of the process, you are unlikely to second-guess anything, because everything already works together and you can hear it for yourself. And while the process can be front-loaded with quite a bit of experimentation in which all parts are in play, the moment good things begin to happen—the moment you begin to react—you'll want to build upon that success.

If the concern over a mono piano is that you want the option to change your mind later, that would have nothing to do with the piano, and only to do with your inability to trust yourself.

Record-making is not a wholly linear process, and it's okay if you're not 100 percent sure of your intent when you record a part. I've spent far more time recording fruitless things than my discography would indicate. And it's okay to leave yourself options if you're on the fence about a part. Just keep in mind that any decision you defer for the now, will have to be made later. Some of those decisions will resolve themselves, which is a good reason for putting them off. Unfortunately, the motivational factor for many recording decisions is fear.

F.E.A.R.

Future Events Already Ruined
False Evidence Appearing Real
Fuck Everything And Run

When it comes to Art, there is nothing more debilitating than fear.

Fear is a constant motivation in our lives. Some fear is good as it helps to protect us from dangerous things. Like bears, for instance. It's totally reasonable for me to fear a large Asheville bear staring at me through my open front door as I wake from slumber on my couch. I can tell you, 25 years in Los Angeles didn't really prepare me for *that*.

Unfortunately, where it comes to a record, most fear is unfounded, overblown, and downright destructive. We all have to face fear in life. Fear of failure and fear of success are probably the most prevalent for us artistic types. They can be especially debilitating when they happen concurrently.

Ain't that some shit? Fear of success concurrent with fear of failure? Who could make a record under those circumstances, let alone a Killer Record? 99 percent of all great performances are born from confidence. And this isn't just about music. I'm talking about life too.

When you believe in yourself you operate without fear. When you operate without fear, you're no longer getting in your own way. As a musician you have surely experienced this mindset. That solo that left the whole room gobsmacked? That was just a momentary burst of confidence in which you operated within yourself, without fear. If only we could summon that kind of confidence any time we needed it. We can. It's just that sometimes our own brain will work against us.

When it comes to Art, fear often manifests as self-doubt, which is the most nebulous fear of them all as there's rarely a specific outcome associated with it. To make matters worse, it all seems so rational at the time we go through it. The way I figure it, self-doubt is just an efficient way to beat ourselves up, as it's the social contract of the Artist to be put down, and if others won't step up to offer a lashing, then we must do it ourselves. Regardless of what you think about that theory, everyone goes through periods of self-doubt, even if it's fleeting.

Exhaustion only serves to magnify self-doubt. It's rather disconcerting to realize your record sucks while you're in the middle of making it. But if the record isn't finished, to proclaim it sucks would be a wholly unfair evaluation, as you don't get to greatness without wading through the shit. Not everything you do will come out great. Which is why we don't release everything we make.

A fellow writer friend once told me that, as an author, I must give myself permission to write badly. The reason for the permission? Because writing badly can't be prevented, and I must push through those times to get to the moments where writing is effortless. And besides, there's an editing process which allows me to address my bad writing, which is often far easier than dealing with a blank page.

Any work of Art in an unfinished state can only be judged on its potential, which is only realized upon its completion. Until the work is finished, it can't be considered a work of Art.

When you listen to your unfinished work in total disarray—as your brain is over-saturated and hyper-sensitive and, thereby, wholly susceptible to self-doubt—this is about the time when you drop your forehead to your desk in exasperation, as you wonder why you ever thought to make a record in the first place.

My forehead has hit the desk in front of me more times than I care to admit. This is about the time I take a few days off. All of those problems that seemed insurmountable at the time are either not as bad as I thought, or easily rectified with a fresh perspective. Even if the ultimate decision is to undo or discard hours of fruitless work, that's a normal part of the process when you build a record with intent. What's important is that you don't tear everything down at a time when you're in a fragile state.

I always chuckle when people freak out about their record in the middle of the process. Is the record coming out tomorrow? Because that would be something to worry about. If you don't waste some portion of your time on bad ideas, you're playing it too safe. Bad ideas often lead to unintended greatness.

I have invested hundreds of hours on creative projects that I've chucked after completion. I've written 40,000 word documents that never saw the light of day. I've recorded entire songs that never made the album. Welcome to the world of Art. You try things, they don't work, you move forward. The bottom line is, you're not going to release your record until it's right. So, there's really no reason to freak out over its current state. It's not done.

Early on in my mixing career, shortly after the success of *Bizarre Ride II the Pharcyde*, I would often take home a cassette reference of the day's mixes. Cassettes were fraught with problems, and a slight misalignment of the heads between the record deck and the playback deck could result in a significant loss of high end. As a young mixer, I would bring home a cassette reference, only to plummet myself into self-doubt because the cassette lost much of the brilliance from the studio. Invariably, I would return to the studio the next day, only to realize all of my concerns were unfounded.

I went through this for way longer than I should have, and at some point I realized, cassette references were only good for one thing–losing sleep. They didn't actually tell me much beyond the fact that I was highly susceptible to self-doubt. The best way to deal with that was to trust myself. Which seems odd. You can cure all self-doubt just by trusting yourself? Why, yes you can.

Rather than continue to bring home unreliable references, I stopped bringing them home at all. Even after purchasing a DAT player for home, it was rare for me to listen to mixes there. My time at home was best served away from the project. Not to immerse myself in it further after a full 12-hour day of obsessing. That required trusting myself.

Self-doubt, while destructive, does have its redeeming qualities. For starters, it can be quite useful for putting ego in check. Don't mistake ego for confidence now. Ego and self-doubt are similar tonics in that ego provides us the elixir of confidence with the side effects of self-doubt. Good things rarely come from ego, as it is merely arrogance born out of conceit which either manifests itself through comparison or delusion. *I'm better than you are* is ego due to the comparison. *I will make a Killer Record* is an expression of confidence as it puts the focus on self. *I will make a Killer Record just like I always do* is ego, because the conceit lies in your attempts to convince yourself that you're infallible.

Whereas ego often puts the focus on others, confidence puts the focus on ourselves. Confidence is where we operate best. It's just an insanely difficult headspace to maintain.

When you operate from a place of confidence, you're doing, not thinking. And you're certainly not concerned with what others might think. That's a great place to be. Yes, you're using your brain power to problem solve and that's surely thinking. But you're certainly not all wrapped up in yourself nor the analysis paralysis that goes along with *over*thinking matters.

When you're confident, you don't second-guess yourself. You don't usurp your own power. You trust yourself, and you work assiduously towards a goal. In confidence, when something is right, you know it's right. When something is wrong you know it's wrong, and all you care about is fixing it. Really, what could be more efficient than that?

In sports, this is called being in the zone. It's the point where your brain and your body are so in tune, that everything you've practiced for years becomes momentarily effortless and automatic. Once self-doubt seeps in, it's over. You're out of the zone.

Sadly, no matter how confident we might be in our abilities, and no matter how good we've become at maintaining our confidence, fear does still come into play. An outside trigger can instantly neutralize all of that hard work, and our worst thoughts can return in an instant. As much as I'd like to supply you with a foolproof method to harness fear in general, that will require an entire lifetime to achieve, and not even then. In other words, I'm still working on it myself. So, perhaps we should address some more specific fears, and try to break them down into their absurdities.

Do you fear that people will hate your record?

That's going to happen regardless. There's no such thing as a universally adored record, and if there was, I already hate it. Therefore, there's no such thing as a universally adored record. You're going to fear something that we can guarantee is going to happen anyway? Do you fear the sun rising? Because you won't stop that either. People will hate your record, and more people will hate it than love it, and the same is true of every record ever made.

As I've already pointed out to you, our goal as an Artist is to cause a reaction. Really, it doesn't matter what that reaction is, so long as it's a strong one. The worst reaction is ambivalence, which is technically no reaction at all. It's a non-reaction reaction in which your work generates nothing more than a yawn. As much as it can be unpleasant to be told how bad you suck, at least you moved someone enough to care.

Do you fear writing a bad song?

It doesn't take long before any songwriter realizes they're playing a numbers game. Most of us record our good songs and let our bad songs fade away from our consciousness. Some of you may record everything that you write as a live to 2-track demo, which is great. But your records themselves should be confined to your stand-out songs. These days there's little room for filler material given the strange slow death of the album as an artform.

Oddly, you're more likely to fear producing a bad record than you are to fear writing a bad song, despite your song being of supreme importance and the production nothing more than a delivery medium. Much of that has to do with confidence. You believe in your ability to write a great song. You like your songs, or at least some of them, which is why you wish to document them. Therefore, it's easy to be confident about them. Your recordings, on the other hand, might not come out the way you intend, and that's going to create self-doubt.

Let me ask you this. Was your first song your best song? Or did you have to write a bunch of songs before you really started to get good at it? Why would it be any different for recording your song? Why would you be good at recording the first time out? Why would you be good at recording the tenth time out for that matter?

You didn't pick up your musical instrument for the first time and play it like a champ. You had to learn scales and chords, and to read musical notation. You had to practice for hours upon hours merely to achieve incremental improvement. Even if you learned to play an instrument by ear, there was still lots and lots of practice involved.

The difference is, of course, aside from perhaps your mother, the world didn't have to sit through all of your awful practice sessions. Yet, once you complete your record, the first thing many of you will do is put it up on the Internet. And you're going to put it on the Internet for the same reason you were so excited to record it. Because you think the song is amazing. Which is exactly the reason why you *should* put it on the Internet.

All that matters are your songs. Those are yours forever. The songs have potential value in the future. Your recordings have none and can be redone. If one of your songs becomes popular, it will be recorded tens of thousands of times by others, and the predominance of those records will be awful renditions of your song. People will still love the song. And if you happen to record the first horrendous version of your own song? That's okay too. A lousy recording is nothing to fear. It's the song that must stand the test of time.

Technology

You know, when it comes right down to it, you can record with any technology you like. Hit records have been recorded live off the floor straight to a wire recorder. They've been recorded live to 2-track analog machines (*stereophonic*). They've been recorded on analog 4-track machines, which then allowed for overdubs. They've been recorded on analog 8-track machines. Analog 16-track machines. Analog 24-track machines. 2-track cassette recorders. 4-track cassette recorders. MIDI. Two 24-track machines linked together outputting to a large frame analog recording console with full automation and complete recall. Three 24-track machines linked together. Digital 32-track tape machines. 48-track digital tape. ADATS. DA-88s. Hard Drive Recorders. Garageband. The DAW, followed by even more DAWs, each of which seem to approach the creative process in their own unique manner.

Before I continue, I would just like to say, if you can make a hit record on an ADAT you can make a hit record on anything. If you didn't live through the ADAT craze, consider yourself lucky.

Okay, so yeah, hit records were mostly made with the technology of the time. And a great act live off the floor to a wire recorder is certainly not going to have the kind of impact we can expect from the same act into a DAW. But I kind of laid out that super abbreviated list in basic chronological order. And

20

you'll notice that right smack dab in the middle of 24-track analog machines is 2-track and 4-track cassette recorders. That's because those technologies occurred concurrently. For me as a lad, 4-track cassette was the accessible technology of the time. And while I can't actually say for sure that a hit record was ever made on a 4-track cassette recorder, Bruce Springsteen's *Nebraska* was, which is an LP adored by millions of his fans.

That's the crazy thing that we tend to lose sight of in all of this. There is an enormous disparity in technology available to us, and we don't actually have to use the cutting edge technology of the time to make a Killer Record. The technology has nothing to do with a hit. People will figure out a way to make a hit record using only the resources available to them, whatever those are. It may as well be you.

Now, let me just address this whole "hit record" concept because I know that some of you just can't fathom why I'm making this about hits and not quality. I mean, there have been lots and lots of terrible songs that have been hits, right?

Put simply: Quality is subjective. Hits are quantifiable.

You see, whether a hit record is even feasible is almost irrelevant, because surely your goal is to cause a reaction. You want people to respond to your music, even if it's only 100.

Hits are just songs that got a huge reaction. The quality is irrelevant. When you think about it, the only difference between a hit record and your record is scale. If the masses love a song, it's a quantifiably great song, because it got a reaction that converts into sales, spins, and streams.

There are all sorts of songs that you or I might believe to be great that aren't hits. But what if we disagree? What if you think my favorite unknown song is shit? Then what? Who's right?

Whereas the quality of any given song is debatable, the popularity of a song renders the quality irrelevant. If the goal of a song is to generate a reaction, then it can only rightly be judged by the size of the reaction it causes.

Let me put it this way to you, because I walk the talk on this. If somehow I manage to produce the worst piece of dog shit record known to man, and it becomes a major hit? That track will go prominently on my discography, forever amen, and motherfuckers will *hire* me because of it. There is no blame to be appropriated for one's participation in a hit song. Just credit.

So, let's not pretend that this whole record-making shit is about quality. It's about tapping a vein.

Exceptions

Every concept that I present to you in this Guide can, and will, have an exception, in some cases more than one. Since musical style, equipment availability, and skill levels will vary so greatly among you, it would be impossible for me to consider every possible hypothetical scenario that you might come across.

At the end of the day, we make Art, and as such, any and all decisions, no matter how fucked, can be defended in the name of that Art. I even encourage that defense. But we must also accept that the Art is not the goal but rather the result. The goal is to cause a reaction, and where reactions to music are concerned, they are largely predictable in nature.

If I seek to cause you to dance with my music, I can choose an upbeat tempo, and place the rhythmic parts prominently in my production. If I want you to feel joyous, I can combine a skippy beat with major chords. If I want you to feel solemn, I can bring down the tempo and combine a low drone with minor chords. If I want to produce a feeling of mystery, I can employ diminished 7th chords. If I want to produce the feeling of anxiety, I can avoid harmonic resolution. There is no feeling that you could name that a clever composer couldn't invoke through music and arrangement. In fact, a film composer will study in school the harmonic and rhythmic combinations that produce specific feelings. Many of us learn them by rote over time. But make no mistake, the Art is in how we manipulate emotions through our music in order to cause a reaction to it. So, while we can surely defend any decision that we make as artistic, if that decision works counter to the goal of a reaction, then your protests are nothing more than a rationalization.

Further problematic, as I attempt to break down the technical information to its core for you, I will have to ignore many exceptions. As much as I'm sure to qualify these with phrases such as: in most cases, usually, in general, predominantly, more often than not, sometimes, and on occasion–those can easily be missed, ignored, or forgotten.

For instance, when I say that dynamic mics have a pronounced midrange, that's a reasonable generalization about a classification of mics. Is it true of all dynamic mics? Of course not. I offer the broad generalization for purposes of recording and purchase strategy. At the end of the day, what matters are the particular traits of the microphones you have available to you.

When I suggest that you won't get big beautiful drums from an undersized room, that doesn't mean you can't record radically cool drums in your bedroom. Maybe you can. But if you don't like what you're hearing on the mics, then you need to problem solve, which becomes exceptionally difficult when you don't understand the nature of the problem in the first place. You can change the player, the instrument, the mics, the mic placements, the mic preamps, the converters, the compressors, and the EQs, and none of those will have addressed the root of this particular problem–the room itself.

Any and every suggestion that I make in this Guide is based on situations that I've come across in my 30 years of record-making. These are generally hypothetical in nature and will not align perfectly with your experiences. Therefore, you need to make all of your decisions based on the reality of your specific recording situation. And you need to operate within your own likes and preferences–not mine. It's your Art. I accept this.

Expectations

The whole purpose of this book is to provide you with a method in which you build an arrangement with intent. It doesn't really matter whether you build your record through the overdub process or the pre-production process as a band. Either way you're still arranging your record with intent.

In many ways, it's easier to arrange for a band than an Artist, because the instrumentation is pre-determined by the lineup. The problem is, you need a bit of space and equipment in order to record a full band at once. And while you could all cram into an empty bedroom and capture it with one mic, the point of this book is to make a Killer Record. Not a demo.

These days, I bring bands into the studio predominantly to capture drums. That's not to say I slough off the rest of the parts. I prefer to capture the full band at the time of my tracking session if I can. But make no mistake, in most instances, on most records, I must successfully capture my drums on that initial session. Any other problem I can fix in the overdub process without incurring great expense.

The overdub process is the predominant method for making a record. Even for bands. That doesn't make it the only method. There are some genres that all but require the band to perform together. And as much as I suggest you keep things simple, including your arrangements, that doesn't neces- sarily translate into simple music. A straight-ahead jazz quartet performing Bud Powell compositions is far from simple music; meanwhile the arrange- ment comprises nothing more than a rhythm section.

Straight-ahead jazz and bebop are about performance and improvisa- tion as much as, if not more than, the songs. As such, the collective musicianship of the group is part of the fan experience. To employ overdub trickery would result in a record far outside of expectations for both the quar- tet and fans alike. And whereas straight-ahead jazz requires a group performance, most modern genres don't.

The overdub process is a contrived process in which we are able to build a record one part at a time. While music programmers often start with a blank screen and build a production from nothing, a band of musicians typ- ically composes a song, works out their basic parts for the capture, and then overdub what's missing. The live arrangement of rock bands is often just a stripped down version of the record.

Just because you only have one guitar player in your rock band doesn't mean you're restricted at all times to one guitar part. If you want a double crunch guitar in the chorus for purposes of lift and contrast, then it merely requires an overdub. It makes no difference that you can't perform the double live. Your fans love the song, and will be too swept up in the energy of the show to care.

Classical music also must be performed. And while it's true a classical record producer will edit a final take between many performances, she still captures those performances as a group in a hall. In a live capture the musicians work together at the direction of a conductor to produce one sound. To record four string players at once in an appropriate room is not the same as to record four string players one at a time. The harmonic interaction between the instruments and the players is lost, which means the subtle tuning and timing adjustments that occur on the fly between the players no longer exists.

As musicians, if we play together, we are reacting to one another. If you play first, and then I play, then I am reacting only to you. We aren't reacting to one another. Not only that, but our instruments aren't interacting in space. When we play together we are creating vibrations in a room, which not only affects how we play, but how our instruments react. This is why piano samples leave so much to be desired. The harmonic interaction between the strings is mostly lost.

When a violinist plays a C and the viola player next to her performs an E, their instruments are interacting with each other, and the sum vibrations of those notes is reacting in the space. You can't recreate that interaction in an overdub process. More importantly, you can't recreate the two-way musical interaction between players, and the more players you add, the more obvious the disconnect.

This is not in any way an argument against the overdub process. The large majority of this book is *based* on that process. For most of you, it will be the predominant process, especially on your earliest records. But if you're in a band, or a group, or in an instrumental section in which the circular interaction between performers and their instruments is critical to the quality of your record, then you cannot accomplish that purely through the overdub process. You need to organize the appropriate space and equipment for the capture, and that often means going to a proper studio. You practice as a group. You perform as a group. You go to the studio and you knock out your record as a group. The capture is the record.

As I said, most modern genres can be built wholly through the overdub process. And in all likelihood you are operating in less than ideal circumstances in which you have limited equipment, limited space, limited experience, and limited money available for your record. So long as you operate within your limitations, none of that will prevent you from a Killer Record.

What matters is the music.

The
Music

There are three elements that make up the totality of every Killer Record. The song, the performance, and the arrangement. It all starts with the song.

The Song

Before streaming sites made all of our records freely available on the Internet, an Artist interested in my services would often request a reel. Not wishing to leave things to chance, I'd carefully listen to all of the Artist's music (past and present), and then tailor a collection of my best mixes within reasonable proximity of the Artist's genre. Of course, I'd include the more well-known records too, and it soon became clear that the Artists and producers who listened to my reel responded most positively to the hits.

Here I thought that my best mixes were the ones in which I had the most influence. You know, the tracks that were all but written off. The ones that proved to be hidden gems that surpassed everyone's expectations. Shouldn't saving a record count for something?

As it turns out, people who weren't involved can't tell that I saved a record because they only hear the results. Go figure.

It wasn't too long before I set my favorite mixes aside and filled a reel with my most well-known tracks. I would even go out of my way to completely avoid the Artist's genre. An acoustic singer-songwriter could conceivably get a reel made up mostly of pop, rock, and hip-hop tracks. And wouldn't you know it? The further away I strayed from the Artist's genre, the more likely I was to win the gig.

In fact, Artists often got nervous when they heard tracks that were too close in presentation to their own. You would think it would give them an idea of what they might sound like, but then that was the problem. They didn't want their record to sound like someone else's. That's what made them uncomfortable. Of course, I couldn't make them sound like someone else if I tried.

Putting hits on my reel only makes sense. This is the music business. People in music want to work with successful people. Hits indicate success. They also tend to be great songs, as evidenced by the quantifiable reaction from a large swath of people.

As it turns out, the Artist and the producer weren't really evaluating my mixes. I mean, they were to some degree, but for the most part they listened as fans. They gravitated to songs that were familiar, which likely brought up fond memories of a particular time and place. That just makes the song nothing short of magical. But make no mistake. It's the song that got the reaction. Not the mix.

I'll grant you, if you write an amazing song, you could deliver a production so atrocious, that no one would ever be able to listen to it. You could also record that song again a year from now if it proved itself worthy. And once you finally publish it on the Internet, any Artist can record your song too. Granted, they have to pay you royalties. But the moment you publish a song, you have issued a compulsory license to everyone in the world. And if one of those recordings somehow becomes a hit? Guess who gets paid on that song? You do.

The Artist will be paid on the Mechanical Royalties from your song, which are technically calculations on sales, although that includes a percentage of your streaming revenues. But the writer collects on the Performance

Royalties. And as the writer you will make way more money on a song than any Artist who records it as their own.

There's no way around it. A Killer Record requires a great song. What isn't required is a top-of-the-line recording studio complete with all the bells and whistles, whatever those are. The personnel? Now that's a different matter entirely.

Look, I was pretty good at this whole recording thing just five years in, and really good just a few years after that, out of a total of 30 years thus far. Should you hire me to produce your record and I choose to accept, I'm going to consistently help you deliver a Killer Record, fast and within budget. It's the consistency in conjunction with the speed that makes me valuable as a professional. It costs way more to do something twice.

While it did take me about five years before I recorded *Bizarre Ride II the Pharcyde*—my first record of note—it most certainly wasn't my first Killer Record. I made one of those two years into the learning process. Believe me, I was producing way more crappy records than Killer ones at the time, but when it comes to jump-starting a career, you need only one of them. And while my first Killer Record back in the late eighties didn't jump-start anything, it's still a great song. I may even record it again. But then that's kind of my whole point. The record is a snapshot in time. The song is forever.

I promise you, anyone can write a hit record, and they can write it on their first try too. It's unlikely. But there is nothing about a hit record that you couldn't pick up by listening to and playing hit records. Great songwriting can be completely innate, and usually is. But for most of us, it also requires practice.

I advise you to hone and sharpen your songwriting skills, for it will make the biggest difference in your success. And if you're relatively new to all this, and you don't believe that your songs are good enough yet, then record some covers. Many new Artists start with covers and there's a very good reason for that. They're typically hits.

Recording a hit song is a great exercise. Not only do you learn what goes into a great song, you start to understand just how critical the song is to a production. Best of all, you'll start to see how *you* fit into a great production. The song that you choose will be a song that moves you, so you'll surely perform it well. If you can figure out an interesting way to present the song, one that is unique to you as an Artist, then you'll have made great strides in your own artistic discovery.

Another excellent exercise is to write a song for your favorite Artist. Like say, a Beyoncé song. The goal being to write it in such a way that the average punter would recognize it as a Beyoncé cover. If you do this exercise right, Beyoncé would be the last person to ever perform it. Artists want to move forward. So, if you want to take it a step further, then don't write a caricature of a Beyoncé song. Write the *next* Beyoncé song.

I recognize that many of you aren't necessarily Beyoncé fans. I'm not even a Beyoncé fan. So, you should choose an Artist who you admire for this kind of thing. The point is, the best way to learn how to produce a Killer Record is to imitate those who make Killer Records. As you do, you'll begin to discover who you are as an Artist.

You know, there's an old phrase that I learned early in my production career. Amateurs borrow, professionals steal. The point being that we all take from our predecessors with impunity because Art is incremental, and as such, we build upon the work of those who came before us. It's just that professionals make money doing it. And when you ostensibly make your money by taking things, the logical jump is you make money by stealing things.

Whatever. It's not actually stealing. It's incumbent upon the producer to understand the line between an allusion and intellectual theft. Unfortunately, I'm not sure that any of us knows where the line is anymore. At least not since the Marvin Gaye estate was victorious in an infringement case against Robin Thicke and Pharrell Williams for their 2013 megahit "Blurred Lines." Without getting into all the nuances of the litigation and who sued who first, the Gaye estate ultimately argued that "Blurred Lines" was too close in *feel* to Marvin Gaye's hit "Got to Give it Up."

Copyright protects Sound Recordings (including samples), melody, lyric, and in some cases riffs that are critical to the song. Like the guitar riff from the Rolling Stones' "Satisfaction," for instance. Yet, here was a case in which the melody, the lyric, and the sound recording were completely unique, and a jury awarded damages based on the similarity of feel and chord changes. But you can't protect feel. And you can't protect the chord changes. So, how in the hell does the Gaye estate win an infringement suit based on something that isn't even protected by copyright? Law is based on statute. But where ambiguities lie, the law is also based on precedence.

Let me tell you, many if not most producers that I've worked with over the course of my career would reference other productions almost as a matter of course before a session. The reference was sometimes tonal in nature, but more often than not, we were looking to derive the feel of the reference. Gaye's "Got to Give it Up," has this certain feel that occurs based on the drum and percussion patterns. Thicke and Williams did a great job of imitating that feel. Regardless of how effective they were, it should have never resulted in a successful infringement case against them. There was just one problem. Robin Thicke admitted in an interview to referencing the feel of Marvin Gaye's track.

Robin has been criticized endlessly for not keeping that information close to the vest, but I'm not so sure the attacks are fair. Frankly, he should have been able to discuss it openly, because he took what he was allowed to take. If you could protect chord changes music would be unrecognizable, as songwriters would have to enter into creative calisthenics to somehow make something new. The creation of R&B songs would have ceased sometime in the eighties. Rock and Roll would've been dead before it even began.

And feel? A four-to-the-floor pattern on the kik drum, which is a staple of Electronic Dance Music (EDM), would constitute infringement. The snare drum build-up from quarters to eighths to sixteenths from early EDM would be out of bounds. Kiks on the one and the three, snares on the two and the four, and the hi-hat on eighths? Infringement. Salsa? Infringement. Silence? Infringement. There's just no way around it, you can't rightly protect feel or chord progressions without completely destroying the integrity of copyright.

The lesson here is not to avoid references for fear of getting sued. I recommend the opposite. The lesson is to shut the fuck up about your sources and influences. In fact, I think that you should go out of your way to take from others in terms of feel and harmony and arranging concepts. That's all fair game. It's record samples, lyrics, and melodies for which you must be mindful.

Imitation is the most efficient way to learn how to write and arrange, which is why there are amazing players who can't read a note. Because music is performed and heard, not read. And if you can hear, then you can imitate. And if you can imitate, then you can learn how to write and arrange a great song 100 percent by rote.

It still requires practice.

The Performance

You can gain notoriety for musicianship that is outside the normal range. Beyond that, your skills as a musician are nowhere near as important as your ability to perform with confidence. For starters, your skills as a player are what they are, and there's no point in waiting any longer for them to improve. Recording is going to improve them, because recording is a sonic mirror. You can hear for yourself where you fall short, which forces you to address those deficiencies.

The world is full of examples of performers that are technically atrocious at their instrument, who have figured out how to play in a unique and interesting way. Some have made their bad playing a feature rather than a bug. Bruce Springsteen is by no means a great singer. Yet somehow, he is the perfect performer for his songs. The Edge was no virtuoso in early days, but he had a style—an identifiable thing that was all his own.

That's the trick right there. Write the songs that fit who you are as an Artist. And if you don't know who you are yet, then you need to figure that out. Your early recordings are the best time to do that, and many of you have surely begun the process. But if you've been recording yourself for more than a minute, and you still don't have a brand? That would be mission critical.

Giuseppe Venuti, a 20th century Jazz violinist of note, famously said, "if you're gonna make a mistake, make it loud so everyone else sounds wrong." The last part seems more of a joke, but the first part—if you're going to make a mistake, make it loud—that's where the wisdom lies. A loud mistake is one made with confidence. So long as you perform with confidence, people will either believe your mistake was on purpose and proclaim you a genius, or they will praise you for your reckless abandon. Either way, you win!

Of course, we must remember, in a live setting a mistake is here and gone and usually forgotten. In a recording, a mistake is forever, but you get as long as you like to correct it. This gives you a tremendous amount of latitude, because the punters understand what a take is. As far as Music Fan is concerned, if you leave a clunker in there, it was on purpose. But if you try to hide a part? You just told on yourself. Show business is an act, even in its most earnest and heartfelt form. Treat it like an act at every stage. If the part is good enough to be in the production, it's good enough to be placed loud in it.

Now, there are plenty of parts that could be considered nuance or texture that are by design meant to be balanced lower than other parts in the production. There has to be a winner when it comes to your balances, and I don't see any reason why the winner should be a keyboard pad meant to offer a little harmonic support. But if it's a part that beckons for attention? You need to place it loud or not at all. Which is exactly what will happen if you send it to me as a mixer. Because when I place a part really loud, no one will ever doubt that it was done on purpose. Confidence sells.

If you're confident live, there's no reason why you shouldn't be confident within the confines of your Womb—that is to say, your creative space, which is a warm and inviting place of solitude in which amazing things grow and take shape. As you would expect, there's no pressure in the Womb. It's totally safe. You can take as many takes as you like to develop parts and lay them down. And you don't ever have to release your record until it's right. You have permission to perform badly until you perform well. It's called practice.

Of course, too much time can be detrimental to the process. There have been a number of big name records to come out over the years with a proclaimed never-ending budget, and most of those projects should have long been aborted. Time is money. So, if money is no object, then time is no object too. Unless you have no money. In which case you really don't have time to fuck around.

Some people find it difficult to finish a record. Or worse yet, they record the same record over and over again in the hopes that it will one day meet their expectations. I don't really get this. Why would you practice by recording the same song over and over again? If that song was really going to be the one for you, it would have gotten some reaction the first time. And if you've got fans, then I'm quite certain they would want to hear something new. If finishing a record is an issue for you, then the most important thing for you to do is to finish your record. Then set it aside and record the next one. Because if you don't finish your records and move forward, your progress stagnates.

The way to finish a record is to aggressively build the production until it's complete. I find the best way to achieve this is to do, rather than to think. When you doubt your early decisions you're acting as your own worst enemy. Those doubts are usually just a distraction, and until you've managed to complete more than a few records, all negative thoughts should likely be observed and then ignored. You don't learn how to make a Killer Record by making one record perfect. Your greatest lessons come from finishing records. But if you seek to make your record production perfect, you're never going to be happy with it. Perfection is unattainable and happiness is a state of mind. And besides, the best records in history are anything but perfect.

Then there's the ADD and ADHD crowd, who see every option available to them and want to try them all. For whatever reason, the musician population got more than their fair share of folks burdened with this affliction. If lack-of-focus describes you, then this must be addressed.

I mean, if you can write great songs, and you have a story to tell, then you should want to tie the production emotionally to the song. Surely, you think about the song and how it makes you feel as you're writing it. Clearly what you write will reflect your mood. Your production should reflect that mood too. It's all well and good to create something unique, but if all you see are possibilities, then unique becomes the goal in a world where people flock to familiarity. So, not only are you focused on the wrong goal, but you're also out of step with what people like.

Once again, your goal is to write and perform the song in such a way that it causes a reaction. It's not to create the greatest, most interesting production of all time. And reaction is best achieved through a production that fits the song.

What feelings does your song evoke? What is the best way to present that song such that it accentuates those feelings? Is the goal to cause someone to dance? To cry? To laugh? Triumphiance? Angst? Is the song dark? Is the song humorous? Your music is designed to cause people to feel a certain way and to move a certain way, or at least it should be. The production should accentuate those feelings.

I know that my production is close to finished when I can't stop singing and moving to the record. Basically, I forget to listen because I can't stop enjoying the song. This is how you know you're getting close to your record too. You judge your record by how it makes you feel and react. Because when the record causes you to react, it will cause others to react in a similar manner. The question then becomes how many people?

Discipline

The Arts require discipline. There's no way around that. If you have none, then you either need a partner to keep you on track, or you're going to have to derive some discipline from deep within. Perhaps set restrictions as an exercise, so as to train yourself to work from start to finish of a record. You already know how to throw everything at the wall to see what sticks. That's what monkeys do. Now it's time to approach your record with intent.

That's not to say you can't wing it. Building a record with intent isn't so much about a plan as it is about trusting early decisions. You can and should experiment to your heart's content as you create an arrangement, but when you come upon a part that works—when you find a part that makes you feel the right way—you need to trust yourself and stick with it. Make the record from top to bottom, and finish it. Whether it's great or whether it's shit, finish the record. Then move on to the next record. And the next. And rather than put overt importance on any particular record, just keep making them one after another.

The worst is when someone on the team proclaims the song a single. I go out of my way to avoid calling out any song as a potential single, and ask my Artists to do the same. It puts way too much pressure on the track. Performances crumble because everyone overthinks everything. Marketing decisions come into play before there's even a vocal. Guitar tones are chosen based on target audiences. It's a shit show every time. You can't determine a "single" until the record is complete. Don't think. Do.

I assure you that my suggestion that you build your record from top to bottom with intent is not made out of some misplaced dogma. Just look at the longer game here. If great songs are a numbers game—and they are— then it makes sense to treat it as such.

But it's my Art!

That's okay. If you want to create great Art, that's a numbers game too. Why wouldn't it be? We've already established that I don't really distinguish between a hit and a great song, so why would calling it Art change the equation? All I ever care about is a reaction. Everything else is for suckers.

There's just no way around it. Success in the music business is a numbers game and always has been. Super-producer Max Martin and his songwriting team spit out songs by committee on a daily basis. Those completed tracks are then heavily focus-grouped in order to find songs that get the most reaction. There's no best song. The goal is not to evaluate quality, because personal feeling isn't quantifiable. The goal is sales, streams, and spins, and those are based on reaction and the personal feelings of many. And if you write enough songs, you start to figure out what gets a reaction. I'd be willing to bet even a computer could do that.

Surely, a supercomputer given enough data and time could learn what humans react to musically. We're probably only a decade or two away from a fully computer generated hit song. It might be sooner than that, even. The good news is, a computer won't be able to perform the song, at least not in the foreseeable future. And as important as the song is to your success, ultimately, it's the Artist who creates the connection with the fan. There's no getting around it. The song must be performed. And people will come to see you perform it.

And here we come full circle back to the crux of the matter—confidence. Performance is about confidence. And if you want to come off confident, then you must approach the making of your record with confidence. Which as I've already pointed out, is a completely safe prospect, because you don't have to release the track if it doesn't come out great.

Let me just pause for a moment, for should I ever say aloud "you don't have to release the track if it doesn't come out great," in a room full of young pie-in-the-sky-eyed musicians and would-be produsahs, the sheer volume of blank stares would be deafening.

What do you mean you don't have to release the track? Why would I spend all that time to make the track and not release it?

37

I understand that people want to share their growth, and it's exciting to post up a song and get a reaction. But you would do well to limit your earliest works, or at the very least reserve them, because you won't be able to evaluate your first records without some distance from them. Even just a few months can be the difference between believing you're genius and deciding you're shit.

Any of you who has more than a few recordings under your belt recognizes the nearly schizophrenic relationship we all tend to have with those early songs and productions. This is normal, and if you find that your first recordings can withstand the aging process, then you're either a total natural or you're completely delusional. Either way, you need some reps to figure out which. And more than just reps, you need to make records without pressure. When you put your early work up on the Internet, you put pressure on yourself. This is a mistake. You want to remove all pressure at the early stages. Then by the time the pressure comes, you're ready for it.

Look, I wrote an entire book, one chapter per day, and posted it online at a time when I'd never written a book before. If you're unfamiliar, it's called *The Daily Adventures of Mixerman,* and an initial audience of 200 visitors per day had blossomed to 150,000 per day by the time I was done writing it many weeks later. The story went viral in the music business before viral was really a thing. So, I certainly get why you might want to put up your early work. I also understand pressure, and the building of that pressure to the point that it becomes difficult to perform.

For me the pressure came from success. Which has its own pitfalls. But what happens when you put up your first track and someone tells you it's shit? Can you take that? Because if you can't—and be honest with yourself—then you need to take some time in the early stages to build your confidence. If you're the type of person that has trouble with criticism, particularly harsh criticism, then at least protect yourself until you're able to take it.

When you learned your instrument, you didn't go out and play a recital without practicing for it first. Did you? Ah, well maybe you did. But you shouldn't have! The point is, you practice, then you perform, and the recital amounts to practice performing. It's also a progress report for parents, which allows them to measure their children to others. Talk about pressure. As if any of those parents would ever want their child to be a musician.

Tell me this. What would happen if you reserved every record that you made over the course of your first year and you released none of them on the Internet? Clearly, if you're a working musician or band and you're in the process of building an audience for yourself, that would be death. Don't do that! But if no one has ever heard of you? And you have no audience? Wouldn't it make more sense to put yourself in a position to attract an audience first?

Feedback is an important part of any creative process, and if the whole goal is to cause a reaction to our music, then it would make sense to test for a reaction. But to the whole world? Do we not understand the operative word *focus* as it relates to the term Focus Group? As in a small group that you can interact with, which will give you an idea as to what you can expect when you release it to the world? The world isn't the focus group. Your friends and family are. And if they aren't tough enough on you (and they likely aren't), then find fellow musicians at a similar stage of development nearby and online. Create a Group specifically for sharing with musicians who take their craft seriously.

Just to say, if you go onto one of these all-call Groups for producers and musicians, don't count on your track ever being heard. No one listens to anything on those Groups, which means you'll get no reaction at all. They're a waste bin. You don't even have a chance at a reaction, because no one is even listening.

In order to get some useful feedback, you need to create a small Group of fellow recording musicians who you've gotten to know, and who are actively recording themselves and willing to exchange feedback. Take control of your personal Board of Advisors. This way, you get positive feedback for your confidence, and targeted criticism for your education from people who can expect the same from you in return.

Some of you are going to totally ignore my advice and post every early brain fart you come up with in a public place. Clearly, that's your prerogative. At least take down the carcasses of your early recordings the moment you realize they suck. It makes no sense to leave up something that even you think is shit. Trust me, every band and Artist has many songs that no one heard before their first official release. There's a reason you never heard them. They suck! And no one in their right mind should leave up something that sucks.

I don't know if you've noticed or not, but the world is a mean place. Most of us sensitive types go through self-doubt in the early stages of record-making. Shit. Forever. But as you prove yourself—not to the world but to yourself—you can combat the self-doubt with the empirical evidence of incremental improvement. You'll get better every record that you make. And you will fall in love with each new song and record. But as time passes, those positive feelings will likely fade. A song that was brilliant just a few months ago, could very well prove an embarrassment today. Which is why I suggest you reserve your productions until you have some distance. When you finally make a track that you still adore three months after completing it? You may very well have produced your first Killer Record.

Congratulations.

Arrangement

You will notice that I will often interchange arrangement, production, and mix throughout this Guide. For all intents and purposes, they are one and the same. And although the mix is often considered its own process, it is really just the fully balanced culmination of the production which is the recorded presentation of an arrangement. Since you're in charge of the production, the arrangement, and the mix, the delineation between them becomes so blurred that they may as well describe the same thing.

Your record.

We have much to discuss in terms of arrangement and production, and it all starts with our parts and how they function.

Musical Function

Every part has a musical function within the arrangement. Or at least it should have. Taking up space isn't one of them. Any part that doesn't inherently make the production better is merely taking up space. Every part in your arrangement should have a purpose, one that becomes readily apparent when it's removed. If you mute a part and the production is better, dump the part. If you mute a part and the production loses something, keep the part. If you're not sure, reserve the part.

There are a total of six musical functions within an arrangement, and any given part can serve more than one musical function simultaneously. When I first wrote these, there were just five musical functions, but I've since added one to the list—bass. Not because music has somehow changed, but rather because people's unbridled adoration of low end has. And while I'm only half serious about that, the fact of the matter is, I should have put bass there in the first place. After the vocal, there's nothing more important than the bass line when it comes to a Killer Record.

The six musical functions are as follows: Melody, Harmony, Rhythm, Countermelody, Response, and Bass.

Melody

The melody, and/or the vocal, has the most important function in the arrangement. As such, it's typically placed prominently in the middle of the stereo field. This isn't a rule *per se*. But how often do you hear a vocal that isn't dead in the center of the stereo field? The answer is almost never, and there's a reason for it. When it comes to placing the melody in the stereo field, this is not the best time to get creative. The melody is what defines the song.

There are productions, of course, in which there may not be a melody, starting with hip-hop. In which case, the rap should be viewed as the melody.

Harmony

Harmony is just a fancy term for chord changes. Any musical part that provides harmonic support to the melody is serving this function. Whether that support is provided by polyphonic instruments like guitar or keyboards, or by a group of monophonic instruments like a horn or a string section, if the role of a part is to provide chord changes, it brings harmony to the arrangement.

Rhythm

Not to overstate the obvious, but the rhythm is what makes us move, and it's a critical part of music. Music all started with rhythm, and if you question its popularity, just listen to some EDM for an hour.

Rhythm is not relegated to drums and percussion. Just about any instrument can provide rhythmic information to your arrangement. In fact, most rock bands are composed entirely of a rhythm section—bass, drums, guitar, and piano. And while clearly, guitar and piano will often provide harmonic information, they're still rhythmic instruments. A piano requires a pedal, and a guitar amplification, in order to sustain.

Response

Response refers to "call and response," which is a device found all over Western music. Traditionally from gospel music, the singer offers the call and the Chorus provides the response. The Who's "My Generation" is a great example of this technique. Roger Daltrey sounds the call: "People try to put us down," and we all sing the response with the band: "Talkin' 'bout my generation."

Response can also be instrumental in nature. Guitar licks that occur between vocal phrases act as a response to the vocal itself. In all but the most frenetic of genres, this kind of musical interjection is designed to momentarily grab the listener's focus and pass it right back to the vocal. And while there can be some minor overlap, for the most part, a response rarely steps on the vocal.

There are some genres in which every part plays a response, seemingly at all times, the most obvious being New Orleans jazz. It's a genre that is frenetic and breaks every arranging rule in the book in terms of subservience to the vocal. That kind of music is more about a celebration through music than the song itself.

Countermelody

The countermelody is a separate melody that plays in conjunction with the primary melody. It's subordinate to the melody, and often operates within contrasting rhythmic phrasing and melodic motion. Put in more simplistic terms, when the melody moves, the counter typically holds, and when the melody holds, the counter usually moves.

If the countermelody doesn't weave its way around the vocal, then there is an inherent risk that the countermelody will compete for the listener's focus. The more effective a countermelody is, the louder you'll be able to place it in the production without pulling focus from the melodic instrument.

Even a beat can function as countermelody. The Genesis song "Mama" is a good example of a beat playing a countermelodic role in conjunction with its rhythmic function within the track.

A countermelody isn't a requirement.

Bass

Bass is the musical foundation of modern productions, although admittedly, not everyone has gotten the memo. I've had a love affair with bass (and low end in general) for my entire career, mostly because it was so often underutilized. Fortunately, that's no longer the case.

I can tell you that as a mixer, when bass is merely holding space on the tonic, you've made my job way harder. It usually offers little in terms of internal rhythms. It's not musically redeeming in any way. Really, if the bass part can't be sung in an enjoyable manner, then, as far as I'm concerned, it's nothing but a waste of space.

I will admit, there have been many Killer Records over the course of modern music in which the bass offers nothing musically redeeming, so clearly this is not the breaking point. We are in different times now, and arrangements tend to be simpler, songs tend to be simpler, and aside from earbuds, even compact consumer playback systems reproduce robust low end. That means your bass part carries more importance than ever.

Obviously, if you are working in a genre like Bluegrass, Mariachi, or Polka (which come from the Southern US, Mexico, and Hungary respectively), then your bass is generally going to bounce between the root and the fifth of each chord on each beat. I suppose that anyone intimately familiar with those genres might take umbrage at that characterization. It just seems to me a square bass line is one of the defining features.

Many rock producers sloughed off the bass throughout the eighties, which partially explains why bass is mixed so low on those records. It wasn't considered important. The motion of the guitars, that was important! The bass often just supported that motion. What a waste.

The current trend is to balance the bass far more prominently in a production than in the past, which makes it difficult to get away with an uninventive part. Good! As such, it makes sense to give it some musical attention. Particularly where rhythm is concerned.

Given the choice between a great drummer or a great bass player, I'll take the bass player almost every time. And if that sounds crazy to you, then you've never tried to mix a track with a weak bass player. It's a nightmare. A weak drummer I can deal with, but the bass part holds down the low-end rhythmic foundation, and if that's weak the whole structure crumbles.

All of that said, not every track calls for an interesting bass part, and not every bass player is up to the task. And besides, a great bass part can be as simple as whole notes in the right production, which can leave a ton of room for other instruments. A part can be insanely simple as long as it means something. There's a fine line between merely taking up space and providing rock solid support. You certainly don't want to write a bass line that over-shadows the song or the vocal. There's no way around it, you have to follow the song.

Mixerman's Five Planes of Space

It may seem strange that I talk about space in terms of your arrange-ment, but that's precisely what we're dealing with here. Think about it. We can absolutely consume a production with low-end frequency information. That would be space. Our panning is limited to the width of our monitors. Also space. We balance our parts in the production, and whatever is placed loudest will appear closest and most up front. Space. Reflectivity, which is achieved through the addition of spatial information (reverbs and delays), creates the illusion of distance and depth. Space. And finally, we use the con-trast between sparse sections and dense sections of an arrangement to create a dynamic that reveals itself over time. Space!

Of course, where it comes to space and time we do have limitations. The space in which we have to operate is contained. We work within a defined range of audible frequencies. The width of our production is limited to the width of our sides. Our balances require some measure of proportionality in order to maintain the illusion of depth. And you can only cram so many things into a dense production before you lose all contrast and find yourself unable to decipher all of the information.

Given that we are operating on what amounts to a sonic canvas, we must be mindful of our space and how we use it. And so, I have defined these as my Five Planes of Space, which first appeared in my book *Zen and the Art of Mixing*.

In a stereo image there are five planes of space that we use to create a four-dimensional image (the fourth dimension being time): panning—left to right; frequency—up to down; balance—front to back; reflectivity—far to near; and contrast (dynamics)—sparse to dense.

Panning—Left to Right

The strongest stereo image is derived from two mono sources panned hard left and hard right. In the case of acoustic guitar, the strongest image will come from two unique players on their own instruments performing their own unique parts. This is a stronger image than one produced by one player performing a true double with the same guitar.

Why is that?

Musicians who have reached at least a modicum of proficiency on their instruments tend to play with some consistency, which creates a subtle sonic fingerprint. If I have the same player on the same guitar perform a true double panned hard, there will be enough slight timing differentials to produce a strong stereo image. There will also be subtle timing and tonal similarities. As such, the guitars will not appear quite as wide as they might were we to switch some things up. Changing out the guitar on the double will serve to widen the image.

The weakest stereo image (aside from most keyboard patches) occurs when you employ stereo miking techniques, mostly because you're collecting both side and center information. It's still a stereo image, but the two sides are not wholly independent, as such, they form an image that spreads across the entirety of the field including the middle.

I routinely pan stereo drum overheads hard left and hard right because the stereo image isn't all that wide to begin with. Meanwhile, others on the Internet proudly proclaim that they toe their overheads in, meaning they soft pan them. But all that does is put even more sonic information in the middle, which both reduces the apparent size of the kit, and increases the competition for space in the center of your production.

When you pan two guitar parts such that one sounds only through the left monitor and the other only through the right, you have defined the edges of your width plane. Make no mistake, you will make your life easier if you use the full width of your stereo field. Why? Because when you muck up the middle you eat valuable space.

When you toe in your two guitars to internal pan positions rather than to pan them hard, and when you toe in your drum overheads rather than to pan them hard, you are purposely choosing to reduce the space within which you have to operate. This would be like moving all of your living room furniture off the wall by two feet for purposes of doing your exercises. You've accomplished nothing other than to make it more difficult to move around.

I have news for you. From the perspective of the listener, it makes no difference where you pan anything. None at all. For starters, Music Fan really doesn't care. You will never hear a punter complain about where things are panned within a production. They might muse about it, but it won't cause anyone to shut off your record.

The fact of the matter is, unless the listener is wearing headphones, she is usually located outside of the stereo image. We can't even really consider headphones in terms of imaging, because the closed ear nature of them prevents the two sides from fully interacting. Headphones also don't align with the three dimensional manner in which we hear. When you play music through monitors the music interacts within a space. Not so with headphones.

I'm not suggesting that headphones should be ignored, or that they're bad, or that no one should ever listen in headphones. There's nothing quite like the solitude of great music in headphones. All I'm saying is the imaging in headphones is unnatural. And so, when you listen in headphones and freak out about the unnatural sound of a hard panned guitar—that's because headphones are an unnatural way of listening, not because it's unnatural to hard pan a guitar. There is no compromise available for dealing with how a track is heard on headphones as compared to how it's heard through monitors. If wide imaging in headphones weirds you out, then you shouldn't ever listen to music in them.

All of this might make you wonder, if it doesn't matter to the listener where anything is panned, then why pan anything at all? Because your panning decisions aren't for the listener. They're for you. This is purely about real estate, which, in terms of a record production, amounts to space. And the more space with which you have to operate, the easier it will be to balance your arrangement, and thereby deliver a Killer Record.

Not to overstate the obvious, but if the punter doesn't care about the panning, but hard panning will make your life easier, then it makes no sense whatsoever to avoid the full width of your stereo image. I can assure you, there is more precedent for hard panning in a production than there is for soft panning, and with almost no regard to symmetry.

Asymmetry isn't something to be afraid of. It should be cherished. Seriously, why would we want everything symmetrical all the time? That would be boring and lack contrast. You're a musician and therefore, an Artist. You do yourself no favors operating in fear of contrast, which is arguably one of your more critical tools. Make no mistake about it, asymmetry is the contrast for symmetry. One doesn't exist without the other. You want to summarily reject one of your most effective tools for dynamic and contrast?

If you find yourself uncomfortable with asymmetry–if you can't fathom the idea of having one electric guitar panned hard, or having a tambourine all the way to one side without anything on the other side to counterbalance it–then you are operating out of an irrational fear.

You significantly reduce your contrast when you require symmetry at all times throughout your production. Meanwhile, I will do everything I can to get lift out of a chorus, even one that has its own natural payoff. It's a powerful dynamic to go from the asymmetry of a single guitar on the left, to two guitars panned hard left and hard right.

I literally shake my head in disbelief when I read how people freak out over panning decisions. Every single day, someone posts about duplicating a guitar and panning them hard left and hard right in order to produce symmetry.

That'll produce symmetry alright. The guitar will appear in the middle.

This fact doesn't seem to prevent scores of other would-be record makers from piping in that they duplicate and pan their guitars with great success all the time. Which begs the question: How is it none of them noticed the guitar was in the middle?

Others will interject how they delay one side by about 23 milliseconds (ms), which is enough of a time differential to throw the guitars to the sides, but not enough to prevent some cancellation from occurring when heard from outside of the stereo field. Still others like to invert polarity on one of the sides (without a delay), which will result in total cancellation in certain situations. Then there's the suggestion to simply re-amp the duplicate, which doesn't actually alter the signal enough to produce a strong stereo image. We'll talk about all of this in detail as it relates to phase coherency. The point is, these sorts of strategies are typically employed for two reasons: to produce symmetry, and to make the guitars bigger.

I can help you with this. If you want your guitars big and symmetrical too, all you have to do is record two of them and pan them hard. It's no more complicated than that.

Most baffling about all of this is how these would-be record makers will do anything they can to avoid recording a second guitar part. That's the fun part! And if the guitar part is slightly outside of your abilities, then it's good practice. You'd rather practice ineffective electronic manipulation?

I don't understand how anyone can listen to music for their whole life, and not realize that hard panning and asymmetry are staples in modern music production. And by modern I mean anything produced in that last 50 years. But then, I suppose that just proves my point. As a music fan, you never noticed the panning. It wasn't until you started working on your own records that panning ever became an issue.

In general, I pan hard or don't pan at all in my productions. I will certainly use internal pan positions on occasion, particularly on dense productions. But I've gone through periods of my career where it was downright rare for me to use an internal pan position other than the center.

You will see discussions online about LCR mixing (Left, Center, Right), which isn't a system or a method, but rather a contrived exercise in which you implement the specific limit of three pan positions, regardless of circumstance. This is a reasonable exercise to establish the discipline, but there is nothing in music that you should do regardless of circumstance.

That said, I can tell you from first-hand experience as a third-party mixer, if you frequently choose to pan hard, you will remove a major impediment from your balance decisions. And that extra space will have an enormous impact on your ability to deliver a Killer Record.

Frequency—Up to Down

The illusion of height in a production is created through frequency. If you close your eyes, and you sit within the stereo field of your monitors, you will notice that the frequencies stack neatly from low to high.

The reason for this is simple. The higher the frequency, the more directional in nature. Low-end information tends to crawl along floors. High-end information will arrive to your ears like a laser given its directionality. This is an important concept, because if you can visualize how the frequencies appear, then you can construct your arrangement as if you're erecting a building.

Consider a garden hose for a moment. When set to "jet," the spray from the hose is focused and highly directional in nature. Very little spray goes to the left or the right. When that jet stream hits a hard object, it immediately reflects. When it hits a soft object like a towel, it's absorbed. This is precisely how high-frequency waves react.

When we adjust our hose to a gentler, wider setting, the spray goes everywhere. It's not directional in nature, and it doesn't reflect all that much, as it generally gets everything in the area wet. This is precisely how low-frequency sound waves react, which is why you can put a subwoofer just about anywhere in the room. Whereas the low end goes everywhere, you need to be in the line of fire of the tweeters or horns in order to get their full brilliance.

The power that frequency has over the listener should not be underestimated. How you balance frequency information in an arrangement can have a direct bearing on how the listener feels. Really, the way that your parts fill the frequency spectrum in an arrangement is equally important to their musical function. Frequencies are the building blocks of music, and as such, we'll spend quite a bit of time on the subject. In the meantime, there are more planes of space to discuss.

Contrast—Sparse to Dense / Bright to Dark

Whereas we can listen to a mix and immediately hear frequency, panning, and balance decisions, we discover contrast over the course of the record—that is to say—time.

Contrast is used to create the illusion of dynamics in modern music. Dynamics, by definition, is a variation in force or intensity, especially in musical sound. Unfortunately, dynamics in music have been greatly reduced over the years. Generally speaking, we've completely eradicated tempo fluctuations from modern music, which affects intensity, and many records use very little of the available dynamic range from the loudest to the quietest parts of a mix. That may start to change as the loudness wars come to a close, but too much dynamic is a problem if you ever hope to hear your record well in the car, or while the dishwasher runs, or the vacuum, or any external noise within our environment. This means we need to create the illusion of dynamic range, and we accomplish that with contrast.

51

When I mixed Ben Harper's "Roses for My Friends" (from his third album, *Will to Live*), I originally sculpted an enormous dynamic range for the mix. The chorus was quite exciting given how much louder it was than the verses. Unfortunately, once I got the mix into my car, I found myself tuning out until the chorus kicked in. And if I started the record at a level such that I couldn't ignore the verse, then the chorus tore my head off. What was an exceptionally effective payoff in the sound-isolated confines of the studio, was too dynamic for a proper payoff in the real-world noisy environment of a car. Given this, we brought the verses up in level.

Now while we had to reduce the actual dynamic range of that mix in order for it to work in a real-world environment we still had contrast in our favor. The verse is sparse and sweet, while the chorus is dense and aggressive, so we get the illusion of more dynamic range than actually exists. Not only do dynamics offer contrast, but contrast is also a dynamic in its own right and, therefore, it increases payoff.

Then of course there's symmetrical contrast. We already touched upon this, but a single guitar in the verse panned hard will contrast nicely with double guitars panned hard in the chorus. If we add a Rhodes in its lower register and place it in the verse opposite the guitar, we will now have stereo symmetry in the verse, which will greatly minimize the symmetrical contrast we had earlier. Where we've lost, we've also gained. There is now a contrast in frequency that occurs between the dark Rhodes in the verse and the presumably bright, gritty electric guitars that take over in the chorus. It doesn't matter where the contrast comes from, as long as it exists.

That said, contrast, while a definitive plane of space, is nothing more than a tool. Just as you can mix a song in mono, and thereby reject all that great stereo width, you can choose to use little to no contrast. How blatantly you use contrast depends on the song.

Reflectivity—Far to Near

Reflectivity is the illusion of space. Whereas we accomplish the three-dimensional illusion of width, height, and depth through panning, frequency, and balance, respectively, we accomplish the illusion of reflectivity within all three dimensions plus the fourth—time.

Sound exists within the context of its surroundings. We don't just hear a direct sound source unless the source happens to be right next to our ear; we hear sound within a certain space. A drum struck in a small room sounds completely different from the same drum struck in a hall, which doesn't sound remotely like a drum struck at the precipice of a giant cavern. We perceive the sound based on our proximity to the source, and we perceive the space by how the sound waves travel and reflect over time. The amount of time it takes for a sound to fully dissipate in any given space is called the decay time. A large hall will have a much longer decay time than a small room, but in either case those reflections occur over time.

The decay time of any given room is determined by its overall size and shape, as well as the nature of the materials contained within that space. A large hall will have a considerably longer decay time empty than it will when filled with people. That's because people absorb sound, and the more absorptive materials present, the shorter the decay time.

Reflections will appear to us as reverb in enclosed spaces, and mostly as delay in open spaces, particularly where there are large obstacles nearby. While reverberation is the quick, successive bouncing of sound waves off reflective surfaces, delay is a distinct repeat caused by a sound traveling for a significant distance, hitting an object, and returning to us.

We've all experienced this kind of delay in real life; whether yodeling across a ravine (who among us can resist this?), or calling out to a friend near a large building, we perceive a one-time direct reflection from a distant object as delay, although that reflection often includes some measure of reverberation, as well. And depending on the environment, there could be considerably more than one repeat.

In order to effectively create the illusion of great distance, we must also take into account the frequency response of the source. The further away the sound source is from our position, the less top end we hear. That's because much of it gets sucked up along the way.

If you want a dog to appear as though it's barking way in the distance within a production (don't ask me why a dog is barking in your production, just go with it), you would have to place it low in the mix, roll off the high end on the barking channel, and send that signal to a reverb unit too. Putting the barking dog low in the mix places it to the back of the sound field, but the reverberation in conjunction with the high frequency roll-off provides the illusion of distance. You can derive the illusion of even more distance by introducing a delay too.

Sometimes reflectivity is contained within a recording. Sometimes reflectivity is added into the mix after the fact to create the illusion of space that didn't exist at the time of the recording. Unfortunately, our control over reflectivity in a production only works well in one direction.

Whereas reflectivity can easily be added, it really can't be taken away. Sure, we can use gates and mutes to cut off the decay the moment a part goes tacit, but we can't effectively remove the audible reflectivity from the part itself. Not without significant and obvious degradation. And while I realize there are some plugins that can somewhat reduce reflectivity and enhance the transients of percussive instruments, it's still not a viable option, especially on instruments that sustain. Not yet, anyway.

This is why so many recordists employ close-miking techniques while recording. When you consider the possible ramifications of your final balances, it's often better to err on the side of too little space than too much.

In general, drums and percussion react well to reflective treatment, since short, percussive bursts don't lose much clarity from the acoustic slap of the space. Electric crunch guitars, on the other hand, lose all clarity within an overly reflective room. There may be a time that's the desired effect. Usually not.

It's not uncommon to mix and match acoustic spaces in a production. The drums can sound like they're in a large, reflective room, and the guitars can sound like they're in an anechoic chamber, with no ill effect to the listener. In fact, this is often the preferred treatment as it allows us to create the illusion of a rock band in a large room while maintaining some immediacy from our guitars.

Reverbs tend to soften sound. When you put a long, sweet reverb on a hard rock vocal, you instantly soften both the vocal and the production. Yes, hair-metal bands from the eighties often used reverb, but hair bands didn't generally perform hard rock; they performed pop rock in the guise of hard rock. The whole point of reverb on a hair band was to soften the tone in order to appeal to a wider audience. That's not to say you can't use reverb in hard rock, but you should consider exactly how that reflectivity affects the overall feeling derived from the production. We will discuss all of this in further detail throughout this Guide.

How you deal with the spatial reflectivity on your record can completely make or break a production. Too often reverb is employed out of some misplaced reflex rather than as a tool for manipulating how the listener feels. Think of reflectivity as a way to create a spatial illusion appropriate to the production.

Balance—Front to Back, Large to Small

Balance is a game of relativity and is the holy grail of the five spatial planes. I've left balance for last since it has a direct relationship with the other four planes of space in the arrangement.

Fundamentally, the balance of a part has to do with how loud it is in relation to all the other parts that are playing at any given moment. A loud vocal doesn't exist in a vacuum. We deem it's loud in the relative terms of everything else in the production. In fact, all internal balances are merely an exercise in relativity. As such, balance is our most effective tool for directing the listener's focus. Whatever you place loudest will capture our attention.

Every adjustment that we make in a production is nothing more than a balance adjustment. A pan knob is a balance knob between the left and the right monitors. A frequency boost or cut to a part alters the balance of that frequency within the context of the part. Reflectivity is the balance between direct signal and audible space. Contrast is the balance between density and sparsity in an arrangement.

Relativity in Balance

It's important to think of balance in purely relative terms. If you bring up the drums, you've also essentially brought down all the other parts. If you bring up every part but the vocals, you've pretty much brought down the vocal.

Relativity also exists between sections. Whatever is currently happening in a production serves to set up what happens next. Balance is the fulcrum you use to push the listener forward. If you bring the entire verse up in overall level, the listener only perceives that level change relative to the sections before and after it. If you bring up a simple snare fill before a chorus, you've effectively added an exciting push forward for the listener. But if you bring that snare roll up too much, you can actually weaken the entrance of the chorus by making it seem small in comparison.

You should give as much weight to how a balance decision affects the current section as you do to how it affects the next one, and this is best considered as you build your track. Two electric guitars blaring from top to bottom of a production offers little to enhance contrast. To bring down the relative level of the guitars in the verse would be a reasonable solution to the problem. Unfortunately, the timbre remains the same. Normally, when you play softer, the timbre softens. As such, a pure level ride isn't always sufficient. Muting one of the guitars in the verse would offer considerably more contrast and help to promote a payoff.

Relativity affects everything in a production. If you bring up the low end on the bass, the kik could sound small. If you place a big, broad, full-spectrum acoustic guitar on top of a gritty rock track, you could very well dwarf the drums. If you pack a production with parts in the upper midrange, you'll probably be forced to place the vocal exceptionally forward as all those midrange parts will compete directly with each other.

Each and every balance decision causes an equal and opposite balance reaction, both in real time and in what lies ahead. If you think along these lines as you build your arrangement, you will improve your results significantly.

Proportionality in Balance

As you build your track with intent you can certainly balance it too. You don't need a professional mixer for that. You know the parts, you know why each and every part is there, you understand what they do, and their function—how could someone else balance those parts better than you? Because the mixer understands great sound? A great production isn't about sound.

As a third-party mixer, my goal is the same as yours. To cause the listener to move and to sing. That is to say, to cause a reaction. All of my balance decisions are based on the needs of the song and the production. All of my arrangement decisions are made based on how the track makes me feel. It has to be. In order to manipulate the emotions of the listener, I must first concentrate on manipulating my own.

When it comes right down to it, we could take the most complicated production and break it down to just five parts: drums and percussion; bass; keys and/or guitars; horns and strings; and vocals. That is to say, rhythm, bass, harmony, countermelody, response, and melody. You can replace that instrumentation with anything, it's still going to break down to no more than five or six functional parts. There's a very good reason for this. The human brain can really only decipher that many parts at a time.

You have the absolute power to direct the listener's focus with your balance decisions. Unfortunately, most people overbalance their parts. There always has to be a winner when it comes to your balances. You can't just put everything in perfect proportion. An overly balanced production disregards contrast, neglects to offer the listener a clear focal point and, therefore, reduces forward motion. Given this, a perfectly proportional production does a poor job of manipulating the listener's emotions. An overly balanced mix would be the exact opposite of a great mix, and this is without doubt a common mistake in a production. It's like a disease.

I've actually been thanked on more than one occasion for my "unbalanced mixes." I don't know for certain, but I think that would insult most mixers. I can assure you it's meant as a compliment and taken as such. Frankly, there's nothing more boring than a perfectly balanced mix.

The louder a part is placed within the production, the bigger it will appear. The lower a part is placed, the smaller it will appear. While high-end and midrange frequencies cut through an arrangement, low-end frequencies need volume in order to generate energy, which appears as size. Therefore, a part placed back in a mix has an inherently reduced low-end push, particularly compared with the more forward parts in the mix. Low end and level are what make a part sound big. Reduce both of those relative to everything else in the mix, and that part will sound small.

Frequency

As you all will recall from physical science class, frequency is produced through vibration. Pluck a string and it vibrates. Hit a drum, it vibrates. The faster the vibration, the higher the frequency, the higher the note.

Now, we measure frequency in cycles per second, which we represent as Hertz, named after Heinrich Hertz who proved the existence of electromagnetic waves. We write the expression as Hz, and for multiples of 1000 we use the term kHz, or kilohertz. Sometimes we get lazy and write the letter K to indicate kHz. I'll stick to the proper terminology for the purposes of this Guide.

The human range of hearing extends from 20 Hz to 20 kHz, but if you're an adult, good luck hearing anything over 18 kHz. That doesn't mean there isn't useful information extending well above our range of hearing; we just can't actually hear it directly.

The low E string on a bass guitar sounds at 41 Hz, which means the vibration of that string cycles 41 times every second. The A above middle C on a piano cycles 440 times every second for 440 Hz. And the top note on a violin, which is E7, cycles 2637 times per second, which would be expressed as 2.6 kHz (with rounding). That's right, the top note on a violin is 2.6 kHz. No wonder it's so annoying. That happens to live in the most present range of our hearing, which also happens to be the fundamental frequency of a crying baby.

An octave above any note is twice its frequency. So, an octave above A4 at 440 Hz is A5 at 880 Hz. An octave above that is A6 at 1760 Hz. All the notes and thereby frequencies in between the octaves define the scale by dividing the octave into relatively equal parts. I say relatively, because we need to compromise a little on certain notes in the scale for purposes of tuning, and that's called tempering. We use 12 steps in the modern Western scale.

All instruments have a fundamental frequency range, and anyone who composes for an orchestra is acutely aware of these ranges, particularly in terms of notes. For instance, a cello has a four octave range that extends from C2 to C6. In terms of frequency, that would translate as a range of 65 Hz to 1 kHz. And while the overtones will extend far above 1 kHz, that is the frequency that we will perceive the loudest by far when C6 is bowed.

Some instruments like pianos and keyboards, acoustic guitars, and even drums, fill an enormous swath of the frequency range. As such, they tend to occupy considerable space in a production. You can only get away with so many parts living in the same frequency range before you get masking, which is exactly as it sounds. You're masking certain frequencies of one part with the common frequencies of a louder part. In other words, you can combat some masking issues partly with how you balance the parts.

The further away in frequency range two instruments are, the less masking will be an issue. An egg shaker is never going to mask an 808 kik drum or vice versa because their frequencies don't cross. The 808 kik lives down around 60 Hz, and an egg shaker's fundamental lives at about 6 kHz. That's a seven octave differential.

Where the problems arise is when you combine parts that predominantly occupy the same ranges. The most common example of this would be the kik and the bass. Those two instruments require some attention in order to derive clarity between them. And if you combine a sub-frequency synth bass with that 808 kik drum? Not only will you get masking, you'll likely get beating too.

Beating occurs when two notes are ever so slightly out of tune with each other. If you've ever tuned a guitar then you're familiar with the sound. That's how you know two strings are in tune with each other. The beating stops. The lower the frequency, the slower and more violent the beating. So, if the 808's low-end bloom occurs at a similar frequency to the synth bass, you could very well get some obvious beating artifacts. This is a tuning issue. Not an EQ issue.

As much as it's good to avoid too much masking, you can't avoid it entirely nor would you want to. You risk too much clarity, and that can actually make us feel uncomfortable. Parts will generally cross frequencies in all but the simplest of arrangements. But the more information that you cram into the same frequency range, the more difficulty you'll have with clarity, and the more EQ you'll require to aggressively carve out and shape the parts such that they can all be heard.

Just to be clear, I have no issue with aggressive use of EQ. But if you consider frequency as you arrange your record, you will have less instances in which you need aggressive EQ. Which means there will be fewer times in which you are dealing with sound rather than the music.

Note duration makes a big difference where masking is concerned. The kik drum and a bass cross frequencies, but the kik has a short duration, which provides us the space that we need to derive some clarity between the two parts. This is true even if the bass is playing whole notes. But if that kik sustained for a few seconds like a long 808 kik, combining that with whole notes from the bass could be considerably more challenging.

A great arranger is judicious in her instrumentation, as well as her chord voicings, and will consider frequency as readily as she will the rhythmic, melodic, or harmonic functions. Of course, we don't seek to fill the full frequency range at all times. There would be no contrast if we did.

I mean, if you want a heavy feeling of foreboding, one way to do it is to drop your arrangement down to just your low-end instruments. If you want a lighter feeling, dump the low-end instruments and add some lilting flutes in the upper midrange. We can directly affect how the listener feels by how we employ frequency in our production.

We choose our instrumentation for many reasons, including availability and musical function, but it's critical to also take frequency into account. A tambourine doesn't seem the best candidate for a hard rock track with a wash of aggressive cymbals and shredding guitars. You need more high-end information, why? It would make far more sense to place your rhythmic overdub in a frequency range that has some space available.

Instruments like the B3 organ can take up an enormous amount of space, or just a little. You don't have to have an organ with all stops at full, nor do you have to use both hands. And if your track has a dip in the lower midrange, then you could do well to voice your chords accordingly. This is why it's so important to view frequency as space. Because it is.

You can't get nearly the low end out of a dense track as you can a sparse one. In fact, if you put too much low end on a dense track, it will sound like pure mud. Conversely, it's far more difficult to overshoot the low end on a sparse track. Frankly, you'd be downright foolish not to exploit that.

Harmonic Series

Everything in a recording interacts, and this includes frequencies. When you bow a violin or strike a piano key, we don't just hear the frequency that defines the note, called the fundamental, we also hear a whole series of mathematically related frequencies above that note. We call these frequencies overtones. Were it not for the interaction of the fundamental frequency with these overtones there would be no timbre. A piano would sound just like a violin which would sound just like the sine wave produced by a test tone. The fundamental in combination with the overtones make up the mathematical ratios that define the Harmonic Series.

The first harmonic of any given note is defined as the fundamental. This is the frequency that sounds the loudest by far and which we perceive as the note. The second harmonic, which would be the first overtone, is twice the frequency of the fundamental, which means it sounds an octave above. In other words, if we play a low E which sounds at 41 Hz, the second harmonic sounds faintly at 82 Hz.

To determine the third harmonic, we multiply the fundamental frequency by 3, the fourth by 4, the fifth by 5, and so on forever, well beyond our range of hearing. It's a little easier to understand with a chart.

Harmonic	Frequency	Note	Interval Between Harmonics
1	41 Hz	E1	Fundamental
2	82 Hz	E2	1 octave
3	123 Hz	B2	Perfect 5th
4	164 Hz	E3	Perfect 4th
5	205 Hz	G#3	Major 3rd
6	246 Hz	B3	Minor 3rd
7	287 Hz	Between C# and D	Subminor 3rd
8	328 Hz	E4	Supermajor 2nd

The Harmonic Series

You'll notice that the further up the Harmonic Series we go, the closer the intervals become. By the time we get to the 7th Harmonic, the interval between it and the 6th Harmonic falls between notes, and is defined as a sub-minor 3rd. I suppose that would be a blues note when you think about it.

You'll also notice how the 2nd, 4th and 8th Harmonics are all octaves from the fundamental. That will prove useful when we get into tone shaping with EQ, because you can bring out the notes of a part by boosting the octave harmonics.

Frequency Range of Instruments

Note range converts directly to frequency.

Instrument	Note Range	Frequency Range
Kik		60 Hz - 100 Hz
Snare		150 Hz - 250 Hz
Toms		60 Hz - 250 Hz
Cymbals		3kHz - 5 kHz
Bass	E1 - C4	41 Hz - 262 Hz
Piano	A0 - C8	27 Hz - 4186 Hz
Guitar	E2 - F6	82 Hz - 1397 Hz
Violin	G3-G7	196 Hz - 3136 Hz
Cello	C2 - B5	315 Hz - 1175 Hz
Tenor Sax	G#2 - E5	104 Hz - 659 Hz
Alto Sax	F#3 - D6	185 Hz - 1175 Hz
Trumpet	F#3 - D6	185 Hz - 1175 Hz
Voice	E2 - A5	82 Hz - 880 Hz

Frequency and Note Ranges

I chose just a few of the more common instruments in the chart above. You'll notice that the bottom note on a piano is A0 and the top note is C8. This produces a fundamental frequency range of 55 Hz to 4186 Hz (~4.2 kHz). A four-string bass starts at E1 and extends to C4 which produces a fundamental frequency range of 41 Hz to 262 Hz.

The note ranges of all instruments are readily available on the Internet, and where it comes to frequency, you really don't need a chart, you'll use your ears.

Notice how the highest fundamental frequency produced by a piano is 4 kHz, which is higher than the top note of a violin which sounds at just above 3 kHz. That means the tiger's share of all harmonic information above 4 kHz are overtones. Which is why when you view a balanced mix on a spectrum analyzer, it's not flat across all frequencies. If it were, the harmonics would be louder than the fundamental, which would be unlistenable. Then there's the percussion, which would be oppressively loud in a perfectly flat mix across the frequency spectrum. As much as our audible range lives below 20 kHz, the bulk of where we operate musically is down under 4 kHz.

You'll also notice that the drums have very low fundamental frequencies, but we know that they also tend to have an attack at a much higher frequency, the fundamental of which tends to fall between 1 kHz and 3 kHz. The attack is very short in duration and therefore it takes up minimal space for any single instance of it.

As musicians, we really don't tend to think about frequency in relation to notes, but it should be one of your main considerations where it comes to your production. It's not just level that you have to balance, but frequency too, because a good balance of frequency within your arrangement provides your production with clarity. Conversely, too many frequencies in the same range at the same level will lead to problematic masking, and a total lack of clarity.

Even with a well-balanced recording, you'll likely want to manipulate and shape frequencies within your production. For that, we use an equalizer, or EQ, which is ubiquitous at this point. You use it in your car, you use it on your amplifier, and you most certainly use it in your DAW.

Frequency Tonality

I first wrote this list in 1999, and it was altered for my book *Zen and the Art of Mixing*, and adjusted once again for purposes of this Survival Guide. We can break down frequency into four basic ranges: Low end, Lower midrange, Upper Midrange, and High end (oftentimes called top end).

Low End

20–30 Hz: This is mostly rumble and subs and is generally not boosted, but rather attenuated. Some people choose to filter these frequencies as a matter of course, but I don't recommend it unless there's a specific problem that you wish to filter out such as air conditioner rumble or trucks driving by.

30–60 Hz: These frequencies are quite low and "boomy" in nature, and will not replicate in most small speakers. While this frequency range is particularly useful in making a production sound big, it can easily overpower everything else if too abundant. The energy down here often needs to be contained and shaped through compression.

100 Hz: This frequency is low but punchy and is easily replicated in a six-inch speaker. It's a far more focused low frequency than the subs, although it's still not by any means directional in nature.

Lower Midrange

200–250 Hz: This is the start of the lower midrange. It can be described as "woofy," as it's not a very clean low end. Too much of this range can cause a mix to sound thick, dark, and muddy. Too little and your mix will sound scooped out and lacking in power. This frequency replicates well in a two- to four-inch speaker, and can be quite useful for making the bass audible in small stereo systems, on phones, and laptop computers.

65

500 Hz: This frequency is the middle of the lower midrange. It is often accused of sounding "boxy," and for good reason—it sounds boxy! You are far more likely to cut this frequency from a signal than to add it. However, there are times that it's a useful frequency to boost for purposes of tone-shaping, as it has some presence attributes to it. It can be used as a thickening agent for tambourines. Or as a presence agent for a vocal. And even as a presence agent for kik drums that sound scooped. Sometimes you need a little boxiness in your life.

750 Hz: This is getting toward the upper end of the lower midrange. This frequency is also boxy in tone and tends to reduce clarity in a mix; however, it can also add presence to a part in the right situation. I use this frequency in a similar manner to 500 Hz, although it's considerably more present in nature. When you cut presence, you begin to reduce clarity. Of course, you can also reduce clarity by boosting this frequency too aggressively. I'm far more likely to cut boxy frequencies than I am to boost them.

Upper Midrange

1 kHz: This is the beginning of the upper midrange. It's an exceptionally "present" frequency as it approaches the peak of our hearing. This can be a very handy frequency for pulling clarity, but can also sound boxy if used too liberally.

2 kHz: This happens to be the basic frequency of a crying baby, which might explain why it's our most easily heard frequency as humans. Too much of this frequency and "harsh" will be an adjective you'll hear when someone describes your mix. I often refer to 2 kHz as "strident," but that certainly doesn't make it useless. When a part doesn't seem to pop out of your arrangement, you can use 2 kHz to help with that. Both electric and acoustic guitars love this frequency as it lives in the heart of their string rake. It's also a really good frequency to cut when a vocal is too strident.

3–4 kHz: This frequency range, much like 2 kHz, is helpful in adding or removing bite from a recording.

6–9 kHz: This is the tail end of the upper midrange. This is where we exit the "bite" range and enter into dentist drill territory. This range of frequencies can give you a nasty headache, and quick.

High End

10–12 kHz: This is the lower end of the high-end frequencies (say that three times fast). The addition of this frequency range can be helpful in opening up a sound and/or offsetting the coloration of a microphone or processing.

12-16 kHz: This is extreme high end, and this range of frequencies will often bring out unintended distortion artifacts as quickly as it will open up a sound, but it can still be quite useful, depending on the overall quality of the EQ. If you were to boost this frequency across your whole production, you would bring up mostly percussion parts. You'll also bring out the overtones.

18–20 kHz: This range is beyond most of our hearing, and while there is definitely information up there, bringing it up with EQ only adds audible spitting and noise. Even if you can hear frequencies this high, you don't want to aggressively boost this information.

We'll discuss frequency and EQ further in the next chapter.

Tempo

Rhythm and tempo affect how the listener feels just as readily as the melody and lyrics. They all work together. The rhythm will generally match and thereby emphasize the feelings evoked by the lyrical content. A brisk, skippy beat can be used to accentuate a positive message. A slow, brooding eighth-note pedal pattern would go with a somewhat darker message. Good songwriters do this innately.

While the song content will mirror the overall feel, performance considerations are paramount when choosing tempo. When it comes to a band, one beat per minute can be the difference between an undeniable groove and an unsettled performance. It doesn't do you much good to record a song at 120 BPM if your band finds the pocket at 121 BPM.

Further complicating matters are the needs of the vocalist. If your singer can't perform the song comfortably, then your tempo is unusable. Of course, if you're writing your track as you build it, then your melody will be written within the confines of the tempo.

Our mood can greatly affect how we hear tempo. On more than one occasion I have been convinced that I recorded a track at the wrong tempo, only to realize the next day that everything was fine. Even if you did record a song at a less-than-ideal tempo, there are all sorts of ways to deal with it through technology and arrangement technique. You can speed up or slow down the overall feeling of a track through internal rhythms alone. In fact, if you're second-guessing a tempo decision, the arrangement could be the main culprit.

Click

In general, it's way easier to work with a click, and if you build your record one part at a time it's practically a requirement. You can do it without, I suppose, but in my view it's prohibitively inefficient. This is true whether you're programming your record, or overdubbing live instruments.

When I work with a band in the studio, I may or may not use a click track. That decision depends on a number of factors, mostly having to do with feel. Some drummers have a better feel without the click track. Which is all well and good when I'm in the studio, because I'm tracking the full band. But if I were to build the track fully in the overdub process, it would make very little sense to operate without a click track.

I produced a record recently with my buddy Garrett Derhofer at Studio 412 for Jeremy Wade of Dead End Parade, a local singer-songwriter. You can find the track on YouTube, it's called "Absolutely." Conceptually, we wanted to produce a modern programmed track, while maintaining the singer-song-writer appeal, which meant recording his acoustic guitar first. The problem was he played his chorus a full 10 BPM faster than the verses, which is a massive tempo disparity. Musically it was a beautiful dynamic that we wished to accentuate. Logistically, it was a problem.

Had we recorded Jeremy playing his acoustic guitar without a click, we would have been forced to program drums to a constantly fluctuating tempo. And although my DAW offers automatic tempo mapping, that would take away from the programmed feel. It made far more sense to set the tempo for the verse, set the tempo for the chorus, and program a ramp in tempo between the two sections that he could perform against. This took a bit of negotiating, but ultimately worked great.

A click track is paramount to produce the feeling of a programmed track. But the tempo change provides an exciting push and a feeling that the singer-songwriter is driving the track. We could have just as well recorded him without a click, but that would have been an entirely different record, and programming over it really wouldn't have been a viable option.

I've made many records without a click track, and still do today, but only when I have a full band available at the time of recording. Although working without the restraints can be a bit of a pain in the ass for edits and overdubs, if the track has a great feel, I'll take the hit. So long as I have the full instrumentation available, I can evaluate how the band performs without a click, and how that works with the song. Should I be left to imagine how the record will feel? Forget it. I'm recording with the click.

Not to overstate the obvious, but the best way to stay consistently on tempo is to practice to a click track.

Instrumentation

Instrumentation is at the very least influenced, if not somewhat dictated, by genre. A typical rock production will include bass, drums, guitars, and vocals. A hip-hop track is often nothing more than a beat, some harmonic samples, a rap, and some ad libs. EDM might include loops, programmed drums, and keyboards. R&B often calls for plenty of kik and bass with some keyboards, perhaps a guitar, along with stacks of vocals.

Even taking genre into account, there is a ton of wiggle room where instrumentation is concerned, and you are by no means locked into the usual. But arrangements do tend to stay within a relatively narrow selection of instruments based on genre. In fact, one instrument can absolutely define a genre, such as the buzzy and aggressive bass part heard in Dubstep productions. If you produce a Dubstep song without the signature bass, you will be the only person who calls it Dubstep.

Of course, genre is just one consideration. But if you know what you're making, then it does tend to point you in the right direction in terms of your instrumentation. Unless you're producing world music, at which point you have a vast array of supremely grating instruments available to you. Should I ever hear another Erhu again, it will be too soon.

If you're in a band, then your instrumentation is nearly built-in. You write your songs based on your personnel, and you operate together to create an arrangement. Those of you who program your tracks may be unencumbered by genre and have a vast array of instruments available to you. Regardless of your situation, my advice is the same. As you build your track— as you consider your instrumentation—take frequency range into account.

Clearly, the instrument and the player are the first consideration. It's all well and good to decide you need a super-expressive violin part to amp up the sadness factor, but if you don't have a player who can pull it off, the part could come off as nothing short of whiny.

Once you've determined the feeling you want a part to evoke, and in what frequency range you need the part to live, you have limited your options significantly. A flute would certainly use a similar frequency range as a violin–but will that produce the feeling of sadness you seek? Tenor saxophone can express a feeling of melancholy, as can trombone, but they both sit in a lower frequency range from the violin or the flute, which could disqualify them given your frequency requirements.

Instruments have certain traits that make them good candidates to produce certain feelings within your production, and a good player understands how to pull those feelings from their instrument. A great fiddle player can express melancholy just as readily as elation, so long as the tempo is in agreeance. Really, you can probably evoke any feeling from just about any instrument under the right circumstances.

The player, the instrument, and the nature of the part, will have the greatest influence on how it makes you feel. But that doesn't mean you should ignore frequency and balance in the decision-making process. I mean, if all you have is a tenor saxophone available for this sad part that you have in mind, then it may make sense to put your harmonic voicings in a higher register so as to make room for that saxophone.

Of course, you may recall that masking can be combated with balance. Should you place the saxophone forward in the balance, it will not be subject to significant masking. Which is all well and good if it's a solo. But if the sax is playing a countermelody or some other part subservient to the vocal, you will be forced to balance it lower in the production. At that point masking can be an issue, and frequency should be considered.

In order to evaluate frequency and any masking that might take place, context is key. Performers might like to hear themselves rather loud in the monitor mix, which provides little context. In order to determine the best register for a part all you need do is attempt to balance it. If you find that you're almost forced to place the part louder than you imagine it, then you have a masking issue that needs to be addressed. The easiest way to deal with the masking is to put the part in another register.

Chord voicings are also important as your inversions can be the difference between masking and clarity. There are also musical reasons to consider your voicings. Both the internal and the top note movement of chords will have a significant effect on the musical strength of a section. The top notes alone provide a melodic musical sub-theme that you can lean on in your production. Your voicings can also be used to create excitement within the production, particularly if you walk them up the register as you approach the chorus.

Simple Arrangements

We discussed keeping things simple where your recording technique is concerned. I'm going to make the same recommendation where it comes to your arrangements.

For starters, a simple production keeps the focus on the song. The song is the Art here. The production is just a vehicle for the song, and the only time that you should ever make the production more important than the song is when the song falls short. If it's your own song, and you find that you must lean heavily on production techniques, then it's time to admit the song isn't strong enough to stand up on its own.

Many musicians try to cram too many parts into their productions. That isn't defined by how many tracks you use. I've mixed productions with over 80 tracks that were masterpieces in which everything went together perfectly. But if you're having a difficult time with your record; if you find that you can't seem to balance everything without the record getting very small; if you find that your dynamics are completely lacking because you've filled every bit of space in all five planes—you probably have too many parts.

I guess what I'm trying to tell you is that it takes tremendous skill to mix a production that's packed with instrumentation in a particular frequency range. It took me years to develop that particular ability. You're trying to make a Killer Record right now. Not a few years from now. So, if you find yourself indiscriminately plugging in part after superfluous part and it seems increasingly difficult to balance your record while maintaining clarity and punch, this would be about the time to consider putting your arrangement under some extra scrutiny.

You're a musician. If you want your records to continually get better, then you need to practice your arranging skills, not your mixing skills because a great arrangement mixes itself. Believe me, if you give me a track in which the parts fit together perfectly in terms of frequency, I can have it sounding like a record in a matter of minutes.

I balance my production before every session. I balance after every session too, because it tells me where I'm at in the production. Every time I introduce new parts, I experiment with my balances. Parts will sometimes interact in unintended ways, and I often seek almost random discoveries as I build my production. The goal is to get the production in a place where my singer is inspired. If that's you, then you'll need to inspire yourself. The best way to do that is to make sure that everything in your arrangement serves a purpose and means something, otherwise you'll have to deal with the arrangement later.

Hey, some of my favorite mixes have come from completely confused arrangements in desperate need of underdubbing techniques and mangling. But I was always coming in fresh as a third-party specialist with license to do whatever I thought was right. Who's your specialist?

As a producer, I rarely record a vocal before I have my arrangement fully worked out. It happens. There can be scheduling logistics that force such a decision. Sometimes the singer is inspired before the arrangement is fully ironed out, at which point I capitulate. But the whole purpose of your production is to act as a vehicle for the vocal performance. And the vocalist is the direct connection to the audience. It's the vocal that sells the song. And if the production is unfocused, or too dense, and lacks any kind of forward push, then it will be difficult to perform. And yes, this is true even if you're the vocalist. You need to get the production in a place where you're just dying to sing it.

The main advantage to a simple arrangement is space. When you have space, your parts mean more, your parts go together better, and your vocalist has more room to fill that space with a compelling performance. Oh, and you can get away with more low end too. Low end makes your record big. It makes your record warm. And it is the foundation upon which you build your production.

There's no doubt, some Artists gravitate towards dense productions, and not every arrangement in the world should be simple. There's certainly room in music for diversity and style. Of course, dense arrangements are also out of style at the moment, but that's nearly irrelevant. Unless you want to make money.

I kid, I kid!

Voice Leading

I think the most useful class I ever took in music was Voice Leading, in which I learned to compose a four-part harmonic opus employing 18th century counterpoint. The four available parts in voice leading are Soprano, Alto, Tenor, and Bass.

As much as Voice Leading is a pedantic exercise in which you must operate creatively within an almost impossibly strict set of rules, it hones your skills, and will help tremendously with writing four parts for modern productions. And maybe you don't need that skill now, but believe me, when it comes time to arrange four parts for vocals, or horns, or strings, you'll be glad to have this knowledge in your back pocket.

You could most certainly enjoy a successful recording career without Voice Leading. But if you want to improve your arranging skills, you might seek out a course.

Forward Motion

Good songwriters, whether consciously or unconsciously, use a variety of tools to force the listener forward in a song. Producers too.

For instance, you can reserve the highest notes for the chorus, which generates excitement and often boosts the payoff. You can use rhythmic acceleration to push the listener through the Pre-Chorus or Bridge, either by shortening your melodic phrases to deliver more frequent rhymes, or by switching up the rhyme pattern from ABAB to AABB. You can also accelerate the chord changes. You can reserve certain vowel sounds for the chorus, which will set it apart from the rest of the song. You can reserve the tonic for the chorus–both the chord and the note. You can even start the song with the hook.

Avoiding the tonic is a big one. We all remember from grade school how the tonic was home, right? Well, when you arrive home all motion stops. So, if your melody lands on the tonic right before the chorus, you've managed to kill all of your forward motion. If you land on a note that requires some resolution, that will sail us into the chorus.

You can use harmony to push forward motion as well. The V chord just begs to resolve to the I chord. The fourth that defines a suspended-chord calls for resolution to the missing third.

We can also enhance forward motion with our production through contrast and balance decisions. A drop (or mute) on everything but a bass slide, or a drop to just the drums provides us a momentary break which pushes us forward. In fact, we have all sorts of ways with which to derive forward motion. There's the entry of an eighth- or sixteenth-note tambourine in the chorus. A contrast change from asymmetrical to symmetrical or vice versa. A riser effect into a chorus. Backwards reverb into the chorus. A denser chorus. A louder chorus. The entry of a counter melodic part in the Pre-chorus. A breakdown. A slight musical alteration to a repetitive bass line. All of these help with forward motion.

Make no mistake, musical tools are never a replacement for a great lyric and melody, which will provide their own natural forward push. If the melody and lyric are less than compelling, the listener has a very effective tool of their own—it's called the skip button.

Prosody

Prosody is the consistency between lyrics and music. For the songwriter, prosody is an important tool. A song like "Wind Beneath My Wings" by design has a melody and a lyric that are both meant to be inspirational in nature (to someone other than myself, I'm sure). The emotional impact of the music is generally going to match the lyric, and this is the most basic form of prosody. Most good songwriters use prosody innately, but there are also more literal examples.

In the Supremes' "Stop! in the Name of Love," the melody does precisely what the lyric says. The word "stop" is sung, and the melody stops on that word. That's prosody. A melody moving up on the word "up" or down on the word "down" is another great example of prosody in songwriting.

Good prosody isn't always quite so obvious. In Johnny Cash's song "Ring of Fire," the melody in the chorus actually moves up as he sings the word "down" three times. He sings: "I went down, down, down, and the flames went higher." While at first blush, the lyric seems to literally contradict the melody, in reality Cash is exposing the inherent contradiction between falling in love as opposed to love being an uplifting experience. This idea is represented brilliantly by the imagery of the lyric and specifically how it works counter to the melody, thereby illustrating musically the contradiction. There's no doubt that this was a conscious decision by a great songwriter.

Stephen Stills' famous song "For What It's Worth," which was first recorded by Buffalo Springfield in the sixties, is an excellent example of how prosody was enhanced by the production. If the song doesn't immediately come to mind, you'll probably recognize the chorus lyric, "Stop children, what's that sound, everybody look what's going down." In the last chorus of that song, the entire production comes to a halt on the word "stop."

Another example of prosody from a production standpoint would be the Genesis song "Just a Job to Do," in which Phil Collins sings "bang, bang, bang" in quick succession followed by two reverberant snare hits and the lyric "down they go." In this case, the snare hits act as gunshots within the production. This is not only effective, it's smart.

Don't go nuts with this. If you add reverb to the snare every time you hear a word like "shoot," or "bang," you risk turning a good tool into an overused joke. The literal translation of a lyric into a production technique is powerful when used judiciously, particularly if the prosody accentuates something important within the context of the song.

The
Basics

Let's face it. You can't convert technical decisions into practical ones, if the technical is constantly getting in the way. So, we need to break down the technical information to the basics. And I do mean the basics.

There are any number of technical decisions that must be made throughout the course of your record. Many of these decisions are debated *ad nauseam* on the Internet, with little regard to the realities of consumers or even musicians for that matter.

I'm a big proponent of making your life easier, but what makes a professional recordist's life easier is not the same as what might make your life easier. It's all well and good to ask the Internet if you should get an analog compressor, but if your main axe isn't up to snuff, then the answer is a definitive no. Fix your instrument situation, and you will improve your performances. This will increase your chances at a Killer Record tremendously.

We've already established that record-making is an Art, and you have to use the resources that you have available to you. As much as I insist that analog gear can, and will, make the life of a professional recordist easier, it's certainly not a requirement for a Killer Record. There are certain things that a plugin compressor is missing that an analog compressor has, and it's difficult to say what exactly that is. All I can tell you is, I don't have to work as hard with an analog compressor, and that's sadly even true of some of the rather atrocious prosumer compressors that are popular right now.

When it comes right down to it, there's nothing about a plugin that's going to hold you back. Whereas I can inject some life into a kik almost instantly with an analog compressor, I can get the same results from the DAW, it just requires more plugins, and therefore, a touch more time. It's always been like this, although the gap has narrowed considerably over the years.

As we move forward in the digital world of recording, plugin manufacturers are starting to figure out how to pull that wow factor out of their products. There are now plugins that I can use that will instantly give me the kind of results that I seek. I like gear that makes a part instantly better.

Really, the power that you have with some brands of DAW in their stock form is ridiculous. All that matters is your song and performances contained in your production.

Sample Rate and Bit Depth

This is the shit that will make your eyes roll into your skull. It's exceedingly technical in nature, and practically speaking, it's not something to spend much time thinking about.

We all know that a CD (going 40 years strong!) reproduces at a sample rate of 44.1 kHz and 16 bits. But what does that mean exactly?

The sample rate describes the number of samples in a second. In the case of a CD that's 44,100 samples every second. And yes, I realize CDs are becoming less common, (I don't even have a CD player anymore), but they are still the format of choice for many independent Artists and bands in the US, and for a very good reason. They can be sold. Besides, the only delivery format that is of a higher sample rate than CDs is . . . I joke! There isn't one. But you wouldn't know that by reading engineering forums. If you read those, you'll come away believing we all listen to records at 96 kHz or higher.

By definition, the top frequency response of your recordings is equal to half the sample rate. In the case of a CD that would be just above 22 kHz, which is 2 kHz outside the human range of hearing. There are some that feel this is insufficient and suggest that the frequencies that extend all the way up to 48 kHz improve the fidelity of the sound. Which is certainly possible. It's also irrelevant when it comes to making a Killer Record.

Another argument for employing a higher sample rate like 96 kHz is that the converters introduce less distortion, which is a dubious argument given the levels of distortion we're talking about here.

Then, of course, there's the bit depth, which describes the resolution of the capture and which determines the dynamic range available. A CD is 16 bits, but for the past 20 years, we all record at 24 bits, mostly because that's what the DAW comes set at, but also because it allows us to record at lower levels.

Why would we want to record at lower levels?

Well, for starters, the moment you go above 0_dBFS (Decibels Relative to Full Scale) in digital you're clipping, which, if you don't know, is rather nasty distortion. Which means we have a ceiling. And I realize there are times that some of you Industrial Artists out there might like to use the sound of clipping as an effect, but there are plugins that will do that for you far more effectively and with considerably more control. Your converters are best used to record and reproduce audio.

While it's very easy to record something too hot, it's actually quite diffi-cult to record something so low that it's unusable. Oh, you can do it if you're really super stoned, but so long as you keep the lower parts of your audio generally above the -18 mark as you record, you're not going to have any problems. And if you have a super dynamic part, then record it at a lower level. I just mixed a track in which the breakdown drops in level to just below -24 dBFS. On the whole mix! If the Internet ever found this out it might ex-plode.

Let's just examine this for a moment. At 16 bits you have a maximum dynamic range from ceiling to noise floor of 96 decibels (dB). At 24 bits you have a maximum dynamic range of 144 dB. That might not mean a whole lot until you consider that every 6 dB of level is equal to about double the volume. So 144 dB is well beyond an enormous dynamic range. It's certainly far more range than you'll ever need. I mean, hasn't loudness been the goal for the past two decades? We have to worry about dynamic range, why? Unless you're recording classical music, and even if you are, your dynamic range is never, ever going to be an issue. I mean, not even close.

Here's the thing. The reason everyone freaks out about recording too low is because you start to lose bits below -18. And somehow along the way, losing bits became worse than clipping. It's not. It's okay if your lowest parts are below -18 if that's how you need to record it in order to avoid clipping. And you don't need to always be up in the yellow of your meters either. The goal is not to get as close to 0 as possible. The goal is to record a magical take that isn't completely fucked because you kept clipping. As a result, many engineers will put an analog compressor ahead of the input to the DAW to protect against overs. We'll discuss compressors in depth later.

You're not going to find many people arguing over optimum bit depth. Unless you're on some sort of legacy system from the nineties, you're operating at 24 bit these days. And if you're operating at 16 bit that most certainly won't negatively affect your results, even if most engineers will snort at the thought of it. Every hit record going back at least 30+ years has been released as a CD in 44.1/16 format. How many Killer Records does that make? And these days consumers listen to MP3s. You're going to worry about sample rate and bit depth?

As I say, the bit depth is hardly a point of contention. It's the sample rates that produce the heated debates online, and I can't for the life of me figure out why. The consumer still listens to MP3s, which are atrocious when compared to CD. They hear MP3s on Spotify. They hear them on YouTube. They hear them on Pandora. They hear them from their iTunes collection.

So, why on earth would anyone be worried about the sample rate? Because you want to be able to deliver a higher fidelity master in the future? Your record is a snapshot in time, and if somehow it's a hit record, it will be recorded again hundreds if not thousands of times. It's the song that will stand the test of time not the recording. Stop worrying about your sample rate. Get a hit first. Then you really won't care about sample rate, because your first big hit was at 48 kHz, so why the fuck should you switch now?

You see what I'm saying?

Now, there are a great many engineers, including many personal friends of mine, who swear that a sample rate of 96 kHz makes their life easier because they feel the plugins are optimized for it, and that's probably true. And some engineers are convinced that if you record at a higher rate, it will dumb down to MP3 more betterer. But if your computer is long in the tooth, or if you're light on RAM, or if you have limited storage, or even slow Internet speeds, then I can promise you, working at 96 kHz is not going to make your life easier. You may not even be able to operate efficiently at that sample rate, and if you can, your track counts could be limited.

Yet another argument for higher sample rates is that time stretching and tuning are more forgiving. I'm sorry but if you need to alter your timings so much that you're getting obvious artifacts at a sample rate of 48 kHz, then you should probably keep recording the part until it's close enough for stretching tolerances. Some call this practice. This is a Musician's Survival Guide, which means you need to think like a musician, and as a musician, you should record a part until it's great because it actually takes less time, it's more fun, and it's what makes you a better musician.

Time stretching and tuning are amazing tools. But there is nothing particularly musical about perfect tuning or timing. With MIDI you have some control over feel because you can adjust velocity and note duration along with timing. It'll take forever, but it can be done. Not so with a recording. And if you're a musician and you plan to perform your record in front of an audience, then it seems worthwhile to invest the time working out the part until you can play it with some feel.

As far as I'm concerned, you should use time stretching and tuning with impunity if that's what's required for the production. But it doesn't make much sense to learn how to play your record after you've already recorded it. And it makes even less sense to record at 96 kHz purely as some kind of permission to play poorly. I would rather record a part for an hour until I can perform it, than to spend an hour moving bits of audio. Wouldn't you?

Just to be clear, although it may appear otherwise, this is not an argument for working at lower sample rates. There are legitimate reasons to choose to operate at 96 kHz, including the ones I've already mentioned along with reduced latency. The latency alone could make it worthwhile to record at a higher rate. My point is if you need to record at a lower sample rate, there's no reason to feel as though you've somehow compromised your recording. You really haven't.

Here's the bottom line on sample rates, and this is really the crux of my argument right here: No matter what you read online, I can promise you that your sample rate will have absolutely nothing to do with your record's success or lack thereof.

No one will ever listen to your record and wonder what sample rate you used. You will never, ever, hear a fan, or even a detractor mention anything about the sound, or the bit rate, or the noise floor, or the sample rate of your record. Those decisions will have no bearing on whether people share your song. They will have no bearing on whether people react to your song, or like it, stream it, or buy it for that matter. The only people who will care about the sample rate and the bit depth are engineers, and they will argue *ad nauseam* on the Internet as if it matters. It may matter to them. We don't make records for them.

The funny thing is, audiophiles—who only listen to sound—go gaga over my Ben Harper mixes. If they only knew that I mixed those records exclusively on the bookshelf monitors of the day. With some of the systems that those numbskulls use, they would have to be able to hear all sorts of shit that I never heard while mixing those records. There is such a thing as too much fidelity, and too much clarity, and I never give a fuck about anyone who puts sound above the music.

I produce my records at 48 kHz. Not only is it the standard for video broadcast, it doesn't overtax my system or storage. Most importantly, it will never, ever, ever prevent me from making a Killer Record.

Gain Staging and Bussing

Gain staging also brings up some rather heated debates online, as if there's any more to it than keeping things out of the red. There is, but that's really about 90 percent of it right there.

We've already established that you don't need to worry too much about the noise floor, but you do have to worry about digital 0 since that's the point of clipping at your converters. That's the ceiling.

Anyone and everyone who is worried about noise floor in the digital domain, should take a day and record on analog tape. There's your noise floor! And don't even think about recording a single coil Stratocaster into a vintage amp. Your head will explode at the level of noise. Seriously, to worry about noise floor at 24 bit in most modern genres would be to worry about the sun going out. We've got like a billion years before that happens. It's not of concern.

So, what is gain staging? It's basically level management and there are stages to this level management, hence the term "staging."

I suppose technically the first stage is your mic which picks up the signal, and which can introduce distortion at the capsule if placed too close to an overbearingly loud source. It's pretty rare for the capsule to distort. But it can happen.

The second stage is the preamp, which amplifies the microphone signal. Not only is it perfectly acceptable to distort at the preamp stage, it's rather common. However, if your preamp is part of your interface, it might not distort all that well. How do you know if it distorts well? Listen to it.

I know that sounds like such a cop out, but come on! It's really that simple. Listen to it. If you like the sound of the distortion then use it to your advantage when it's appropriate. If you don't, don't. You can always derive your distortion from plugins if it's not working at the preamp stage. How much distortion you introduce is a matter of taste. Just understand that distortion compounds over the totality of your production, which means a little can go a long way.

The point is not to distort everything all the time. Some, if not many, parts should be relatively clean. But most mic pres tend to shine as they get close to distortion. Many mic pres thicken tonally before they break up, and it's that thickening that you want to mostly take advantage of, and technically speaking, that's distortion. The best way to determine the line is to cross it. As such, you should push the preamp into overt distortion and then back it off until it has just the right dirtiness, if any at all.

From out of our preamp we go into our converters, specifically the AD stage, which converts the Analog signal from the preamp to a Digital signal for your DAW to process. If you hit this stage with too much level you'll clip. And I realize we discussed recording levels already, but if you take my advice and record at moderate levels? Gain staging issues are almost completely eradicated. Here's why.

Once your audio is in your DAW and playing through the channel, which is the next stage, you don't have to worry about distortion. So long as you're not distorting at the stereo bus, you're good. For all intents and purposes, there is no unintended distortion introduced at the channel. And you can't clip there either.

You can literally put a test oscillator on a channel, add a Gain plugin, and set the oscillator signal at 30 dB over 0 (or more), which will put the channel deep into the red. This assumes your DAW operates at 32 bit floating point (and I believe all current DAWs do), but so long as your stereo output levels are good, there will be absolutely no distortion introduced. All you need to do is bring your Master Fader or your Stereo Output down more than 30 dB to compensate for the extra signal. *Voila!* No distortion. Try it. And if it doesn't work? Your DAW software is probably a bit long in the tooth.

You understand what this means, right? If you record at a modest level, you're pretty much home free after that. The only other place you can clip is at your stereo output. And any distortion you introduce at the plugin is going to be intentional distortion. It's part of the design of the plugin.

So, why bother worrying about overs on the channels if it can't distort? Because the moment you output the individual channels to a console, that 30 dB of extra signal is blowing up the individual DA converters. Possibly literally. I don't know for sure and have no intention of trying it.

I suppose if you always work internally to the DAW, then technically it makes no difference if you're creaming every channel, because you can just bring down the master fader to prevent the stereo outputs from clipping. But it's not a very good habit.

You need to be sure that you understand what you're looking at when it comes to your DAW meters. You can typically set your meters to pre-fader, which shows the level that's hitting your converters, or post-fader, which shows the level after the channel fader. You must have your meters set to pre-fader in order to see your record levels. Otherwise, you could be very surprised later.

There will be times when you may record things a little hotter than you intend. This is nothing to freak out over. Even if you managed to clip your audio once or twice in the process, it's not the end of the world. Are you really going to re-record the best take your drummer has ever laid down because you managed to clip the snare drum a couple of times? You can just replace those two clipped snares with two good ones from elsewhere, and no one will ever be the wiser. You could even ignore the clipping as far as I'm concerned.

I mixed a record for T-Bone Burnett some years ago, and he asked the mastering engineer to purposely clip the kiks and snares. There was literally a nasty momentary distortion on every kik drum. I won't pretend I was happy about that nor that the record was successful. The point is, if one of the most heralded producers can clip on purpose, then you can most certainly clip by accident.

It's important to note, if you record a signal too hot, you can gain it down after the fact, but that won't remove the clipping that occurred on the way in. If it was recorded with clipping, then the clipping is there forever amen.

Many of us like to add an extra layer of gain staging between the channels and the stereo outputs. We call this a bus, and it's nothing more than a signal path for combining audio. If I record two kik drum mics to their own channels, then a bus is absolutely essential as it allows me to process both mics as one signal. The channel faders allow me to balance the levels between the two mics, which goes to the bus for processing.

As I pointed out earlier, whenever you have two mics placed in close proximity they can, and will, interact. If you compress the signals individually, that interaction can become dynamic and, therefore, apparent. You could conceivably get frequency cancellation that differs from kik to kik throughout the song. Given this, it's far more effective to compress those two kik drum mics as one signal. And the best part? Now your kik drum is on a single fader.

Snare drums are also good candidates for a bus, as they are often recorded with a top and bottom mic. Really, I put a layer of bussing on everything. Toms get a bus. Overheads get a bus. This reduces my drums down to just five channels.

You might be asking what's the difference between bussing and a group? A Group locks the audio together for purposes of editing, and locks the faders within the Group together such that one fader controls the others. But there's no way to process the Group signal, because every channel in the Group has its own output. Groups can be useful, and even necessary when it comes to editing parts and keeping them locked together. But busses are how you combine signals for the purpose of processing them as one.

The 2-Bus

The 2-bus, or the stereo bus, or outputs 1 and 2, is the final stage of your monitor mix, and ultimately your mix. If you want to compress or EQ the entire mix, this is where you do it.

I would suggest you are very cautious about what processing you put on your 2-bus as it affects the entire record. There could be rare occasions that it might make sense to put an effect on the 2-bus, like a reverb or a flanger. And if you program EDM you might choose to strap an LFO plugin, perhaps even an automated filter on the 2-bus. In general? I would recommend you avoid inserting plugins to the 2-bus, and that includes compressors.

For a professional mixer such as myself, a proper 2-bus compressor can make mixing much faster because it helps to contain the low end and control the dynamics of the mix. It's also an exercise in tail chasing. As your levels creep up over time—and they do—you will hit the compressor harder, which will attenuate your low end and greatly reduce your overall dynamic range, thereby making your mix small. This is easily remedied by bringing down the input (or threshold) to the compressor, at which point your low end will reappear, and your mix will open up in a far more inviting way. Unfortunately, your balances will also change, and you'll need to trim your levels in an effort to rebalance. Then the cycle repeats itself as you start to edge up your faders again. If that sounds like madness, it probably is, and as you would imagine, it requires quite a bit of practice and finesse.

Further problematic, not all compressors are good candidates for the position. Many compressors are far too aggressive for the 2-bus, and you will find yourself unable to control the dynamic or prevent unwanted artifacts. At which point you will remove that compressor and wonder why anyone would ever compress the 2-bus? My question would be, why would anyone use that compressor on the 2-bus?

If you go online and ask the Internet whether you should employ 2-bus compression, you'll get every answer you can imagine, and some people will even claim that most professional mixers don't use a bus compressor, which just isn't even close to true. 96 percent of top mixers use a compressor on the 2-bus. And yes, that's a made up statistic, but so is theirs, that's the point.

Where it comes to young mixers, I insist that they at least learn how to mix into a 2-bus compressor. In fact, I've been advising this online for the better part of 20 years now. But as a musician mixing your own record? Unless it's for purely artistic purposes of effect, I don't think musicians should put anything on the stereo bus at all. That's a difficult recommendation to make. But as I consider what will make life easier for most musicians, I have to wonder: should there even be a mix process at all?

Sacrilege, I know!

The mix is the production which is the arrangement. They all go together. As far as I'm concerned, by the time you've completed your last overdub, the mix should be done. Granted, you may come back to touch up a few balances when you're fresh. But for the most part, you can save yourself tremendous time and frustration by viewing the mix and the arrangement as one and the same process.

If you'd like to experiment with a compressor on the 2-bus come mix time, I wouldn't try to dissuade you, but you most certainly don't want to deal with a stereo bus compressor while you're tracking. You're changing your balances far too drastically for that. Besides, a compressor on the monitor mix while you're trying to record puts the focus on the sound rather than the performance and the part. When you're thinking about sound, the music is suffering.

You know, if you're almost finished with your record, and you like how it sounds, but maybe you want to add some compression to see if it will make your mix pop, then by all means, put a compressor on your 2-bus and experiment away. It's a brickwall limiter you want to avoid until the record is fully done.

I've been reading about all sorts of people who work with a brickwall limiter strapped to their 2-bus. I'm here to tell you, that's just madness. There is no reason why you should seek to severely limit your dynamic range at a time when you're trying to maximize emotional impact. And while a compressor limits dynamic range too, it works in conjunction with your balances and is part of the mix. The brickwall limiter just makes things louder, which will prove nothing short of exhausting over the course of your work.

First a brief history in regards to loudness.

When CD carousels were all the rage, you wanted your CD to have more level than the next one, because then it would get noticed more readily by the listener. Then there was the perception that your record would sound louder on radio, which is a myth, but that didn't stop people from believing it. As you can imagine, major labels were super interested in any mastering engineer who could make records really loud. The louder the better. And the guys who could make your record the loudest? Some of them were paid as much as $10,000 to butcher an album in under six hours' time.

How on earth the myth came about that louder records sound better on radio is baffling to me. All one had to do was to listen to realize that wasn't true. Besides, radio stations must contain their bandwidth to strict FCC standards, and so they already employ brickwall limiters to their broadcasts. In reality, records with a reasonable dynamic range sound better on radio than super loud records. These days, we listen to streaming sites, and they now set all the music to the same level, which leaves some room for dynamics. In other words, you gain no advantage with a super loud record. In fact, you're penalized.

It's not that dynamic records automatically sound better than loud records. There's a reason to use a brickwall limiter. If your dynamic range is too large, you will force most listeners to adjust their volume throughout the song. If you've ever listened to classical music in a car, you're familiar with how annoying this is. Because most people listen to records in noisy environments, parts of your music can utterly disappear if your record is too dynamic. For the most part we seek to bring up the level of our records with a brickwall limiter. The question just becomes, how much limiting is appropriate?

Many mastering engineers (MEs) still deliver loud masters, despite the changes with streaming. I can understand this. For twenty years, the ME's job was dependent on her ability to make a record loud. Most MEs who resisted loud records lost gigs in the process, and ultimately had to fold to the reality that absolutely everyone wanted their record loud, even if few would openly admit to it. So, there's a bit of PTSD there, to be sure.

Currently, the big streaming sites have set the optimum level to between -16 and -12 LUFS. I can't even tell you what LUFS is from a technical perspective. All I know is there are LUFS meter plugins on the market that will tell me my level, at which point I'm just optimizing numbers by rote. From a practical perspective, -14 LUFS isn't all that loud.

Ultimately, once you're done with a record, you'll want to bring the level up. That's a large part of what the mastering process is for—to bring the level up. It's also to compensate for any frequency anomalies, and prepare the master for its final delivery destination, which in the case of a CD, that would be a DDP image file or WAV file. But it's the loudness that causes the confusion.

The great thing about brickwall limiters is, when used with some modicum of restraint, they don't tend to dramatically alter your balances. The same is not true for compressors, which is why mixers often strap a compressor to the 2-bus—it protects the balances from changing during the mastering process.

That said, if you're going to apply 20 dB of gain reduction with a brickwall limiter because you just love your production to have so little depth you could practically hang it on a wall, and because you absolutely adore attenuated and crunchy low end, then I would suggest you spend no time whatsoever on your balances. They really don't matter when you limit your mix this aggressively. A little goes a long way in terms of bringing a production up to level with a brickwall limiter. Used judiciously, they don't dramatically alter your balances. Used aggressively, they will serve to eradicate all that is musical about your production.

While brickwall limiting your production is helpful for the consumer who must deal with the excessive background noise of life. It's nothing short of exhausting in an isolated studio environment—even a modestly isolated one.

I can assure you, that if you work on your record with a brickwall limiter strapped on the 2-bus, you'll absolutely exhaust yourself and everyone who works with you. Loud records are not generally warm and inviting in nature. Dynamic records are. Even if your goal with your record is to irritate, you'll be able to work for far longer clips of time if you're not working at level. Of course, a compressor used poorly will exhaust you too, which is why I advise you to avoid strapping anything on the 2-bus. That just keeps things simple.

Monitoring

Your monitoring has everything to do with how your record will sound to the outside world. Quite simply, what you hear in your room needs to translate outside of your room, and your choice in monitors is only one small part of the equation. The shape and size of your room and how you treat that room acoustically will greatly affect what you hear. As if that's not enough, where you place your monitors in relation to the room, and where you place yourself in relation to the monitors *and* the room will also make a huge difference in what you hear. Fun times!

In general, space is your friend, mostly because low-end waveforms require distance to complete a cycle. It takes 18.15 feet for a 62 Hz soundwave to fully develop. That's not to say you need twenty feet behind your listening position, but the smaller the room, the more problematic, mostly because that low end needs space to develop, and then has nowhere to go. Frankly, I've found that the ceiling height has more to do with how well a room translates than any other factor, but let's not pretend that I'm anything more than a hack when it comes to acoustics.

I treat my room with tapestries, rugs, acoustic panels (made from Owens Corning 703), and some bass trapping. I can mix like the wind in my current room, mostly because it's got some size to it, including nine-foot ceilings. It's also a dedicated space for mixing, which I find to be super helpful. But I'm a professional mixer, and I literally chose the house that I'm in based on the size and overall isolation of this one room.

I posted a picture of my room online recently, and all sorts of people freaked out, mostly in regards to the Persian rugs covering the floor. That's supposed to be a big no-no for good control room acoustics. Whatever. I like dead rooms.

I used to walk into world class acoustically designed rooms and hang tapestries from top to bottom. As you can imagine, this significantly alters the acoustics of the room and runs counter to most control room design these days. I've got news for you, acoustic recommendations are often subject to fads like anything else in this business. So, there is some element of taste involved here. Budget too. There's really only one thing that matters when it comes to your monitoring, and that's how your work translates outside of your room.

When it comes to translation, the problem isn't so much what you're hearing as it is what you're not. As sound travels in your room, it can create null points, that is to say locations where certain frequencies disappear from audibility due to cancellation. This cancellation happens because frequencies can interact negatively in a space, which we will discuss at length in regards to microphones. I can assure you, if you can't hear a frequency, you can't adjust for it even if you know the null is there. Your acoustic treatment is just one part of the puzzle in this regard.

How and where you place your monitors will also greatly affect matters. In fact, your monitor position in relation to your location in the room is likely the first thing to address in terms of a problematic null point.

If you're in a relatively small room, the recommendation by most acousticians is to bass trap as much as possible. Bass traps aren't particularly cheap, although they are considerably cheaper than a buildout. They also take up quite a bit of space because you need bulk in order to trap the low-end frequencies. So if you're in a small room as it is, you're going to then fill it up with bass traps? That's not optimal. Especially if your room is dual purpose. Headphones might be the better option.

People will yell at you on the Internet if you use headphones for mixing and there is some merit to the protests. The low end doesn't react the same as it does in monitors. The imaging is unnatural. And you can hear things like reverb more readily in a closed ear system. In other words, they pose significant challenges where translation is concerned.

Which is all well and good, but if the monitoring in your room isn't reliable, or if you have isolation issues that prevent you from using monitors at certain times of the day, then headphones may be your only option.

Not all headphones are equal, and you may want to invest a few hundred dollars in a separate headphone amplifier with designated converters. There are a ton of people mixing at home these days, which has created a market for more accurate systems. That said, I can't personally vouch for any of them.

If your room is problematic, but you'd still prefer to listen on monitors, you can use your monitoring levels to mitigate some of the damage the room imparts. While you really must push some air to properly judge the low end, you're better off operating at modest monitoring levels for purposes of fine-tuning your balances. This is true when recording too.

Surely, when you're laying down a part, you want some volume from your monitors. I like to feel that kik drum in my chest, as it makes it easier to play in time. But in order to judge tuning and timing, you're far better off monitoring at low levels. It's easy to miss a tuning issue when you're listening too loud. In fact, be sure you listen at various levels as you build your record. This way you're less likely to miss something.

You can literally spend days online researching the best way to set up your monitoring environment only to get nowhere with it, mostly because every space poses its own unique challenges and no article can cover all of the possible issues. Anytime I have to set up a new room (I've managed to move twice in the past two years), it takes me a full year to find the optimum monitor placement and to learn the room such that I can mix aggressively with absolute confidence. Most of this is done through trial and error.

If you're expecting me to write a whole chapter here about what you need to do to make your room usable, that's not going to happen. Oh, I could tell you that you probably want your monitors fairly close to the front shortest wall, and you need to somehow reduce the parallel nature of your walls, ceiling, and floor, and you want to form an isosceles triangle between your listening position and the monitors. And some of that may even be helpful. But I got all of that from the Internet myself, and some of those things don't work for my room, and you may not even have a designated control room, so I'm not sure why any of that matters. All you can do is work with what you've got, and that is going to require the same trial and error process that I have to go through whenever I move to a new space. Welcome to the new world of record-making.

All of that said, let's get one thing perfectly clear. You do have to make your room usable. It's mission critical, and it's the only mission in this book in which you may have to stop being a musician for a moment, and you may have to pony up some money. Because if you can't hear what's happening, then how on earth can you make a Killer Record?

Of course, there are computer programs that can be used to measure your room. I'm sure that some are probably better than others, but at the very least you can get some idea of what you're dealing with. There's no way around it, any nulls and overt peaks must be addressed, and you may have to invest some money on modular acoustic panels and bass traps in order to get there. Frankly, you might do well with some acoustic consultation.

Many of the Insulation Pimps will offer their consultation, but beware. That arena is littered with charlatans and snake oil salesmen, to the point that I recommend you seek out GIK Acoustics for assistance with your acoustic needs. Tell them Mixerman sent you.

Your room does not have to be perfectly flat in its frequency response, nor will it be. It won't even react the same at different monitoring levels, which is to our advantage, really. So, if you find that there's a mild bump in a frequency, just knowing it's there could help matters tremendously. My room has a little bump at 125 Hz. That means I'm hearing 125 Hz louder than it actually is. And since any linear frequency issue that occurs in a room will translate in an equally opposite manner outside of that room, that means my mixes will come out of my room 125 Hz light if I don't compensate for it. Of course, if I don't deal with it, then the mastering engineer will, so slight bumps or dips in frequency, especially in the low end, aren't going to pose too much of a problem. In my case, I like to hear the low end nice and loud while mixing, so the bump actually serves me well.

Eventually, as you listen to your work outside of your room, your brain will actually adjust how it hears inside your room. How do I know this? Because I used to mix in a different room every two weeks, and I did that for a number of years. It would take me a full day to learn a room the first time I worked in it. Once I returned to that room, my learning curve decreased considerably. And if I returned again to mix a third and fourth project, I would compensate for the room automatically. The most remarkable thing? Years could go by between repeat visits, and my brain would still remember the room. The power of the brain never ceases to amaze me.

If you're working out of a dedicated room, even if it's a spare bedroom, then you must learn exactly what you're hearing. This requires some pain. You have to listen to your work outside of your room to understand how your room translates. Which is a headfuck of epic proportions, because you're comparing sound. Unfortunately, it's a necessary process. If you notice that your snare drum is too loud outside of your room, then your brain will start to adjust how it hears that snare drum in your room. So long as your room can translate, it will, and eventually you'll trust your room more than any other environment. This takes time and persistence.

As important as the room is, your monitors do matter. Most of you will select your monitors within a certain price range. If it's your first set of monitors, that's a reasonable way to choose them. If you really have no idea where to begin in regards to your monitors, reach out to a Gear Pimp who offers consultation. This is far superior to asking the Internet its opinion.

When it comes to monitors, your biggest consideration has to do with the amplification. There are two kinds of monitors—active and passive. Active monitors have amplification built in. Passive monitors require an external amplifier. The advantage of a passive monitor is you can custom match your amplifier to your speakers. The advantage of active monitors is you don't have to deal with any of that. Unless you already own a really good amplifier with sufficient power, you're far better off with an active set of monitors as they will greatly simplify your setup. They also travel well. I use active monitors.

For the first half of my career, there was a particular brand of bookshelf monitors on the bridge of every console in Los Angeles. I rejected them for years, but once I learned them, they became my primary monitor. I can assure you that they are, and were, atrocious monitors, that lacked low end, and could never be described as pleasing. But they did have a particularly aggressive midrange, and once you learned them, your mixes translated. The best part? They weren't expensive monitors.

That said, I would recommend against bookshelf monitors at this stage of the game. We use considerably more low end in our productions these days, and although you can learn to judge the low end in a bookshelf monitor by watching how the woofers crinkle, they're nothing short of exhausting. You're far better off with something more full range.

When it comes to judging low end, size matters. That said, an 8-inch woofer is usually more than sufficient to provide you with full low-end extension, and many powered monitors will offer you some top and bottom EQ adjustments on the back.

If your cones are 6 inches or smaller, you might consider implementing a subwoofer, especially when you're recording. Small monitors will literally wear you out, as they can't reproduce the full extent of the low end. I can assure you, it's way more enjoyable to record for hours with a healthy low end.

Subwoofers can cause you to mix bass light, so be mindful.

The Interface

Your interface is how you get audio to and from your computer, and it contains both your AD and DA converters. The ADs convert the Analog signal to Digital. The DAs convert the Digital signal to Analog, which means they affect what you're hearing and are, therefore, part of your monitoring. It's rather difficult to find subpar converters in anything but consumer devices these days. Even prosumer converter units generally won't get in your way.

Twenty years ago a top-of-the-line converter cost as much as $5000 per channel. Today, there are units that are perfectly acceptable at just $50 per channel. My current converters cost about that per channel.

For the most part, manufacturers include an equal number of AD converters as DAs in their interfaces, but unless you have a console or a summing box, you really only need two DA converters for stereo playback. How many ADs you require depends on how many channels you wish to record at once. If you're unlikely to record more than two channels at a time, then you really only need two channels of AD conversion from your interface. Four mics would require four DA converters. Four preamps too, but many interfaces come with those these days.

Interfaces are designed so that you can get audio in and out of your computer easily, and typically include a control panel that allows for software routing, along with input and output metering. The routing panel that comes with your interface will allow you to monitor directly off the input to the converters, which will eradicate latency. What's latency? The bane of your existence in the studio, that's what.

Conversion of audio takes time. It's not a lot of time, but for a player, the difference between being on top of the beat and behind it can be as little as 3 ms. Depending on your converters and your settings, your conversion can introduce even more than 3 ms. And while it's not the end of the world to hear even as much as a 5 ms of latency on the part you're trying to record, it's certainly not optimal. Some will find it intolerable.

You can reduce latency by adjusting the buffer in your DAW. The buffer gives your computer some time to process things. The bigger the buffer, the greater the latency, the more difficult it is to record. A buffer size of 1024 samples generates a nearly 60 ms delay in my system, which is fine for mixing, but not for recording. It would be outrageously difficult to effectively play against 60 milliseconds of latency.

As much as it would make sense to set your buffer to the absolute lowest setting at all times, your computer must work considerably harder, which can manifest as digital pops on your recordings. Or your computer could just stop playing and crash entirely. If the lowest buffer setting of 32 samples is problematic, switch to 64. Once you get above 64 samples, the latency starts to become unbearable.

The more RAM you have installed in your system the lower you'll be able to set your buffer. 16 gig of RAM should be sufficient for most users, but I can assure you, if I were able to put 32 gig in to my MacBook Pro, I would. RAM is not the place to skimp on your computer. And yes, I do all of my mixing from a laptop. It plugs into all sorts of other fancy things, but the entire operation is indeed powered by a laptop.

If you're able to monitor from your interface control panel, you can get the latency down to 0, but this isn't necessarily ideal, because you won't be able to monitor any of your plugins. Personally, I prefer to just live with the latency.

Most DAWs offer some sort of low latency mode, which will shut off the plugins that cause a delay. Unfortunately, if the plugins you're using introduce latency, then you won't be able to monitor them as you record using low latency mode. At which point, you'll either need to choose less taxing plugins for monitoring, or perform without them.

Make no mistake, there is no latency in heaven.

Microphones

When it comes to microphones, it's more important to understand how and where they shine. The brand of mic is of far less consequence than the type. Therefore, you need to understand certain aspects of mic design, because they relate directly to your decision-making process.

The Capsule

Microphones have a capsule, which is simply a membrane suspended in a housing. Basically, that round thing inside the microphone grate reacts to the sound waves, which are then somehow converted into an electrical signal. Don't ask me how. I still haven't figured it out. But that's what it does.

Pick-Up Patterns

Every capsule has a pick-up pattern, which describes the overall manner in which a mic collects and rejects sonic information. What the hell does that mean? Well, sometimes you want a mic to pick up lots of information around it. And sometimes you want a mic to pick up just the sonic information directly in front of it. The pick-up pattern is what determines this. On some mics the pick-up pattern is selectable. On other mics the capsules are modular and can be swapped out by the end user. Most mics have only one available pattern, which is usually all you'll need. They call it cardioid.

Cardioid

You've probably heard people call their mic a cardioid mic. That's not a brand. It's a pick-up pattern, and it's the most common pick-up pattern around. Cardioid really just means heart shaped.

Cardioid patterns are relatively tight in nature, which means they mostly pick up information directly in front of them. They're also subject to something we call "proximity effect." When you place a cardioid microphone in close proximity to a source, like a singer, you will get a boost in low-end information. You may also get some measure of distortion, but that's not always a bad thing. In fact, you can use proximity effect to your advantage. If you want more low end out of your capture, just move the mic closer to it. If you want less, just pull the mic back. Do you see how simple recording is when you don't clutter your brain with too much useless technical information?

For the most part, the mics that you have will employ a cardioid pick-up pattern. But there are other patterns available. There's hyper-cardioid and super-cardioid, which are even tighter and, therefore, more directional in nature than cardioid. These aren't as commonly used in the recording studio. The most prevalent alternative pick-up patterns would be omnidirectional and figure-8.

Omnidirectional

Basically, when a capsule is set to omnidirectional, it picks up sonic information in all directions evenly around the microphone. This is particularly useful for "gang vocals" as your crew can surround the microphone, which will then pick them up evenly around the mic.

It's important to note, omnidirectional patterns are not subject to proximity effect, but given the 360 degree pickup pattern, you'll collect considerably more room information than with the more directional cardioid patterns. For most recording applications, omni is not a desirable pattern. But it can be exceptionally useful when you want to surround the mic with performers, or if you seek some level of ambient information in your capture.

Figure-8

A figure-8 pattern picks up information from the front and the rear of the capsule, and rejects the side information. This can be useful for recording two performers facing each other. Keep in mind, both sides of the capsule go to just one preamp, so you need to get the blend between your performers right at the mic.

Nearly all ribbon microphones are figure-8 by design. Some condenser microphones allow you to switch between the cardioid and figure-8 patterns. Some mics even allow you to select varying degrees of those patterns.

Powered Microphones

Some microphones require a power source as part of their design. Most powered mics accept 48 volts of phantom power, which you can typically send to the mic from the preamp. This function is usually labeled on the pre-amp as "48V" and should include a bright red light to let you know when it's activated. There are two very good reasons for that red light. You can fry many ribbon microphones with 48 volts of power, and a mic that requires power won't reproduce sound without it. Really, it's not advisable to plug any mic into 48 volts hot. It will cause your monitors to pop violently.

The inclusion of a powered transformer in a microphone has to do with design considerations, and should have no bearing on mic selection. If it needs power, send it power. If it doesn't, don't.

Tube Microphones

Some condenser microphones incorporate a vacuum tube for purposes of amplification and derive voltage from their own dedicated power supply. The mic won't sound without it, nor will it operate on phantom power. In general, tubes are warmer in tone than solid state microphones, which can be beneficial on strident instruments.

Plugging a tube mic into a live power supply is a great way to give yourself a nasty shock. Do yourself a favor and make sure the power supply is off for at least 30 seconds before connecting or disconnecting your mic to it. You've been warned.

Microphone Types

Now that we understand the pick-up patterns, let's talk about the types of microphones. For the purposes of this Survival Guide. there are five types of mics that you will come across: small diaphragm condensers (SDC), large diaphragm condensers (LDC), ribbons, dynamics, and speaker mics.

Condenser Microphones

Condensers have a fast transient response, full frequency range, and robust gain, all of which is just a fancy way to say they're sensitive to sound. That means condensers don't require an especially loud source to excite the capsule. There are two basic kinds of studio condenser mics—small diaphragm and large.

Small Diaphragm Condenser (SDC)

Small diaphragm condensers tend to have a wide cardioid pickup pattern, which means they excel at capturing off-axis information, and can offer a detailed sonic image when used in pairs for stereo miking. If you want to get a nice aggregate stereo image of a drum kit, a pair of SDCs overhead can be an excellent choice.

Large Diaphragm Condenser (LDC)

The large diaphragm condenser is probably the most widely used studio mic there is. The LDC capsule is larger than that of the small condenser, which seems to make a whole lot of sense given the definitions of large and small.

LDCs, like SDCs, are sensitive microphones, but aren't as good at picking up off-axis information as their smaller counterparts. The size of the capsule leads many to believe that LDCs have a more extended low end, which is a myth. Generally speaking, you will get a full frequency response from any studio condenser.

LDCs are often the first choice for vocals, drum overheads, room mics, stringed instruments, etc. Seriously, these bad boys are a good choice on just about any source, so long as there's space to fit the mic.

Dynamic Microphones

A dynamic microphone diaphragm operates similarly to the woofer in your monitors in that the diaphragm is connected to an induction coil and magnets. That's about as technical as we need to get.

These are workhorse microphones that are less susceptible to damage from abuse and moisture, which is why they are so commonly used for live reinforcement. Make no mistake, dynamics are a staple in the studio, as well, and they can take downright oppressive sound pressure levels without ill effects.

Dynamics also exhibit excellent rejection properties, which means they don't pick up information on the sides all that well. This can be an important consideration when choosing a mic. Like those times when you've got a microphone pointing at a snare drum in close proximity to a hi hat and cymbals. In most cases, you'll want lots of snare drum and not a lot of that brass on the mic. As you can imagine, good rejection properties would be a useful feature for a mic placed in such a precarious position.

Dynamic mics don't have the full transient response of condensers and, therefore, aren't used for purposes of fidelity to the source. If you want to capture a tom drum tone accurately, you would be better off with a condenser placed a foot or two off the head. Unfortunately, this kind of placement would pretty much make it an overhead on a full drum kit. Even if you place condensers in close proximity to the toms, you'll still pick up a ton of cymbal information. Dynamics in close proximity will pick up more low-end information from the tom than top-end information from the cymbals, often making them the best choice.

In general, we use the close mics on a drum kit to fill in missing information. For instance, if you place a pair of SDCs in a stereo configuration (which we'll discuss shortly) over the drums, they will pick up a rather accurate image of the drums in that space. But because the SDCs are several feet from the toms, you won't benefit from proximity effect. As a result, there can be a definitive lack of low end. We can fill in that low-end information by placing dynamic mics in close proximity to the toms and snare, and then blending them in with the overhead image.

Here's the thing though. While it's true that dynamic mics aren't as sensitive to sound pressure levels as condensers, they are way more sensitive to placement. The dynamic mics' general lack of sensitivity and capsule speed virtually requires proximity to the source. Therefore, the tiniest movement in any direction of a dynamic mic can, and will, result in a notable differential in tone. This is important to understand, because in certain situations, a dynamic mic can make you work harder than you should. There are many engineers who enjoy dicking around with dynamic mics in front of a guitar cabinet. Personally, I prefer the far more forgiving ribbon or condenser for that application.

Since dynamic mics lack sensitivity, they aren't the greatest choice for miking from distance. A dynamic over the drums is going to sound quite trashy, which is great if you're making a punk record, or if you want lo-fi drums. But in general, your dynamic mics work better close to the source.

For whatever reason, there are times that a dynamic is the optimal vocal mic. That said, they can be a major pain in the ass for this application because of their sensitivity to position and the general mobility of singers. Given this, dynamic mics are often preferable on stationary sound sources, but this is by no means any kind of rule.

Singers use dynamic mics almost exclusively for live performance, but it's generally better if you don't hold the mic while performing the record. Hey, if it makes for a better performance, go for it. But you very well could get a ton of noise from the handling of the mic.

Dynamics are exceptional at rejecting ambient room information, particularly when placed in close proximity to robust sound pressure levels. Lastly, dynamic mics do not generally require a power source. Nice.

Ribbons

The capsule from a ribbon mic is made from an extremely thin strip of corrugated aluminum suspended in a strong magnetic field. Ribbon mics are technically dynamics because they employ an induction coil, but we don't ever refer to them that way because they have such unique capture properties. As such, ribbon mics get their own classification–quite simply, ribbons.

Due to a generally steep rolloff above 16 kHz, ribbons have a rather smooth top end, and can often be perceived as dark in nature. They also have a rather slow response to transients, which can have the effect of rounding off those transients. Given this, ribbon mics are used to great effect to capture drum overheads, guitars, and even vocals. And there is nothing quite like a good ribbon for capturing your more strident brass instruments.

Many ribbons can't take an excessively loud source. An aggressively played kik drum can disintegrate a ribbon membrane in an instant, so be mindful of where you place them. That said, some of the relatively newer lines of ribbon microphones can handle just about any source at any level, including a blaring guitar amp. In other words, if you have a ribbon mic, make sure you understand its design tolerances.

As I pointed out earlier, the large preponderance of ribbon mics are bi-directional, which means they have a figure-8 pattern—the rear pattern often brighter than the front. And although a surge of 48 volts can disintegrate the ribbon membrane under the right circumstances, there are some ribbons that require phantom power.

The longer I produce, the more ribbons I employ in my recordings. Ribbons may have a steep roll-off on the top end, but that just means you can brighten the shit out of them without bringing up annoying sizzle distortion that some cheap condensers introduce. As much as I'm a proponent of distortion, top-end sizzle is particularly exhausting, and should be avoided when possible.

If you're a musician recording at home, in all likelihood you don't have a ribbon mic available to you. I've recorded all sorts of records without a single ribbon, so they are by no means a requirement. They are, however, a great addition to your arsenal over time.

Speaker Mic

Okay, now it's time to blow some minds. Remember how I told you that the woofer of your monitors operates just like the diaphragm in a dynamic mic? That's because a speaker is basically the opposite of a mic. What goes into the mic comes out the speaker, right? So it makes sense, that if you were so inclined, you could use a speaker as a great big microphone. And you can.

Essentially, a speaker placed in front of a sound source will act like a massively large dynamic microphone. It doesn't matter really if the speaker is still housed in its cabinet complete with the crossover, or if it's a single woofer outside of the cab, either way, they can be a bit unruly as microphones.

The bigger the speaker, the more low-end information it will pick up. A 15-inch woofer will pretty much only capture the subs, but when combined with a condenser mic on a kik drum, this can provide desirable results.

You need only connect the rear terminals of a speaker to a male XLR connector in order to convert it into a microphone. If you aren't particularly handy with a soldering iron, you can just do what I do. Cut the male end off of a mic cable, strip the white and red insulated wires, and connect them to the appropriate terminals.

Speakers are not efficient as microphones given the size of the diaphragm, which is referred to as a cone when used as a monitor. They are, however, great at supplementing the sub-frequency information in your capture. Speaker mics can also produce interesting results on their own, particularly when they're smaller in size, and especially when they're still in their housing complete with tweeter. A small speaker cabinet placed in front of an amplifier can produce some rather interesting guitar tones.

I often use speaker mics to supplement the sub-frequency information from bass cabs and kik drums. Keep in mind, a 15-inch woofer may be a great way to extend the sub-frequency blossom of a kik drum, but you need to be careful with frequencies that low. It's really easy to blow out your monitors if you're not prudent with how you introduce the speaker mic into the blend. The tiniest amount of that sub-frequency goes a long way, and a sudden burst of subs could send your cones flying across the room. I'm being hyperbolic, of course. If for no other reason than so you remember it.

Headphones can be used as microphones too. And they're stereo! I can't say I've ever used headphones this way in the studio. They are, however, a great way to record a rehearsal.

Stereo Mic

A stereo mic has two capsules mounted one above the other. Some stereo mics allow you to rotate the top capsule 45 degrees for purposes of tightening the width of the image.

Stereo mics are typically condensers, and can be extremely handy as the capsules are phase-coherent within the housing, meaning it makes it difficult to fuck things up. Unfortunately, you're not going to come across many of these unless you visit a commercial facility, or unless you purchase one yourself. Which isn't a bad idea, because you aren't required to use both capsules all of the time. You can use them as a mono mic too since most of them are just two-capsule versions of an existing model.

USB Mic

USB mics aren't a type of mic at all. They're just mics that connect to your USB port on your computer rather than directly into a mic preamp. Most USB mics are likely condensers, and can be useful for podcasts and the like. Generally speaking, these are not high-quality microphones. If it's all you have, then you need to figure out where they shine. But if you're trying to capture a drum kit with seven USB mics, there's not much I can offer you other than encouragement. Good luck with that.

Direct Box / Direct Injection

A direct box, while certainly not a microphone, is used to plug an unbalanced line level signal into a balanced microphone input. A direct box is often referred to as a DI, which stands for "Direct Injection." Guitars, basses, and keyboards—anything with a 1/4-inch unbalanced jack to be recorded directly without an amplifier—require a DI.

A DI often has a thru-port, which will allow you to daisy chain the signal to an amplifier. This way you can record both the direct and amplified signals at the same time.

The point isn't to use the DI signal in conjunction with an amp, although you wouldn't be the first, and that can even be a cool trick on occasion. You record the DI as backup. If the amp doesn't work out then you can use the DI to send to a virtual amp. Or you can bag the amp and use a virtual amp exclusively. Just remember, it's best if you can get that guitar tone right before moving on. Otherwise, all of your subsequent decisions are dubious at best.

A microphone requires far more amplification than a line-level instrument. So, if you were to put an XLR adapter on your ¼-inch cable and plug it into your preamp, you will introduce copious amounts of preamp distortion to the signal. Which might be kinda cool every now and then. But in general? You need to step down the level with a direct box that goes to the mic input of your preamp

That said, many mic preamps and audio interfaces include a line-level input, which will often live right smack in the middle of the XLR mic input. If you can plug your ¼-inch jack into your interface, then this will negate the need for a DI box. In fact, most of you will record your direct signal this way.

Pad and Roll-Off

Some condenser microphones include a pad, which allows you to reduce the output of the microphone before the signal hits the preamp. Should you place a mic in front of an outrageously loud guitar cabinet, the preamp could produce overt distortion even at its lowest input setting. You can use the pad to reduce the signal. The preamp often has its own pad, which will work the same as the one on the microphone. Essentially, if you're getting unintended distortion, insert the pad. If not, don't.

A roll-off switch employs a selectable low-frequency filter. We use this to reduce the low end from proximity effect, or to deal with a source that's a bit heavy in the low end. I rarely use the roll-off because I can just use EQ, but it can come in handy at times.

Seemingly Arbitrary Notes Section

Microphone Attributes Cheat Sheet

Since this is a Survival Guide, I should probably give you a microphone attributes cheat sheet for reference.

Dynamic Mics: Don't require power. Tend to be relatively small in size. Operate best in close proximity to the source. Have generally good rejection qualities. Good for skinned percussion instruments including toms and snares, some vocalists, and electric guitar amps.

LDC Mics: Require power. Have fast response to transients. Tend to be bulky and may need some space for placement. Are sensitive and could require a shock mount. Work well from distance or in proximity. Have great proximity effect in cardioid. Often have selectable polar patterns like omni or figure-8. Don't have great rejection properties, but aren't the best for collecting off-axis information either. Tend to be the first choice for vocals, regardless of whether it's the best option.

SDC Mics: Require power. Have fast response to transients. Tend to be small and narrow and can fit in small spaces. Are sensitive. Work well from distance or proximity. Have proximity effect in cardioid. Often have selectable polar patterns like omni or figure-8. Have superior collection of off-axis information. Good for stereo miking. Drum overheads, acoustic guitar, vocals, percussion, room tone, hi hats, snare drums in isolation, horns.

Ribbon Mics: Generally don't require power, but can. Almost always operate in figure-8. Have a significant drop in frequencies above 16 kHz. Have decent rejection on the sides, but no rejection from the back of the capsule. Prefer a robustly powered mic preamp. Good for recording anything.

Speaker Mics: Work like a giant dynamic. Great for capturing sub-frequency information. When there's a crossover and a tweeter present, they can produce interesting capture results.

Mic Preamps

Mic preamps are without a doubt the most overrated part of your signal chain. There are many preamps on the market, all of them have their own unique tone to them, and while many professional recordists may have a favorite, or even lots of favorites, you just need preamps that will stay out of your way. That's a rather low bar.

Very few people have gone into the depths of mic preamps quite like I have. When I was recording Ben Harper's *Burn to Shine* album, I had an enormous variety of mic preamps available to me, including all sorts of rare shit that producer JP Plunier and I were buying off of eBay. This was back when eBay was strictly an auction site. I mean we even bought old Ampeg tape electronics to use as preamps. It was stupid.

We also had lots and lots of mics available, and let me tell you, it's easy to fritter away time when your goal is to determine the best microphone preamp pairings for each and every instrument on every song. We recorded one song at a time on that album, and we used different drums with different mics in unique spaces to record each song. There wasn't a combination of mic and pre that I didn't use.

I'll never do that again. What a wank! From distance, I can tell you that we got absolutely zero benefit from pairing mics with preamps like that. I can't even listen to that album. That has mostly to do with how long it took to make it, but then that's why it's a wank.

Look, we would have spent six months on that album regardless. I was filling time. Not spending it. Believe me, I would have never done this were Ben not absolutely exhausted after years of relentless touring. He needed six months in the studio just to rest!

You can record an entire record with just one variety of mic pre. I've recorded many albums using only the preamps from the console. Engineers can argue all they like about whether pairing preamps with microphones like wine with food is a worthwhile endeavor, but as musicians making a record, we have bigger fish to fry.

The odd thing is, as much as mic pres are overrated, you can't just slough them off either. A crappy mic pre can introduce unintended distortion and frequency holes. So, you need a preamp that's going to stay out of your way. The good news is, if you have mic pres in your interface, they're probably good enough for now. At some point, however, you will likely want to upgrade to some solid analog preamps, and where it comes to new-stock preamps, price point is a decent indicator of quality. At the end of the day, I choose my preamps based on how they distort.

Distortion

Distortion is your friend.

Play me a record with no distortion, and I'll play you the most uninspiring piece of crap recording you've ever heard. Seriously.

This really has nothing whatsoever to do with the current trend to aggressively and audibly distort nearly everything in a production. Distortion does not necessarily mean aggressive distortion nor does it mean apparent or overt. All distortion means is to alter or change something, ostensibly in an unflattering manner. Which is kind of weird, seeing as we like distortion.

Dictionary.com defines it thusly: Distort - 1. to twist awry or out of shape; make crooked or deformed.

There are, of course, degrees.

Don't ask me why it is that we love everything distorted. I couldn't tell you. But we do. If we didn't, Picasso would have been a pauper. Electric guitar tones would have never evolved beyond a little bit of unintended breakup. And all analog gear would have plummeted in value long ago.

Perhaps we just find reality too boring. And let's not pretend that the contrived nature of a network television reality show could ever be classified as real.

Distortion does fall into trends, and like most fads in music production they have everything to do with technology. I'm convinced that the current near overuse of distortion in productions has mostly to do with one particular saturation plugin, which distorts like no other plugin I've ever heard. Before that plugin was available, you pretty much had to derive your quality distortion from analog gear. Once we could distort in the box (ITB) in a convincing manner? A trend was born. And why not? Do you know how long some of us have been waiting for good ITB distortion? Of course, it's been available for about eight years now, but it was also way ahead of its time.

I may be wrong about assigning credit to one plugin. There could be more factors than that, but I can assure you it had an effect, and this would not be the first time that a specific piece of gear changed the direction of record production. The drum machine is largely responsible for the programmed drums of the eighties. Digital effects units were responsible for the gated reverb of the same period, which was merely a model of the organically derived gated drum reverb from Phil Collins' mega hit "In the Air Tonight." Sampling drum machines allowed hip-hoppers to loop beats from records, which became the dominant production style in that genre in the late eighties and early nineties. Audio quantization programs brought us the groovy rock productions of the *aughts*. Ahem. Autotune brought yodeling back into fashion. There's no way around it, we all use the same gear and plugins, and when a record comes out that has a fresh sound, the technology used to derive that sound will be used to death by everyone. May you be the person responsible for the next big production trend.

Despite the fact that overt distortion is having a renaissance period (one of many over the years), that is not the reason that I insist distortion is your friend. Forget about trends. Externally derived distortion is probably more important than ever given the abundance of interface mic preamps in home studios. Many of those interface preamps are lacking in useful distortion properties. I have nothing against mic preamps found in your interface, but they just don't tend to distort all that well. Not the ones that I've heard.

That said, our improvements in recording software technology are occurring at such a breakneck speed, I fear that by the time this book comes out, someone could release a virtual preamp tomorrow that distorts in a way that would make Buddha smile. If you use interface preamps, listen to how overtly they distort when you push them. If they don't distort in a useful manner, you'll need to derive your distortion from plugins.

Distortion Flavors

Have you ever listened to a Motown record from the sixties and heard the obvious distortion on the vocals? That distortion is from the preamp. How do I know? Because I know analog preamp distortion when I hear it. It has a particular sound.

I mean, there are a ton of different kinds of distortion. There's breakup. There's gain. There's crunch, spit, buzz, sizzle. There's low-end distortion which can be woolly in nature. There's bit distortion, and there's clipping. And each of these distortions is useful in its own way, and when you have control over the kinds of distortion that you introduce, you have control over your record.

The distortion properties of a vintage preamp is probably the single biggest factor in their value. If you wonder how a preamp could be worth $4000, it's because no other preamp distorts like that one, and there are enough people who have benefited from that distortion over the years to justify the expense.

It's not just the overt distortion that occurs from pushing the gain all the way. It's the subtle thickening that occurs moments before breakup that is often so desirable. And while this is technically distorting the signal, it's not necessarily heard as distortion.

As far as I'm concerned, no preamp is worth that kind of money, that is, unless money is no object. And if money were no object, I'd own all sorts of expensive things. But let's be real here for a moment. The preamp won't fix a shitty song. It certainly won't fix a lackluster performance. Besides, we are finally entering an era in which digital distortion algorithms are convincing and pleasing, even when sickly aggressive in nature.

Now, there are five reasons to introduce distortion to your production: sustain, clarity, obfuscation, thickening, and agitation. First, let's define some flavors of distortion, and explain where they shine.

Clipping

We generally seek to avoid clipping from our hardware, as it manifests itself so nastily it can reflexively cause you to duck. There are times when controlled clipping distortion might be desirable, but in general, I only use this kind of distortion if my goal is to agitate. As I pointed out earlier, it's always best to derive your clipping from a plugin and not your converters so as to maintain control over it.

Bitcrusher

Bitcrusher distortion is also exceptionally nasty distortion, in which the audio is downsampled in order to produce a lo-fi tone. The lower the bit rate, the more obvious the artifacts of aliased high-end frequencies, which present as spitting and noise. The bitcrusher can offer a very cool effect, but it's exhausting to the listener, and even if your goal is to agitate, you might want to demonstrate some restraint with how much bitcrushing you apply to any given production. That said, it's a very cool effect. The more low end in your production, the more tolerable this kind of distortion will be.

Total Harmonic Distortion (THD)

This is the measurement that manufacturers tout to get you to purchase their gear, and it's more commonly expressed as THD. It's not a particularly meaningful number, since we often go out of our way to distort things. Anytime someone points out distortion specs, my response is always the same. Distortion, dismortion! Yeah, we want to limit distortion when it's a problem. These days you're more likely to introduce it than to avoid it.

Overdrive

Overdrive is probably the most useful and common distortion of them all as it's not overtly aggressive in nature, which allows you to retain some modicum of your dynamic range within the part. In other words, you're not obliterating the signal as you break it up. Overdrive is often used in conjunction with filters, in particular LPFs (which allow the low end to pass), in order to reduce the strident nature of the distortion. High frequency overdrive is meant to be grating. Low-mid and low-end overdrive acts as a thickening agent.

Crunch

Crunch distortion is used to describe high-gain electric guitars. Oftentimes a crunch guitar plays power chords which requires sustain. This distortion is typically derived from an amplifier or pedals–virtual or otherwise. Crunch distortion shines in the upper midrange. The rock, metal, and pop genres often call for crunch guitar.

Buzz

Buzz distortion acts like a separate layer over the source. As such, it typically only affects a somewhat narrow frequency band. Its resonance puts a definitive edge on anything that sustains, and is used to provide clarity. Buzz distortion is especially useful for clarity on low-end instruments like a clean synth bass, or even a sustaining electric bass part. The buzz brings out the upper harmonics, which helps the notes remain audible throughout the production. This is a particularly common distortion in Industrial music.

Fuzz

Fuzz distortion affects the full range of frequencies, which makes it somewhat more complex in nature. Unlike buzz, the delineation between the tone and the dirt is not so evident. Whereas buzz offers clarity, fuzz can offer either clarity or obfuscation, since it distorts the entire signal. When it comes to bass, you can add copious levels of fuzz distortion for purposes of edge and clarity. Fuzz distortion introduced in a subtle way can appear woolly in nature.

Woolly

Distortion of the low frequencies often comes off woolly. Used aggressively, it can start to sound unstable, as the low-end energy causes an especially dirty breakup. Used judiciously, woolly distortion can be relatively inaudible beyond a slight bit of breakup in the low end, which is often masked. Rock Bass guitars love woolly distortion, although they can consume your entire mix when used too overtly. Kik drums react well to woolly distortion too. While it's true that woolly distortion can add clarity for transient instruments, it can also obfuscate instruments that sustain.

Tape Saturation

Tape saturation plugins are merely distortion plugins. The effect is supposed to emulate the sound of hitting tape too hard, but they've become almost cartoon-like in their modeling. The sound of uber-aggressive levels to tape was typically used as an effect, not as a matter of course. Most of us used tape for purposes of fidelity. But there were some engineers (especially in the nineties) who virtually claimed the overt sound of crushing tape on all of their records. As if that was ever a popular sound.

Tape saturation distortion supposedly models odd harmonic distortion which is, indeed, the kind of distortion you can expect from a tape machine. Basically, a saturator distorts the early odd harmonics. Don't ask me how or why the early odd harmonics distort from tape. I couldn't tell you nor do I care. All I know is I've never heard a tape saturation plugin that actually sounds like tape, likely because they're all way too overt in how they schmear the sound.

Some people claim to put tape saturation plugins on nearly everything, and that's a great way to turn your production into a woolly mess lacking any kind of clarity. Don't believe for a moment that tape saturation plugins have anything to do with the sound of analog tape. They really don't.

I adore the sound of tape given that it reproduces far more musically than the digital platform. Yet, I can't stand the sound of most tape saturation plugins given how unmusical they are. Call me crazy, but I don't typically go out of my way to be unmusical in my decision-making. My advice is to use tape saturation sparingly, purely as a way to add distortion.

I would be remiss were I not to mention, there are some tape machine modeling plugins that are meant to offer the sound of tape. These can offer good things, and should not be lumped in with tape saturation plugins, which are designed to mangle the tone.

Saturation

Saturation distortion is like tape saturation on steroids, which is actually far more useful as it gives you considerably more control over the tone. It allows you to absolutely drench a part in overt distortion, but it can also be used in more subtle ways. Saturation plugins can be extremely useful, and are a staple in modern pop music at the moment. Don't let that dissuade you from using one.

Spitting

Spitting distortion can be derived from any frequency range and produces a feeling of instability as the breakup is almost random in nature. The spitting distortion can at times sound like digital pops, mixed in with some other kinds of breakup distortion.

Tube Distortion

Tubes, sometimes called valves, introduce even-order distortion, which is supposed to be less musical than odd, but I'm not even sure I know what that means anymore as I personally find tube distortion to be rather pleasing in nature. The beauty of tubes is they can absolutely sing if given enough level, making them excellent for sustain. Valve distortion is often described as "warm," as it resonates most apparently in the lower midrange, and therefore, acts as a thickening agent. It's particularly effective at providing sustain, without overt top-end distortion, although you can certainly get a tube to buzz if you desire.

Tube Screamer

Tube screamer distortion is an emulation of valve distortion, and is derived from a pedal. They are often used to inject more gain to an amplifier for purposes of sustain. Tube screamers tend to filter out the top and bottom end, placing them squarely in the midrange. As a result, they can make power chords sound downright small, but they can be quite useful for apparent midrange.

Breakup

Breakup is mild distortion in which there is minimal sustain and resonance. Breakup is effective on virtually any instrument, including vocals. Electric guitars that are too clean in tone can sound downright anemic, and often do well with a touch of breakup. It's still a clean guitar, it's just that now you've added a little spice to make it pop in the production. Breakup can be derived either with a guitar amp, preamp, or plugin.

Distortion Levels

Now that we've established the importance and diversity of distortion properties, we should probably discuss levels of distortion. How much distortion is too much distortion?

It depends on the production, of course. Some productions call for distortion on virtually everything. Others call for very little overtly audible distortion. But you always want to introduce some measure of distortion.

So, where's the line? You can make the track pure white noise if you think it's going to sell records. Excess distortion is a matter of taste and would fall under artistic license. Too little distortion on the other hand is a technical issue. Because you never actually want too little distortion. A record without distortion is like food without seasoning. It lacks flavor.

Throughout the history of recording you would have to go way the hell out of your way to record too cleanly. You would need preamps with exceptionally low distortion specs, which you would gain super conservatively. You had to avoid most EQs, or at least you had to avoid EQ boosts, particularly in the high-end frequencies. You had to choose compressors that had super low THD specs. Of course, none of that changed the fact that you introduced distortion when you went to tape. And then there was the consumer's turntable stylus, which would also introduce distortion. For most of my career it was actually difficult to avoid distortion.

When it comes to distortion, the mic pres that come in interfaces generally don't help matters. I'm not going to malign interface pres as a group as they're not unuseful for home recording, and they're rather prevalent to boot. You just need to understand how they distort, if at all. That said, as much as you might prefer to introduce some distortion at the mic pre, there are other stages from which to derive it.

You should choose your distortion based on your production needs. If I'm mixing a dense production, and I find it difficult to make the bass note movements audible, then I can use distortion for purposes of clarity. If my part is transient in nature, and in need of either some thickening or punch, then saturation can help with that. Gain on a guitar amp will provide distortion for purposes of sustain and edge.

All distortion can be made to agitate, which probably has more to do with the ratio of top-end information than any other factor. Pleasing distortion tends to roll off at the top end, and the distortion of the upper harmonics provides us with clarity. If copious levels of upper midrange and top end are a part of the distortion makeup, agitation will undoubtedly be the result.

Kik drums are routinely distorted in my productions, and you might not ever even notice. That's the thing about low-end distortion. It's not necessarily audible in context, and often acts more like a thickening agent. Sometimes I want to hear the distortion on the kik drum, but then that's often for purposes of edge. I'm also often using distortion in conjunction with compression to assist with punch.

I suppose the big takeaway is this: If your equipment isn't introducing enough distortion, and your production sounds anemic, lacks edge, punch, or clarity, then you can use distortion to help with any and all of those maladies.

Processing

Processing is anything that you do to alter the nature of the signal. Equalization, compression, limiting, distortion, reverbs, delays, modulation, tuning, timing, sample replacement—all of this alters the original signal and is, therefore, considered processing.

Purity is not your friend where it comes to processing. There are no rewards for minimal processing, and there are no penalties for aggressive processing. It's just how we manipulate and shape the sound for the benefit of the music. In other words, processing is an important part of making a Killer Record. And the most commonly used processing tool of them all would have to be EQ.

Equalizers (EQ)

Our best weapons for shaping frequencies within our production is EQ. There are a number of varieties of EQ available, but the only one that we need to concern ourselves with is the parametric EQ—the most commonly used EQ in record production.

Bell Curve

There are two types of EQ adjustments on a parametric EQ—bell curve and shelf. A bell curve EQ places the selected fundamental frequency in the center of a specified range of frequencies, which taper off to make the curve.

The width of the bell curve is determined by the Q factor, and the wider the Q the more frequencies affected by your EQ. We call that range of frequencies the bandwidth. The center frequency is the loudest frequency in the bandwidth, and as the frequencies extend outward, the curve dissipates.

A bell curve looks like this:

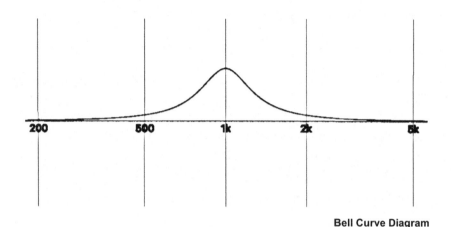

Bell Curve Diagram

Shelf

Shelving EQ, of which there are only two—high shelf and low shelf—also affects a range of frequencies, but the selected frequency is the starting point, not the middle point. For example, a high-frequency shelf set to 10 kHz will affect all frequencies from 10 kHz up, regardless of whether you're applying a cut or boost. Conversely, a low-frequency shelf set to 100 Hz will affect all frequencies from 100 Hz down.

All of that said, the Q Factor also affects shelves, and if you widen the Q all the way, your starting frequency becomes the middle frequency as you soften the curve of the shelf. The widest Q factor setting on a shelf is relatively useless as it affects way too many frequencies. A narrow Q affects frequencies above the Q point, which is generally what you want from a shelf.

A shelf looks like this:

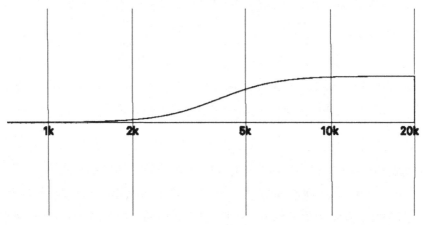

Shelf Diagram

Which probably has you wondering when to use a shelf, and when to use a bell curve. Well, if you want to bring out or cut a particular band of frequencies, then you would use a bell curve. If you merely want to adjust the totality of your top or bottom end on a part, then you use a shelf.

That said, there's really no right or wrong way to EQ. All that matters is what you hear. And if it sounds right, it is right.

Filters

There are two kinds of filters on your parametric EQ: the high-pass filter (HPF), which allows the high frequencies to pass unabated, and the low-pass filter (LPF), which allows the low frequencies to pass unabated. That's right. The high-pass is used to eradicate low end from a part. And a low-pass is used to filter out top end from a part. That doesn't make things confusing at all!

A high-pass filter set to 100 Hz will eradicate all frequencies from 100 Hz down. A low-pass filter set to 10 kHz will filter out all frequencies from 10 kHz up.

I've seen some engineers, particularly outside of the United States, put high-pass filters on all channels as a matter of course. This is at the mic pre, mind you, which means it's recorded that way, and when you eradicate frequencies on your capture, there is no getting them back. Unless there's some low-end artifact from the room that you need to remove, I would generally recommend against this. You really can't determine how far down you want the bottom end to extend until you have the entire arrangement at your disposal.

When viewed from the totality of my entire career, I surely implement high-pass filters far more often than low-pass, although I now use low-pass filters more frequently than ever before. Why is that? I'm not exactly sure. But I don't believe it's that I've changed. I think more people tend to record with overly bright microphones.

I should tell you, a low-pass filter can really dull things considerably, and it's not usually the best way to shape the top end of a part. Oftentimes, if I apply a low-pass to a guitar part, it's because I want to diminish the sizzle on the top end, in order to make the upper midrange more apparent. This can help to derive more presence out of electric guitars. It can also assist with any masking caused by the cymbals. If you find a filter too aggressive (and the LPFs often are) then try a shelf set above 16 kHz. This will allow you to attenuate the top end without eradicating it.

High-pass filters can be used to tone-shape the bottom end, particularly if you want to get control of the subs in your bass or kik for purposes of clarity. But if you use a high-pass to basically eradicate all the sub-frequencies from your low-end instruments, you could remove valuable information. Remember, an overlap in frequency between instruments is natural. You don't want to eradicate masking. You want to control it through tone-shaping and level.

Keep in mind, it's your sub-frequency information that helps a track appear big. You want to shape your low-end information so that it all works together in balance, but you don't want to kill your subs in the process. As difficult as it is to balance a robust low end, it can actually be more difficult to balance your record without it.

The Q Factor

Your Q factor allows you to select the range of frequencies that you'll affect with your adjustments, and you have the ability to narrow and broaden the bandwidth substantially. As a rule of thumb, overly broad bandwidths affect far too many frequencies to be useful, and overly narrow bandwidths address too few.

According to Wiki, Q factor is a parameter that describes the resonance behavior of an underdamped harmonic oscillator. Uh huh. That's all well and good, and it's even interesting, but in practical terms, the Q factor ranges from the broadest range of 0.10 to the narrowest of 100. The broadest setting will affect nearly all octaves, while the narrowest can literally generate a whistle within your part when boosted. As much as I hate to put values to these sorts of things (as they get taken as gospel), a Q factor of 0.71, which affects a two octave range of frequencies, is probably a good starting point. And in general, you don't want your Q factor above 2.0 as it starts to get a bit narrow. Mind you, that's out of a possible 100.

The narrower the bandwidth, the more surgical your EQ. Super narrow bandwidths are referred to as a notch EQ, and this is used to fix a resonance in your capture. You literally notch out an overabundance of a narrow frequency curve.

Aggressive EQ techniques are used to fix and to mangle. Subtle to moderate EQ techniques are used to tone-shape. The more command you have over your production and recording, the less you should need aggressive EQ techniques. I mean, if you're hearing a problem at a time when you have control over the source, that would be the best time to fix it.

Tilt

Some EQs come with a tilt function, which is a handy dandy little mode that is likely to become more prevalent in plugins over time. Visually, the tilt looks like a seesaw on a frequency fulcrum in the middle of the bandwidth. Tilt the seesaw to the left and you attenuate the low end as you boost the top end. Tilt the seesaw to the right and you attenuate the top end and as you boost the low end. If all you need is to gently open up a tone, the Tilt function is a great way to do it.

Frequency Analyzers

DAW EQs usually provide the mixer with a visual representation of the frequency manipulation, which allows you to see the range of frequencies you're affecting. While the visual modeling is useless for EQ decisions (those are made purely by ear), it's quite useful in accelerating your understanding of frequency and EQ in general.

Most DAW EQs include a frequency analyzer. I advise young mixers and engineers to keep their analyzers off because it's important that they develop their ears and not depend on visual crutches. For musicians? A visual representation could be useful, so long as you understand what you're looking at.

Analyzers can be a bit deceiving since your parts will not generally appear perfectly flat, nor should they. Even your mix won't look flat, and you could very well find yourself boosting outrageous levels of top end just to get the analyzer to look right. Don't do that.

An analyzer displays the general frequency makeup of a part, including any buildup of a particular frequency, but that buildup doesn't automatically indicate a problem. I mean, I'd expect an excess of low-end information on my bass guitar or kik drum. So, if your goal is to make the frequency response look flat on every part, that would be a very bad goal indeed.

It's best to use the analyzer to confirm what you're hearing, not to define it. A visual bump at 750 Hz on an acoustic guitar could be readily apparent on the frequency analyzer. But that 750Hz bump that you see on the analyzer could potentially offer a sum positive within the production despite the appearance of a boxy tone. And while you will cut 750 Hz far more often than you'll boost it, if the overall production benefits from the 750 Hz bump in the guitar, it would make sense to keep that frequency, even if it appears out of balance on the analyzer in relation to the guitar itself. This is why it's best to trust your ears, and use your eyes to verify, not the other way around.

The most effective way to find offensive frequencies by ear is to boost and sweep. Don't be shy. Boost as much as 4-6 dB if you like, and even more if you need because you're on a fact-finding mission. You want to purposely make frequencies sing and then search out the most obnoxious frequency by sweeping across the spectrum. When a frequency range sings in a particularly unappealing way, cut it. How much you cut is determined by ear, but when you blast yourself with an overabundance of a frequency like that it can take a moment to reset. You may even have to return to further adjust your cut. If you notice there are problematic frequencies in close proximity to one another, then widen the Q. If you notice another problematic frequency elsewhere in the spectrum, open up another bandwidth, and cut that one too. You can even put EQ modules in series if it makes life easier.

EQ Strategies

Many of you have probably read the claims online that it's better to implement an EQ cut than an EQ boost. Which is somewhat true when it comes to notch EQ, but some go so far as to suggest that a professional mixer will never apply an EQ boost. Nothing could be further from the truth.

In terms of technique, I give no thought whatsoever to whether I'm cutting or boosting. That's a decision that's made based on the realities at hand. And while there are many general rules that you would do well to follow where it comes to record-making, there are other rules that are so downright archaic they may as well be myth. This is one of them.

The advice all stems from the days of tape, which also introduces hiss. And when you boost top end off tape, you boost the hiss too. So, if you were to boost top end on the playback of every channel from an analog 24-track recording, the result could very well be an unbearable level of noise.

Further, many analog EQs introduce top-end distortion which is exhausting for the listener. As a result, engineers from analog days would actively avoid top-end EQ boosts when possible, so as to limit the compounding of added hiss and distortion. It's not that the mixer wouldn't ever boost. Sometimes a top-end boost is the best approach. But there was some strategy involved.

The EQ boost myth was the same myth 30 years ago as it is today. It's just that it wasn't totally bad advice back then, given the artifacts of analog tape. But now? It makes no sense whatsoever, particularly when you consider that DAW EQs don't tend to model the overt top-end distortion properties of shitty analog EQs. Therefore, you can pretty much boost and cut your EQ with impunity.

Many of your EQ tonal decisions will have to do with swapping frequencies. For instance, when it comes to the kik drum and bass, you want one of them to live lower than the other in terms of frequency. If the kik drum is blooming at 50 Hz, and your bass is also living down in that range, then it can be difficult to derive clarity between the two low-end instruments. You will have a far easier time blending the two if you give your kik and your bass their own fundamental low-end territory. In this example, you can bring the fundamental frequency of the kik up an octave by cutting 50 Hz and boosting 100 Hz, thereby providing more room for your bass. Sometimes, you want the kik to live under the bass, all of this is program dependent.

I go out of my way to encourage aggressiveness when it comes to recording and producing, because timidity is a terrible mindset for creating Art. If a part requires an outrageous EQ curve to work, there's no reason to hesitate. But many parts may only need a slight bit of EQ shaping, if any at all. So, yes, mangle with EQ when it's called for, but if a part seems to be working within the context of the arrangement, leave it be.

EQ in Solo

Another one of my favorite myths is the idea that one should never EQ in solo. Or better yet, the claim that a professional would never EQ in solo. Laughable.

I'll grant you, if you solo every instrument and EQ each of them in isolation with absolutely no regard for how your parts work together, you're going to have a tough go of it. Clearly, you should make your EQ shaping decisions based on how a part works within the context of the production, not in isolation. But when it comes to implementing those decisions, there's no reason to restrict yourself from monitoring in isolation.

In our kik and bass example above, the decision to alter the shape of the kik had nothing to do with the quality of the drum tone itself. A kik with a 50 Hz bloom could very well sound fantastic in isolation. We want to change the low-end shape purely so that it will play well with the bass guitar.

Not to put too fine a point on it, but the issue isn't the act of soloing in and of itself. The solo is there so that you can isolate a signal in order to magnify problems and remove distractions. The issue is ignoring the interdependency of all your decisions while in isolation.

The solo deniers believe it best to EQ a part as you listen to it in the context of the track. Surely that technique has merit, and if it proves preferable for you, then by all means use it. But don't believe for a second that you should limit your use of solo as a viable method for applying processing. Solo all you like.

Exciters

Exciters can be used to boost the upper harmonics from a selected frequency point. They are particularly useful for purposes of audibility as they also introduce some distortion. In general, they're used to fix problems of clarity, and I will often have one on bass, and will sometimes use them for vocals. It would be unusual to use more than one or two exciters in a production, so don't go crazy with these. As much as I love distortion, if you put an exciter on every channel that would be nothing short of overkill. If you're struggling to get a part to sit right with EQ, insert an exciter and see if that helps matters.

Sub-Frequency Generators

It's always dicey to add subs, but if the low frequencies have somehow been eradicated from a part, like your kik drum, or if you're working with a loop that needs some low-end assistance, a sub-frequency generator can save the day. I'm not sure how the hell they work, but practically speaking, they take the existing fundamental frequency and generate an undertone an octave below it. If your kik drum has a sharp drop-off below 100 Hz, a sub-frequency plugin can generate the missing frequencies. It's really super easy to add too much sub-frequency, which can put your low end completely out of whack. Use sub-frequency generators judiciously.

Compressors

Compressors are used to reduce dynamic range, shape tone, boost output, and control low end. They are useful and effective tools. Much like microphones, analog compressors are quite disparate in both tone and reaction, which many plugins model. Ostensibly, if you understand how the analog designs react, then you'll have an easier time choosing the right plugin for the job.

Used to the extreme, compressors can create fantastic effects. Used more judiciously, they can reduce your workload by allowing a part to sit within context of the track without losing important musical information due to masking.

Unfortunately, most DAWs offer just a single stock digital compressor designed to control dynamic range with little to no tonal benefit. That may not sound like a big deal, and it won't prevent you from making a Killer Record, but it most certainly won't make your life easier.

As if that's not enough, many 3rd party plugin companies don't reveal what they're modeling, or if they do, it's expressed through a graphic of a particular brand and model of compressor. If you don't know what the popular vintage compressors look like, you don't know what you're using. That's not the end of the world, but it does make it far more difficult to select a plugin based on analog design properties.

Ultimately, you need to learn your compressor(s) that you have available to you whatever they are.

VCA Compressor

Solid-state VCA (Voltage Controlled Amplifier) compressors impart minimal color to the tone, and they tend to have very responsive attack and release times, which makes them handy for dealing with transients or peaks like you'll find on drums. They are generally clean compressors, but will distort when set to the fastest attack time.

FET Compressor

FET (Field Effect Transistor) compressors are quite colored in nature, and are useful for both dynamic control and the shaping of tone. They tend to sound aggressive because they impart distortion artifacts, which is probably what we love most about them. FET compressors are likely the most useful of the bunch.

Valve or Tube Compressor

Valve or tube compressors impart obvious color and pleasant distortion qualities to your tone. They have generally much slower attack and release times than solid-state VCA compressors, and as such, aren't all that effective for the quick transients produced by drums.

Optical Compressor

Optical (or opto) compressors use a light source and sensor to compress. In general, optos offer relatively slow attack and smooth auto release curves. As a result they tend to shine on bass and vocals. Optical compressors are also more susceptible to some distortion. Sometimes they are referred to as leveling amplifiers.

Compressor Operation

There are just two ways to use a compressor. Audibly and inaudibly. Whether you choose to use a compressor in an aggressive and obvious manner, or in a subtle and transparent way, is an artistic decision, not a technical one. Aggressive use of compression can cause blatantly heavy breathing and bring in distortion artifacts—a tone that at times has artistic merit as a production technique.

The decision to use audible compression should make sense within the overall vision and context of the production. There are a number of ways in which to make compression more apparent. You can lop off the initial transient with a compressor. You can put a part in a steady state, such that it has no apparent dynamic whatsoever. You can increase the apparent size of a room. You can cause obvious breathing artifacts. You can create a sudden dynamic change called fortepiano (*fp*). You can introduce distortion. You can make a part feel aggressive. Or, you can simply control the dynamic range to prevent a part from disappearing into the arrangement. I'm going to explain how to accomplish all of these.

The overall audibility of your compression will be largely dependent on your skill with a compressor. That said, if you understand how the compressor settings and controls work, you'll have a far easier time compressing with intent. Put simply? You need to make that compressor your bitch.

Ratio

Most compressors have selectable ratio settings. The higher the ratio, the more aggressive the compression as it relates to the threshold. A ratio of 4:1 will attenuate the level of the signal to 1 dB of output for every 4 dB of signal above the threshold. Yawn.

Here's the bottom line. A ratio of 2:1 is mild compression, 4:1 medium, 8:1 heavy, and a ratio of 10:1 or above means your compressor is technically functioning as a limiter, which just means your compression settings are super aggressive.

So what ratio should you use? That depends on the nature of your program material and the overall attributes of the compressor. Higher ratios will tend to be more audible, that's for sure. But if you're just looking for some dynamic control, then 4:1 is a good place to start.

Sometimes 4:1 isn't sufficient, at which point you can either increase the ratio, which will make the compression more audible, or put another compressor in series. In fact, I often have as many as four compressors in series on a vocal, with EQs before and after each of them. Maybe more if I need it. I can assure you, for someone like me who started in the analog world, I find the idea of putting four compressors in series absolutely ridiculous. Unfortunately, the modeled artifacts tend to occur way too early on plugins, and as a result, more layers of mild compression are needed in order to achieve inaudible compression.

Now, I'm not suggesting I put compressors in series on everything. I don't. Nor am I suggesting to avoid higher ratios. A high ratio doesn't automatically translate as audible compression. That would depend on the threshold, attack, and release settings. They all work together.

You certainly don't need to feel as though you must accomplish all of your compression with a single unit. If one compressor isn't enough, then go ahead and insert another one if you need it, and another one after that. Or you can use a higher ratio if you like. I pass no judgement on the aggressive nature of audible compression. It's a great way to bring some edge to a production. Just keep in mind, too much of it can be exhausting to the listener. Pick your spots.

Threshold

The threshold is how you set the level at which compression is applied. On an analog compressor the threshold could also be the input. Plugin compressors often have both an input and a threshold. The input will help to deal with any gain-staging issues. Use the threshold to adjust your compression.

As much as I'd love to give you values to help you set your threshold, that's not going to help all that much as it's wholly dependent on the level you're sending to it. I couldn't even tell you how aggressively to move the needle, because on some compressors the answer would be a little, and on others you can peg the meter. And besides, who the hell knows what you're really looking at in terms of metering on a plugin. That's up to the guy who programmed it.

The best way to learn a compressor is to constantly push it to its limits and back off, which will demonstrate where your compressor shines. This is true of all compressors, virtual or analog.

The Knee

Some compressors include a knee control, which determines how abruptly the compression takes hold after the threshold is passed. A hard knee is more abrupt and more audible. A soft knee is more gradual and less audible. So, if your compressor feels a little grabby and that's not working for you, try a softer knee. If you want your compressor more audible, try a harder knee.

Attack and Release Times

The most significant tonal settings on a compressor come from the attack and release times. And while it's true that some compressors don't include adjustable attack and release settings, they still have reaction times.

It's often your attack and release settings that determine whether a compressor is a good fit with the program in need of dynamic control. Parts that are transient in nature require a much faster compressor than long drawn-out parts.

The attack time of a compressor has to do with how quickly it can reduce the level of the source feeding it. The faster the attack setting, the more likely you are to lop off the initial transient. A slow attack allows more of the initial transient to pass before the compression fully takes hold.

An attack time of 0 ms, which is ostensibly immediate, will not only lop off any transients, it will also introduce obvious distortion artifacts. This is not a setting you should use often even if you generally prefer audible compression. Even an attack time of 1 ms will open up the tone considerably.

I have all of my compressor plugins set at a 50 ms default attack time, which isn't particularly fast, and I adjust from there. That's probably a useful setting more times than not as it's enough time for an initial transient to pass, but not so much time that we can readily hear the compressor grabbing hold.

The release time has to do with how quickly the compressor resets after compression takes hold. A fast release time allows the signal to pass unabated almost immediately after the initial compression takes place. A slow release will cause the compressor to reset slowly over time.

Slow release times result in a less dynamic part and less audible compression given the gentle ramp. That said, a sudden transient can become quite apparent—especially with a fast attack setting—as the compressor can react almost violently to it, such that the sound will all but disappear before it slowly ramps back up. That seems downright useful.

A cymbal crash overdub pushed into a compressor with a rather fast attack time of 20 ms and a full five seconds release time, can result in a loud initial attack of the crash, followed by a sudden near-null, at which point the cymbal slowly ramps back into audibility. You can literally put a hole in your audio using a compressor like this. Of course, if your cymbal naturally dissipates too quickly, then you may have to shorten that five-second ramp. Everything is source dependent.

Whereas a slow release time on a kik drum will tend to attenuate the low end significantly as the compressor clamps down on the low-end bloom, a fast release will allow the low-end bloom to pass unabated. So, if you have a kik drum with a problematic sub-frequency bloom or an overbearing ring, you can contain those maladies by slowing down the release time considerably. If you just want to compress the initial attack of the kik drum without attenuating the low end, then a fast attack and a fast release would be your best setting. It's impossible to give specific values on this because there are far too many variables.

Auto Release

Most plugin compressors will include an Auto release function which allows the compressor to react to the program material in a dynamic manner.

When Auto is selected, there is a fast initial release for purposes of loudness, followed by a slow release to help smooth the transition. It's both a fast and a slow release in one, and it can be exceptionally useful for inaudible compression, as the ramp in release time greatly reduces the chance of pumping and breathing artifacts.

Where it comes to inaudible compression, Auto is probably the safest setting. That doesn't always make it the best. But it's not a bad place to start. The Auto function allows you to be aggressive with the compressor with less chance of artifacts. And if there's a problem that's best addressed with a more aggressive release time, all you need do is deselect the Auto.

As much as I'd love to tell you specifically how to set up a compressor for any given situation, my settings correlate with how the compressors in my DAW react. Seeing as a millisecond is clearly defined by the atomic clock, you would think the attack and release settings would be identical in all DAWs. Unfortunately, we can't count on that. A model is not electronics reacting to sound. A model is someone's programmed version that may not show an accurate visible representation of what's happening. There's just no getting around using your ears.

Audible Compression

If it's audible compression that you seek, you can use your attack and release settings to great effect. For instance, if you wish to extend the apparent size of a drum room, you can do so with super-fast attack and super-fast release setting. This will attenuate the initial attack of the direct signal, while allowing the ambient information to pass unabated. Set the attack to 0 ms and you will also introduce copious amounts of distortion. This is an exceptionally effective treatment for drum room mics, as you can increase the apparent size of the room with the extended reverb time, and introduce distortion at the same time. While it's true the 0 ms attack setting will lop off the transients from the room mic(s), we can derive our transient information from the close mics. That said, this doesn't work all that great in a lousy sounding room, as all you end up accomplishing is bringing out everything that's bad about it.

A snare drum compressor with an aggressively fast attack setting of around 5 ms or less will result in a lopped off transient, which is somehow the championed snare tone of Indie rock bands the world over. It has a very particular sound to it, which may or may not be appropriate for a particular production. I'll let you figure that out.

The long attack and release times of valve compressors can be used to great effect too. Used aggressively on a piano, for instance, you can significantly boost the overtone information, thereby creating an exceptionally rich steady-state tone. Don't be shy with threshold or ratios when seeking this effect.

It's important that you are aware that altering attack and release times will often require a threshold adjustment. Going from a slow attack to a fast one will immediately increase the compression. In fact, everything on a compressor is interdependent, so any aggressive alteration of one control will likely require adjustments to the others.

When to Apply Compression

So, when should you apply compression? Any time you're having issues with dynamics. A part that dips in and out of audibility in your production would be a good candidate for a compressor, as it will even out the dynamics and allow you to more easily balance it without automation.

That said, it is not a great tool for evening out the dynamics between sections. A verse guitar on the same track as the chorus guitar might require a level adjustment between sections. That kind of dynamic is best dealt with through automation not compression. You could also give the chorus guitar its own track for processing, which would be my preferred method for dealing with that sort of issue.

No matter how well you think you know your compressors, there is still some measure of randomness involved in the selection process. If a compressor is imparting a tone that is counter to your goals, switch it out for something more appropriate or take it off completely.

Regardless of your best guess or the counsel of others, compressors should ultimately be set by ear. There are no general rules or presets for which to rely upon. You should, and will, use every combination of attack, release, and ratio settings available over time, and there is no ideal setting. It's all program-dependent.

A vocalist singing a long drawn-out melody, in which the tails of her notes all but disappear, will require a far longer release time than an MC performing a more percussive rap. So, your release times are often set based on the nature of the part. Further complicating matters, if you're applying aggressive compression on a vocal with a fast release, the tails of phrases could actually come up in level as the compressor resets. Conversely, a slow attack time on a vocal can result in the first word of every phrase popping out. You can deal with both of these issues with automation, but wouldn't it make more sense to adjust the attack and release times? There is some measure of critical thinking that is required with all of this.

Let me lay out the procedure for you. First, you listen to the part in the context of where you'd like to hear it in the balance. Then you evaluate how it falls short, if at all. Then you apply the processing that you believe will assist with the problem. If that doesn't make things better, then you try your next best guess, and you continue to do this until you've fixed the problem.

Compression in Series

Layered compression can be useful for controlling dynamics without bringing out artifacts. That said, the only instruments that tend to get any kind of compression in series are the ones that have low end and appear in the middle of the sound field, which is pretty much kik, bass, and vocal. Nearly everything else typically only requires one compressor, even the plugin variety.

The kik and the bass form the foundation of the track, and it's critical that they stay rock solid in your production, and the best way to accomplish that is with compression, perhaps even in series. That said, if your kik is programmed and has no dynamic, there's not a whole lot of point to compressing even for purposes of tone-shaping, which can be handled by EQ. An organically recorded kik on the other hand, could require copious compression in order to keep that foundation rock solid.

We tend to put enormous low end on records these days, which is how it should be, but that requires practice. The low end is what separates the men from the boys in this business, and if you want a big low end, you need to be willing to push that low end into the compressor, allow the compressor to attenuate it, and then add it back in on the other side of that compressor. And if that's not enough, add another EQ and compressor on the bus. I can assure you, if you get that low end dynamically contained, the rest of the record will fall into place.

Of course, it's the vocal that's the main focal point in the production. As such, you certainly don't want that vocal dipping out of audibility on one phrase only to tear your head off on the next. And while we don't necessarily want to put the vocal in a steady state, that's likely better than an overly dynamic vocal, and that's saying something.

Typically, I put an EQ in front of and behind every compressor on my vocal. I also often set unique attack and release times for each compressor in series. How I set each compressor is totally program dependent, of course, but I'll often employ varying attack and release times to my advantage. And if I want the compression audible? I'll hit at least one of them hard with a high ratio.

The EQs between the compressors can be quite handy for tone-shaping. For instance, in the case of a strident vocal, I can either attenuate the excessive 2 kHz frequency causing the strident nature of the vocal, or I can boost somewhere between 100 Hz and 200 Hz into the compressor. The boost of low end in conjunction with a slow release time will cause the compressor to attenuate that strident tone. It isn't a requirement to put an EQ between every compressor. I have them inserted like this on my sessions purely for speed. If I need EQ before any given compressor, the EQ is already there. If I don't, it just stays in bypass.

In general, it's not a bad idea to do surgical EQ before the compressor, and broad tone-shaping after the compressor, but as I already pointed out, your release setting can be just as effective as an EQ cut for problematic frequencies.

Multiband Compressor

The multiband compressor allows you to compress multiple frequency ranges individually. Typically there are five compression bandwidths spread from 20 Hz to 20 kHz. There could be more bands, there could be less. The individual bands can be narrowed or widened which will affect the width of the other bands. At all times, the five bands cover the full frequency range.

Not only can you adjust your compression for each band, you can also boost or cut the frequency range before the compression. You can adjust your attack and release settings for each band too.

All of that might sound rather handy, if not enticing. But as powerful as multiband compressors can be, they're aggressive tools, often best reserved for problematic parts. Some mastering engineers prefer to derive their loudness through copious multiband compression. But even as a mixer, I rarely use them as I find them too aggressive, and far too complicated for most situations.

Limiters

Limiters are basically high-ratio compressors, which prevent the audio from passing a certain threshold. But when we use the term limiter, there's more than one kind.

Many compressor plugins include a Peak Limiter, which, when engaged, turns the output control from the compressor into an input control to the peak limiter, which will react to transients by knocking them down. This will often introduce some distortion to the signal.

In general though, what defines limiting is the ratio. A compressor set above 10:1 is limiting, and below 10:1 is compressing. There is nothing magical that happens when you cross the threshold of 10:1 to indicate you're limiting rather than compressing. That said, limiting is considerably more aggressive because of the high ratios.

Whereas compression tends to react to the bottom of the mix by pushing it up, limiting reacts to the top of the mix by pushing it down. That very well could be a ridiculously, stupidly, over-simplified explanation that has nothing to do with how a limiter actually works, but practically speaking, if you think about it in those terms, you'll have a better idea of when to use one over the other.

Limiters should not be confused with brickwall limiters, which have a ratio of infinity to one and will prevent a signal from passing a certain output level regardless of the sonic consequences. Brickwall limiters are what we use on the entire mix to make it loud. It's a tool used for mastering a record for its final delivery. Really, you shouldn't use a brickwall limiter for any purpose other than to give yourself level on a mix or a reference.

Surely you won't die if you insert brickwall limiters throughout your production. You will, however, fuck up your record, and maybe the record after that, and perhaps even the record after that until you finally realize that maybe brickwall limiters are too aggressive for purposes of production. The problem is, they tend to put your parts in a steady state which provide you with instant satisfaction, as if you've figured this whole recording thing out. Then you listen to your track months later only to wonder why your record sounds so small.

Aggressive tools have their place. But I am compelled to warn you to be judicious with your aggressive tools, because if you use them in the normal course of your processing, you will cause yourself problems. What kind of problems? I don't know. It depends on the tool and what you're trying to do. But my goal isn't to keep you ignorant. My goal is to have you concentrate on the music and not the engineering. If you use your aggressive mangling tools for the usual course of processing, the engineering is all that you'll ever think about.

Limiters are too aggressive for most processing, unless you really want to hear the artifacts of the compressor. At which point you should use a limiter because the artifacts are useful for a record in need of a little bit of edge and dirtiness. But that becomes an artistic decision and not a technical one.

Here's the thing. You could apply some modicum of compression to every single part in a production and deliver an amazing track that does everything it should. But if you do that with limiters and multiband compressors? I can guarantee that your production is going to come out small, and you will spend far too much time on technical manipulations rather than on your music. I probably use a limiter once or twice on every mix.

And if I really want to hear audible compression, limiters can be great for that. So they do come in handy. Just not for everything all the time.

Stereo Compressors

Obviously, stereo compressors are useful for compressing stereo things. When you use stereo miking techniques, it's best to use a stereo compressor because it will deal with the sides together, thereby preventing strange interactions between the mics. In the analog world, stereo compressors require their own design characteristics. In your DAW, your mono compressors operate as stereo compressors too. It's really that simple.

Sidechain

Many compressors include a sidechain function, which allows you to compress a signal based on the input of another signal.

Radio stations use the sidechain as an easy way to automatically attenuate the music when the DJ speaks. A compressor is inserted on the music channel, and the DJs mic goes to the sidechain of the compressor. This way, when the DJ speaks, the compressor reacts, which then attenuates the level of the music. The attack and release times are used to set the fades, typically rather quick for both. When the DJ speaks, the music immediately drops 10 dB in level. When the DJ stops talking, the music ramps back in.

A sidechain can also be used to cause a synth pad to pulse by running a hi-hat signal into the sidechain of a compressor inserted on the synth channel. The compressor reacts to the input from the hat, which results in compression of the synth. If you want a more aggressive pulse, you can use the sidechain of a gate, which can be set to close momentarily based on the input from the hat.

Some engineers like to send their kik drum to the sidechain of their bass compressor, which will attenuate the bass every time there's a kik. If you read audio forums online, then you might be under the impression that engineers routinely, perhaps even always, sidechain their bass to the kik drum.

Somehow I've managed an entire career without ever doing that. Not even once. And I think if you listen to my records, you might find I have a pretty good command of my kik and my bass. So, it's okay to use this technique if it interests you or if it works for you, but don't believe for a moment that it's any kind of requirement to get a kik and a bass to play nice.

The relationship between the kik and the bass can be one of the more difficult balances to get right, and this seems to cause people to seek out more complicated ways of processing them. There is no magic bullet or technique that will make it easy to balance two parts in the same frequency range. There is only time and practice.

Parallel Compression

Parallel compression is achieved through combining an uncompressed signal with the compressed signal. Why would you want to do that? Because aggressive compression will attenuate low-end information, which for certain parts, like a kik drum, can be problematic. An aggressively compressed signal combined with the uncompressed signal will provide you the full blossom of your low end, in conjunction with the punchiness of an over-compressed transient. This is a particularly useful trick for hip-hop kik drums, as it can be difficult to get a huge low end while retaining the attack. Punch too.

I would recommend using an *efx* send for this, and we'll talk about how to route this shortly, but you can absolutely annihilate that kik drum through a compressor on your *efx* return and blend it back in to your phat kik to boost the attack. You can literally reduce the tone of that compressed signal down to nothing more than the tiniest pop if you're aggressive enough with the compressor. And you'll be shocked at how little of that pop you need.

You can also apply some EQ to your compressed signal which will allow you to dictate the nature of the attack. You can boost the presence range (750 Hz to 3kHz) into the compressor. And if you want to derive punch, you can push about 200 Hz into your parallel compressor. That's all a matter of taste.

Distortion is probably your best tool to derive punch, and you can use distortion in conjunction with your parallel compression. If you choose to distort, you might want to lighten up significantly on the compression, as the distortion will react best to the low end. Again, a little goes a long way on this.

Most plugin compressors now include a "mix" knob which essentially offers you parallel compression right from the compressor itself. Essentially, the mix knob will allow you to blend your uncompressed signal with the compressed one directly from the channel. I recommend the *efx* send method, because it allows you to mangle that compressed signal and blend it back in from the mixer, which can speed things up considerably, especially if you introduce other processing.

Some rock mixers are known to routinely place copious amounts of parallel compression on all of their drums. Some claim to use it on nearly everything. Personally, I don't tend to use parallel compression all that much. Kick drums, absolutely. Maybe even bass. But rarely will I parallel compress an entire drum kit, mostly because I compress my stereo bus. My purpose is not to dissuade you from parallel compression. It's a totally useful tool that you should have in your arsenal, even as a musician. I just don't want you to think that you should use it as a matter of course as some suggest on the Internet. Try parallel compression so that you know what it does. Use it when it makes sense for you. It's not something to live by.

Analog Compression

I had a conversation with my Sound Odyssey partner Ryan Earnhardt last week, and he pointed out that, although he finds his prosumer analog compressors nothing short of woolly in nature, he still finds them way better than any of his plugins. Sadly, I must agree with him.

This is not to say that the compressors in his DAW are bad. But they still don't react quite the way that an analog compressor does. I can be far more aggressive with an analog compressor than a plugin.

Of course, this was on a kik drum, which loves distortion, as do drums in general, and it's not surprising to me that a compressor with woolly distortion could offer a benefit. But that doesn't change the fact that a compressor that neither of us thinks is all that great, and which sells like gangbusters to the DIY crowd, is somehow better than the plugins. As Ryan describes it, he can put his analog compressor on a kik drum and it sounds instantly better. That's what we want from our compressors if we can get it. From any processing, really.

My purpose is not to bash plugins. There are plenty of plugins that make things instantly better when you insert them on a channel. They just don't tend to be the compressors. For whatever reason, analog compressors just don't react quite the same as the models. This is even true of the plugin models that I really like. That doesn't prevent us from making a Killer Record.

That said, analog compressors are useful, especially on the way in. When you have opportunities to use a quality analog compressor, take it.

De-Essers

Essentially, a de-esser is a compressor, which operates on a narrowly selected bandwidth that can fall anywhere within the range of 2 kHz to 16 kHz where the esses reside. The de-esser is designed to attenuate the problematic frequencies, but first you have to find them.

Most de-essers have a "listen" function, which allows you to solo the high-frequency bandwidth and sweep in order to find the problematic resonance. Once the offensive frequency presents itself, you can then attenuate that narrow band, which will reduce the level of your esses without necessarily dulling your vocal. That said, it's not a bad idea to introduce a slight boost with a high-end shelf after the de-esser.

A de-esser is used to remove overly-aggressive esses, which amount to annoying high-frequency bursts. The best way to reduce esses is through mic placement technique, but that's not always sufficient. Some singers have a deadly ess, some mics accentuate that ess, and compressors only bring those esses up in level. Cue up the de-esser.

I'm exceptionally aggressive with de-essers, as I find esses nothing short of annoying and always have. Some people like them, and as with anything, how aggressive you are is really a matter of taste. But you need to control the esses to prevent them from becoming a distraction.

De-essers used aggressively can cause a lisp, and can even eradicate the esses completely, neither of which is particularly natural. Personally, I find esses so annoying that I'd rather hear the occasional artifact than to be cut by 100 esses. Fortunately, the current trend is aggressive de-essing. I'm all for it.

You can usually be far more aggressive with the de-esser on background vocals. In fact, I often ask background singers to avoid sounding their esses at the beginning and the end of phrases as they sing, since those are the ones that tend to flam. This is especially so with stacked harmonies. Too many esses are nothing short of sloppy.

As a mixer I'll often remove the esses by hand from the beginning and end of phrases of stacked vocals by applying aggressive fades. Esses within the internal phrasing tend to be more in time, and as such can be dealt with by placing a de-esser on the vocals bus. You can de-ess the background vocals individually if you like, but you'll save time if you apply the processing at the background vocal busses.

De-essers can be frustrating to use, and as with anything some are better than others. But even the best de-esser can take some time to dial in. Generally, you don't want your de-esser audible, but you may have to make some compromises. You might even cause the occasional lisp.

Esses react well to reverb as the percussive nature of them results in a splash of space. This tends to soften the esses somewhat, but that doesn't necessarily supplant the need for a de-esser. Even with the splash of verb I can't stand esses. As with everything, that's a matter of taste, but currently, the trend is to aggressively remove them, sometimes to the point of sounding unnatural.

As you learn your de-esser, push it to its limits. There's no point in being timid with esses. Those short bursts of high-frequency distortion will blatantly stick out from the next room and will generally annoy the listener. You want to contain those.

efx Sends

Some of you might know them as Aux Sends but for whatever reason, it seems to confuse the shit out of people these days. Some DAWs refer to them as *efx* sends, which is perfectly fine by me since the whole point of them is to send to an effects unit from multiple channels all while keeping the direct signal in the stereo bus. That's why I like using them for parallel compression.

There are a number of ways to introduce effects. For example, you can insert an effects plugin last in your vocal chain and adjust your wet/dry balance at the reverb unit itself. Which is perfectly reasonable if you want to put reverb on a single lead vocal channel. But what if you have 20 vocals? Do you really want to insert a reverb on every channel and adjust the parameters on each of those reverb units individually? I'm thinking not. Even using copy and paste, that would be nothing short of inefficient.

Rather than to run 20 discrete reverbs with the identical settings, which would be quite processor intensive, it would seem to make more sense to send all of those vocals to one single reverb unit. This way, if you want to change your reverb patch, you only need to do it once.

Now an *efx* send is really just a bus. Whether your DAW refers to it that way, I couldn't say, but it's a path for audio which can be assigned and that makes it a bus. There are two main ways to send to a bus. You can bus through the output section of the channel, which is what we did when we made a kik bus by sending two kik drum mics to one channel for purposes of compression. Or you can bus with an *efx* send, which is basically a little volume knob located on each channel that you can assign to a bus and use to send the signal to your effects processors.

Let's say you want to send 20 vocals to one reverb. You might want to have some control over the blend of vocals sent to that reverb. Perhaps the high harmony part is exciting the reverb more readily than the low harmony parts. That little volume knob on each channel allows you to balance how much signal you're sending from each channel.

The *efx* send provides you with control that is generally semi-independent of the channel fader. Why is it semi-independent? Because by default the send is located after the fader (at least it should be), which means how much you send to the reverb is also affected by the fader. This way, when you lower a part in the balance, the reverb level comes down with it, which leaves the ratio of wet to dry signal intact regardless of how you balance it. This is generally how you want your sends to react, but not always.

There will be times when you may want the channel fader to have absolutely no influence on the *efx* send whatsoever. We call this pre-fader, and it allows you to remove the dry signal from the stereo bus entirely without killing the reverb in the process. In fact, the most common reason to set a send to pre-fader, is so that you can fade out a channel to reverb or some other effect.

Then there's the pan knob, and this is where things get interesting. Typically, the send is before the pan. So that means a tom drum panned hard left will excite the reverb across the entire stereo image as if the tom was placed on the left side of a reverberant room. This creates the illusion that your tom is in a room, and the stereo field forms the boundaries of that room.

Sometimes we want the pan after the send (post pan) which allows the reverb to follow the direct signal wherever it goes in the stereo field. A tom panned to the left will only excite the reverb on the left side, rather than across the entire sound field. This creates the illusion that the tom is coming from distance outside of the confines of a room.

Conceptually, were you to record an electric guitar with reverb coming from the amp, that captured space will remain married to the guitar part regardless of where you pan it in the stereo field. This would be the same effect as sending a dry guitar to a *mono* reverb post pan. The reverb stays married to the part.

Of course, some of you are beside yourself at the idea of recording a guitar with reverb because you've been chided into recording everything dry and adding reverb later. Sure. If you want control, that's how you do it. But if you want to capture a vibe, you record the reverb from the amp.

There are some things that a canned effects unit can't recreate. There are guitar amps that have magical spring reverb units built in that a plugin can't rightly match. There are pedals that have a certain vibe to them, and these things can affect how you play. It's not critical to maintain full control of your reflectivity at all times. What's going to happen? You'll get fired? You have no one to answer to but yourself. If you like how something sounds go ahead and capture it that way. It'll be okay, I promise.

When a tone has a vibe it causes a certain feeling, and if you'd rather not risk losing that feeling, then this would not be the time for timidity. There are no rules, but were we to make one, it should probably be this: if what you're hearing has a vibe, record it like that. This would be similar to, "if it ain't broke, don't fix it."

Now, there's a reason why I'm spending some time discussing post and pre pan when it comes to your *efx* sends. When you send all of your mono instruments to stereo reverbs set such that they take up the entire sound field, you begin to wash things out with masking. Except you're masking the entire production, at which point you've made the whole thing sound soft. It's the sonic equivalent of an airbrush.

Mono delays can also be problematic. If your left and right panned guitars are both hitting delays that appear in the middle, then you've completely usurped the directionality of those guitars. You've also managed to muck up the middle. As such, you might consider marrying the location of the guitars with their delays in order to provide yourself a considerably wider image. This, in turn, will provide you with more clarity.

When it comes to an arrangement, clarity is the name of the game. There is absolutely no reason to keep a part that has no purpose other than to occupy space. If you place a part such that you really can't hear it, then the part shouldn't be in the arrangement. All you're doing is taking away clarity from everything else. Beethoven didn't put superfluous parts into his arrangements. Neither did Mozart or any other composer that you've heard of. So why should we?

Cuz it's creative, man.

I can't argue with your creativity, but I can tell you that, when you muck up the middle with delay returns from your sides, you mask the vocal, which will make it more difficult for you to balance that vocal given all the competition for center space. It's often a good idea to use pinpoint side instrument delays and verbs in your arrangement, because it gives the illusion of a wider sound field, which then provides more clarity in the middle.

Of course, if you want to maximize clarity, then don't introduce a ton of space. There's a reason why most rock productions introduce space on the drums, but not on the guitars. Because it allows us to provide the illusion of space without losing the immediacy of the guitars.

I would be remiss were I not to mention that it's important to set your reverb units output fully to "wet" when using an *efx* send. If you have any of the dry signal at all coming from your reverb, every time you increase your send, you'll also increase the dry signal in the balance, which will alter your wet to dry ratio. That's just going to make you hate life in a very special way.

Stereo keyboards also tend to muck up the middle, and many patches include reverb. Many producers like to stack their keyboards for texture, which is totally legit. But keyboard patches produce a generally weak stereo image and are often laden with stereo reverb. You will have a far easier time if you place your keyboard orchestrations in more specific locations within the stereo image. Moreover, you would do well to take full control over the space with *efx* sends, rather than to allow your stacked keyboards to oblite-rate clarity with internal stereo reverbs.

Reverb

There are really only two purposes for reverb. To create the illusion of space. And to mask imperfections.

We've discussed how reverbs will reduce clarity, but how would that be any different from masking imperfections? The answer is it wouldn't. It's just that if you're too aggressive in how you mask imperfections, the result is a reduction in clarity. There's a line.

In those times when you're feeling uncomfortable with your production, many of you will almost instinctively smother it with reverb in order to mask the imperfections. And your instincts could be well-founded. I mean, if you sound like a dying seal, then copious amounts of reverb could be exactly what you need. But if you smother everything in your production–even most things–with reverb, you're revealing to the world that you're not comfortable with your own record. Blatantly obfuscating your entire production only makes the imperfections more obvious.

Believe me, people know when you're trying to hide something. You're far better off to place your apparent weaknesses loud and proud, as no one will ever doubt your intent. In other words your confidence, or lack thereof, is revealed through your record. So, how do you deal with that? You fake it until you make it.

Whenever you catch yourself attempting to hide a part, either remove it entirely, or place it loud, regardless of its quality. If placing it loud is impos-sible because it completely fucks up the feel, that's not a confidence issue. That's a definitive problem with the part.

The decision to hide a problem part or to smother it with verb, or both, won't fix a thing. In some ways, excess verb makes matters worse, because the listener will focus on that fucked up part. This is why it's better to place your problem parts boldly in the production. Of course, that may include placing the reverb boldly too. You just can't have too many instances of prominently placed reverbs as they tend to mask each other. A vocal smothered in verb can be perfectly acceptable, so long as that space doesn't compete with other boldly placed reverbs.

A little reverb can go a long way. It's by no means a requirement to put copious levels of verb on all your drums. If you want that kik and snare in your face, you may want them dry and without any reverb at all. The absence of space is just as much an effect as the addition of it.

If you do apply reverb to the drums, the kik, snare, and toms are probably sufficient. In general, reverb on hats and cymbals tend to wash out the mix. And you certainly don't have to match your drum space with your vocal space, or any other space for that matter.

Bone dry drums in need of some slap do well with a gated reverb. You can place a gated verb prominently in the balance for a big canned drum tone. But used subtly, that gated reverb will often sound more natural than even a room patch. In general, the shorter the gated verb, the better. The trick is in how you balance it. You can also use a slapback delay as a tail to achieve a similar effect. We'll discuss delay tails shortly.

String patches and pads are often treated with verb, but we really only notice the space when there's a break in the action. Long sustaining parts that move fluidly are best served with less reverb, not more, as that verb mostly just eats space. Where it comes to added space on sustaining parts, there's a point of diminishing returns. By the time the reverb is obvious, you've masked your entire mix with it.

Crunch guitars–particularly sustaining ones–are best left dry as the reverbs tend to soften their tone by smoothing out their distortion properties. To soften tone is to mask imperfections. The problem is it's the imperfections that we happen to like about the distortion. We want to obfuscate those imperfections, why? That seems to be cross purposes. As per usual, there can be times a reverberant treatment on a crunch guitar is totally appropriate. For the most part, it's the tone of rookies.

There's just no way around it, there is a balance that must be achieved between space and clarity. I guess what I'm trying to say is, I can't really teach you taste. You have your taste, and I have mine. Considering I spent the first three years of my LA career mixing without any reverb whatsoever, and these past three years mixing with more reverb than ever before, I believe that answer might depend on the production trends of the time more than any other factor.

So, while I can't tell you where the line is, I can tell you this: When you find yourself wondering why there's no clarity to your production, or if you find the whole thing just sounds soft, you might want to reduce your overall reverb levels.

Natural Space

Sometimes, we use reverb purely to create space that wasn't there at the time of the recording. Sadly, there is no canned reverb that will adequately and naturally mimic an organic room. Halls can be remarkably convincing. Rooms, not so much. So, if your goal is natural room space, it's best if you can mic up a natural room as part of the capture.

You can also derive your space after the fact by blasting the part through a PA and capturing the room tone. You can turn any space into a reverb chamber, so long as there's enough action to it—that is to say reflectivity. Tile bathrooms make interesting chambers. Open living rooms with wood floors and vaulted ceilings make good chambers. Even stairwells make good chambers. In fact, I often open up the back stairwell door in my favorite recording room. This way, I can record the player in the room, but capture some beautiful reflectivity with a stereo mic in the stairwell. The closer I put the player to the stairwell, the more she excites the space.

The size of the space in conjunction with the material used to create it will dictate the action or reverb time. If you don't have spaces in your home that have action, then consider a field trip to a local church, or a rec center, or an empty house. Most recording rigs are mobile these days, and if a natural space is going to help set off a recording, then it's probably worth taking a field trip.

Intimacy

When it comes to reverb or lack thereof the main consideration should be intimacy. The more intimate your production, the less space.

The most intimate space occurs when you're wrapped up in the arms of someone you love. There is no reverb when your partner is singing in soft tones inches from your ear. And there is no intimacy at the back of a stadium filled with 20,000 adoring fans.

You achieve an intimate tone by close miking your singer in a neutral space. The addition of reverb would only serve to destroy that intimacy. Should you introduce a small room from your favorite reverb, you introduce the illusion that we're in the room with the Artist. As we increase the size of the reverb, we will reduce the level of intimacy.

Delays, on the other hand, provide the illusion of great distance. A delay combined with a large hall will place the singer in a stadium. There's nothing intimate about that.

Your song should dictate the level of intimacy you choose to present. And while some songs will require an obvious treatment, others could be more oblique. Seeing as you wrote the song, you would know better than anyone what your intent is, and I would say follow that first and foremost.

Choosing a Reverb

Where it comes to choosing a reverb, your first consideration is the nature of the space. Halls tend to be dark and large. Rooms are more contained with generally shorter reverb times. A room can be large, of course, but there's a point where a room becomes so large, that it would have to be defined as a Hall. For whatever reason, canned plate reverbs are often overly bright, and I have no earthly idea why seeing as real plates are generally warm. Spring reverbs are somewhat trashy sounding, or at least they should be, but not always. Gated reverbs supply a burst of space followed by the near-immediate dissipation of it. Used aggressively on drums, a gated reverb will deliver the big bombastic tone of eighties drums. Used sparingly, they can actually sound like a natural room.

Now there are some reverb units that you'll have to program from scratch. Those can do some really cool things, I'm sure. I almost never use them. I have so many more important things to think about than to spend time dicking around with a reverb unit, I can't even fathom it. I just fire through presets.

I realize that people will absolutely scream at you if you ask for a preset online. You can't use a preset! Sure you can. I mean, they're useless for EQs and compressors as there's way too many variables involved. But when it comes to reverb? It would seem to make far more sense to scroll through presets than to spend time trying to program one. Not only will you usually find a reverb that works really well, you'll also learn what your arsenal of reverbs sound like.

You may not know where to even start, in which case you can go through a process of elimination. Do you want a Hall? A Room? A Gate? Or a Plate? Sometimes when you're unsure of what you want, the best thing is to figure out what you *don't* want and go from there. As you familiarize yourself with your available reverbs, you'll start to have an easier time selecting the appropriate space.

Delays

Whereas a reverb provides us the illusion of space, a delay can provide the illusion of space and distance.

In general, I tend to stick to mono delays, which I prefer due to their pinpoint placement in the stereo field. Stereo delays have their uses, but they are better served with shorter delay times of under 250 ms. Otherwise, they tend to muck up the whole production.

A mono delay, on the other hand, can be set to offer you what sounds like a reverb tail, without eating up space in the process. How? First we need to discuss the settings on your typical mono delay.

Time

The time value dictates how long it takes between the initial signal and the delay. This value can be set based on note values, (i.e. quarter note, eighth note, sixteenth note), or as absolute time expressed in milliseconds.

Back in the olden days, you needed to use math to figure out what tempos went with which note values. Or you pulled out your handy dandy delay chart. These days, a delay unit will do the math for you. I'm going to explain it just the same.

Let's calculate the delay times for a tempo of 90 BPM (The Devil's Tempo). There are 1000 ms in a second, which means there are 60,000 ms in a minute. To determine the length of a quarter note in milliseconds, we divide our 60,000 ms by 90 beats to get a value of 666. Therefore, at 90 BPM a quarter note occurs every 666 ms. Which means an eighth note occurs every 333 ms. And a sixteenth note every 166 ms. And a quarter-note triplet is, well, erm that would require some more math. A quarter-note triplet occurs over the course of two beats. The half note value is then divided by 3. That would be 1332 ms / 3 = 444 ms. Fortunately, we rarely need to do these kinds of calculations anymore. Just set the delay to the note value you want and you're done.

Feedback

Before digital delays, we had tape delays. On a tape machine, the playback head (repro) is placed after the record head. It was the original version of latency, because you could monitor input off the record head, but you couldn't monitor the playback of the tape without a 50-60 ms delay caused by the physical distance between the heads. Somewhere along the line, someone realized they could use that latency to their advantage.

Tape machines also have speed settings, and if you slow the machine down, you will extend the time differential between the two heads. Whereas you could expect a 60 ms delay for a tape playing at 30 inches per second (ips), that became a 120 ms delay at 15 ips, and a 240 ms delay at 7.5 ips.

If you send the signal from your vocal to the tape machine, it will record the signal on the record head, then play the same signal delayed from the play head, the value of which is determined by the speed of playback. But that just offers us one repeat. In order to get more than one delay, we send the tape machine return back into the tape machine again, which will then be recorded and played back, multiple times depending on the level of the return. If you send so much that the return goes into the tape machine louder than the original vocal, then every subsequent repeat will get louder, at which point you lose control over your feedback. Which is why they call it feedback, because you are literally feeding the return back into the delay unit.

The beauty of tape delays is that each subsequent delay will lose fidelity and, therefore, get darker, grainier, and noisier in nature. A tape delay plugin will typically offer you the parameters needed to model these attributes.

Delay Filters

The filters are critically important when it comes to delay, because part of the illusion of great distance is caused by a loss of top end. A trumpet played in proximity to your position is going to sound considerably more brilliant than a trumpet played a mile away. That's because top end is absorbed more readily than low end, and by the time the sound reaches you, the top end has been sucked up by the environment.

The filters allow you to shape the tone of the delay. A high frequency roll-off helps with the illusion of distance, and the low frequency roll-off can help the delay cut through. The further away you want that delay to sound, the more you should filter the top end.

I suppose there could be times that you want your repeats to have the full frequency spectrum of the part, but it's rather unnatural and offers you no contrast between the part and the repeats. A roll-off of the top end will allow you to blend that delay into the part, and if it's a relatively short delay time, anywhere from 80 to 250 ms, you can use that darker delay to thicken a part.

It's almost routine for me to filter some amount of the top end from delays. That said, the part will dictate how aggressively you use your filters. But use them you should.

Mono Delay Tails

If you apply a robust feedback of 50-60 percent in combination with a rather short delay time between 50-200 ms, your mono delay will start to sound more like a reverb than a delay. This effect isn't ideal on super percussive parts because the delay starts to sound like a machine gun, but on parts like vocals or electric guitars you may find this spatial tone nothing short of useful.

As you increase your delay time, the repeats become more apparent, but with such a robust feedback setting, it will still sound rather reverberant in nature. Go ahead and filter off some top to enhance the effect, as that will serve to attenuate the apparent attack of the taps. Once you balance the delay with the dry signal, it can sound like a natural reverb.

The beauty of a mono tail, is it provides the illusion of space, without eating space in the process.

Short Delays

A 60 ms delay is super quick and is often referred to as a doubler. This effect will cause chorusing, and all sorts of wonderful masking. As a result, it's often used to obfuscate the unevenness of a part. It can also sound downright robotic, and if you seek a more natural tone, you would do better to just record an actual double of the part.

A slapback of 120 ms with absolutely no feedback will manifest as space too. Mind you, a short delay requires some modicum of percussiveness for the part to be effective, and this includes certain vocals. In other words, unless your goal is to obfuscate, slow-developing keyboard pads would derive little benefit from a delay this short.

A 250 ms delay with minimal feedback, or none, set back in the balance with a filtered top end is an excellent way to give a part the illusion of distance without losing any definition or clarity from a wash of reverb. A prominent 250 ms delay is useful too. But if the delay is too loud, it no longer feels like distance.

Once you get higher than 250 ms, you start to get into eighth note and quarter note time values, depending on the tempo. At a tempo of 120 BPM, that 250 ms delay is the equivalent of an eighth note. And at 90 BPM, an eighth note is equal to 333 ms. Once our times get up that high on a delay, it's more about the taps than space.

Taps

Taps are repeats, which occur at the higher delay times. I can tell you, a delay which manifests as taps can get a bit distracting when used as a tail. Stereo taps even more so. In general, when you get above an eighth note in time, and especially when you get as high as a quarter note, you'll want to automate your taps such that they only occur on certain words.

There are any number of ways to automate a tap, since you can automate just about any parameter in your DAW. I use *efx* sends to get to my tap delays, just like any other effects unit. This way, I can automate the send to open whenever I want to introduce the taps. I can also automate the level of my send.

You'll hear this effect all the time on the lead vocal. The last word of a vocal phrase will often get a repeat, typically a quarter note, but any value that you like, really. It's the automation that makes this work, because we can make far more out of those taps if they aren't sounding all the time.

Now, if you're wondering why I would automate an *efx* send rather than to just mute the return of the delay, there's a very good reason for that. It's not clean. If I'm sending to the delay all the time, then when I open the return, I will hear the previous phrases. The point of the automation is to send the words that I wish to repeat with precision.

If your track isn't cut to a tempo, then you'll have to adjust the delay manually, and you may never get it in perfect time, nor should you try. Frankly, productions without tempo restraints don't typically call for delay taps. I use taps fairly regularly, but I also often mix commercial music. Not all productions call for this.

Dry delay taps can stick out, which can be useful, but if you want to blend them more into the production, you can always add a splash of verb to them. It wouldn't be unusual for me to apply a little of the vocal reverb onto taps.

You can get as creative as you like with how you mangle and manipulate the delay. Distortion, tonal modulation, pitch modulation, flangers, automated panning, filters—all of these can be used in conjunction with the taps to create fascinatingly complex effects. Which can be called for and totally great if you want to invest the time on that sort of thing. Just be sure not to lose sight of the song and the production in the process.

Stereo Delays

I have received sessions from clients in which every vocal had a stereo delay on it, with the left set to a quarter note and the right set to an eighth note. In my 30 years of making records, that treatment has yet to work. This is often the stock setting of your DAW's stereo delay, and it does nothing other than to distract when set forward in the balance, and to obfuscate when set back.

I can promise, you almost never want a quarter note bouncing around all the time, even if it's to the side. There could be trippy sections with this sort of treatment. There could even be a trippy production. But, in general, you're far better off using automated delays than to just let a quarter note delay ride like that. As I said before, where it comes to stereo delays, you're far better off with shorter times.

As far as I'm concerned, the best use of a stereo delay is what we call ping pong, which basically pans the delay back and forth on the sides, but this too would be a candidate for an automated send.

Programmable Delays

Sometimes, you want the first delay to hit at a different time interval from the repeats. For example, you might want to repeat the last word of a vocal phrase such that the initial delay sounds at a dotted quarter with subsequent quarter note repeats. You can accomplish this in one of two ways. You can use a fully programmable delay unit, which allows you to manually place the repeats, the filter dissipation, and the panning. Or, you can insert two delays in series such that the dotted quarter delay goes to the quarter note delay for the repeats. This sort of effect is way easier if you have a fully programmable delay.

Modulation

Modulation includes choruses, flangers, Leslies, ensembles, phasers, tremolos, ring shifters, and the like. Each of them does its own thing, but they all do one thing the same–they add motion.

Chorus is the effect that occurs naturally when two instruments are playing the same part. The slight differences in tuning cause the parts to react, which provides subtle motion to the part. A chorus effect modulates the tone in a linear manner, which makes it less interesting than a natural chorus caused by double tracking a part, but that doesn't make it unuseful. If you want to obfuscate tuning issues, a chorus is a great way to do it.

Modulation units like chorus, ensemble, flangers, and phasers often also introduce distortion, and that's very handy for providing clarity in terms of balance. In other words, you can hide tuning issues and make the part more apparent at the same time.

Ensembles add harmonics, which add distortion, and essentially sound like a more filtered version of a chorus. Ensembles, choruses, and phasers can all be useful for background vocals, even ones that are in tune, at which point it's their distortion properties you seek. Used judiciously, the distortion can help stacked harmonies cut through a dense production, even if placed several dB below the lead vocals. Used aggressively, you can make the harmonies swim in motion.

Tremolo plugins can be used to provide motion either in volume or pan position. A stereo tremolo will ping pong a part back and forth from left to right. A mono tremolo oscillates the volume. Used lightly, they can sound like vibrato. Used aggressively, they provide rhythm and width.

Leslies are the speaker cabinets that make a B3 grind due to its spinning horns. Flangers sweep through the point of cancellation to produce a psychedelic motion.

Modulation can help set a mood, can cover tuning discrepancies, and can help to push parts forward due to their distortion properties. They can also make a boring part more interesting. Be careful with modulation. You can absolutely destroy the integrity of a production with too many instances of motion.

Tuning

Tuning plugins are a great way to kill everything musical about your production. They're also a great way to fix tuning issues. Go figure.

I said it before, I'll say it again. I can't teach you taste. As such I can't even teach you how to tune because you can be as aggressive as you like. Really, there is hardly a production that goes by these days in which the vocal tuning isn't obvious. Even a total lack of tuning is apparent. Just listen to an Adele record.

As far as I'm concerned, if no one is going to care about obvious tuning artifacts on a vocal, then there's no need to worry about the artifacts. Of course, it may date your record once that goes out of style. But I'm not sure that matters too much. That's true of nearly all records.

Some DAWs have tuning functionality built in, and it won't be long before they all do. For those without, if you want to tune parts by hand, then you'll need a third party package in order to do it.

More often than not, tuning is performed on vocals. Used with impunity, tuning acts more like an effect. Used judiciously, they can provide your production with some polish. Frankly, I'm not sure anyone even bothers to hide tuning anymore. And it most certainly doesn't require skill to perform a tuning job with obvious and apparent artifacts. Just set all the pitch controls to stun and let her rip.

If, on the other hand, your production calls for you to be somewhat more discerning, then you may wish to keep your tuning inaudible. Not only will invisible tuning require time and practice, there are tolerances. You can only pitch a note so far without hearing the artifacts, even with the formant parameter, which is used to tamp down on chipmunk tones through vowel manipulation.

Tuning is a slippery slope, especially on vocals. The moment you tune one note you've exposed tuning discrepancies on subsequent and preceding notes. It's like a cancer in the way it spreads. To tune one note will often force you to fix three. And then even more notes need tuning. Before you know it, you're on your way to a T-Pain sound-a-like competition.

That last statement is hyperbolic, of course, but make no mistake, the moment you start to tune, you'll find plenty more notes in need of tuning. The problem is, most people tune to a chromatic scale, which isn't all that natural, because there are certain notes that are meant to be flat or sharp based on the scale in conjunction with the harmony. Then there are some singers who naturally sing three cents flat as a matter of course. To bring them fully up to pitch is to destroy the sonic fingerprint that makes them unique. We aren't really meant to sing in perfect tune, and the effect of perfect chromatic tuning is changing the way that we hear in general.

I tell you this, not to dissuade you from tuning, but rather to make you aware. Not every note has to be dead on the pitch. And if you get the performance right, you shouldn't even notice the tuning discrepancies, and you might do well to keep the tuning natural. So, if you tune your vocal, perhaps compare it to the untuned vocal, to be sure that your manipulations have had a positive effect on your production. It never hurts to compare the before and the after of a tuning job.

The pitchier the performance, the more likely you are to introduce artifacts. In other words, the best way to get good at invisible tuning is to put yourself in a position to avoid it in the first place. The good news is, we have methods and means with which to record an amazing vocal performance that's also in tune, and it doesn't have to happen in one take. We will discuss those momentarily.

Tuning is not relegated to vocals, and there are even polyphonic tuning packages now, which are nothing short of a miracle. I can promise you though, if you use tuning as a matter of course on everything, your chances of a Killer Record plummet. You'll strip it of everything human.

I look at tuning like this. If a tuning issue jumps out and pulls me from the production in a negative way, I fix it. If I don't notice the tuning, I leave it. Just keep in mind, when you place your tuning under a visual microscope, issues that were unnoticeable before can become downright intolerable.

Tuning issues are often made manifest from monitoring problems. If your entire take is out of tune, and that's unusual, then you need to address the balances. Either you're too loud in your headphones and you're not deriving enough pitch from your monitor mix, or you're too low, and can't adequately track your own pitch. And if you're constantly out of time, then you can't hear enough of the rhythmic instruments. Many, if not most, vocal tuning and timing maladies are a result of a problematic monitor mix.

Many DAWs also come with Autotune, which will pull your parts into tune automatically based on a manually set time value. Autotune can be useful in a pinch, or for a part with minor tuning issues, but if you put Autotune on every harmony in a set of stacked vocals, things could get a little phasey and weird. The same is true if you hand-tune any kind of section, whether stacked vocals or a horn section, you can only get away with so much tuning before it's really obvious.

Again, obvious tuning can be precisely the effect you seek. In which case, tune with impunity. Otherwise, it's best if you get your performances right at the time of recording.

Comping and Punching

As much as we like to perform a part from top to bottom and move on to the next, that's rarely how it works. There are two basic strategies to over-dubbing—comping and punching.

A comp (short for composite) is a take that is compiled from several performances. Most DAWs have a system for comping takes, which allows you to take the best parts from multiple performances and stitch them together to make one new fabulous performance. Some DAWs place your takes in an expandable folder, which will allow you to quickly select among sections, phrases, words, and possibly even syllables, although those can get a little tricky.

Suppose we have a vocal in which you performed three takes, none of which are perfect on their own. You could use Take 1 (T1) for the first line, T2 for the second line, back to T1 for the next few words, and then to T3 for one word, and then back to T1 for the remainder of the phrase. This procedure continues down the track, and by the time you're done, you have a performance. Now, whether that performance is good enough or not, that's up to you. But this is a very effective procedure for constructing a take, as it keeps the integrity of the performance.

A great singer doesn't often need more than a few takes. A less than great singer could require considerably more than a few takes. So, if you don't like your first three takes, then you can always sing it another three times. You could sing it ten times if you like, but then you have to go through all of those takes, and that can get rather time consuming and draining to boot.

Once you construct your comp, it's not a bad idea to go in and try to beat it if you think that you can. You're warmed up. You have a vocal down, which will boost your confidence. And the pressure is off, which often manifests as a looser more compelling performance. You may beat the vocal comp out-right, or you may beat none of it. And if you only beat some parts, then you can comp the new takes into the existing comp.

Now, there's not much point to recording an entire part from the top if there's only one tiny little problem at the end of the song. For that we can simply punch in, which means we go into record at the point of our choosing. Of course, in many DAWs a punch-in will merely create a take folder wher-ever you're at in the track. So if you record a part on that section multiple times, you'll be able to comp it too.

When you're recording by yourself, a tight punch-in can be difficult if not impossible. Most DAWs will allow you to set an automatic entry and exit point, which will make the task considerably easier. You can also pick up a footswitch controller, if you like. Or you can even put your DAW into a loop which will allow you to record the same section multiple times without hav-ing to reset. That's a great way to shed a part, but at some point, you need to stop and give your brain a moment to process. There's a big difference be-tween playing notes and performing music.

It's important that you get into good habits in regards to how you over-dub. The more efficient you are in this regard, the better, as it allows you to concentrate on your performance rather than on the logistics of recording. Location points can speed things up considerably and help you to quickly find your spot in the production. Adequate and consistent preroll is helpful. And don't forget to give yourself a breath. Every now and then stop for a few seconds to mentally prepare for your next attempt.

When I'm running the session for my Artist, I tend to punch in at the precise entry point. This is habit caused from years of recording to analog tape. I realize we don't record in a destructive manner in our DAWs, but if you're recording someone else, it's still not a bad idea to perform your punch-ins with precision. It really helps the player with the transition from playback to record.

When it comes to vocals, I prefer to capture a performance from top to bottom, although that's not always possible. Occasionally, there's overlap between sections which requires a separate track. And sometimes there are sections best reserved for later, especially if the part is physically difficult to perform. I avoid screaming parts until the end of the day, possibly the end of the project, unless for some reason I want more rasp from the vocalist. Although, that can be a dangerous game to play.

If a vocal part is particularly tough, I might choose to record in sections rather than to ask my vocalist to perform the entire song. Some transitions can be challenging and some parts just a touch high, and these are two very good reasons for working in sections. Absent those possibilities, I'd much prefer to record a vocal performance from the top. I mean, if you can't sing it down for the record, then how the hell are you going to sing it live? If it's just a matter of practice—and I know this is going to sound crazy—just practice it.

Editing

There will be times when you have recorded a take that requires some editing in order to place it in better time. How aggressively you choose to edit has everything to do with how you want to present your production.

The edit process is a tough way to derive feel, but a great way to put things in time. You can also strip feel away if you're too aggressive, and that's rarely of benefit. If you want your production to sound programmed, then surely you should edit aggressively to the tempo grid. If you want the record to feel raw, then leave in all the mistakes other than perhaps the most distracting of them. It's the in-between that requires some modicum of taste.

There are two ways to edit. You can time stretch, which allows you to slide notes through compromise. Or you can cut and slide. Parts that are way out of time will require you to cut and slide them because time-stretching will introduce obvious artifacts.

An organic drum kit can be a bit of a pain in the ass to edit because you have to group those mics together and phase lock them. If you don't, you'll hear some rather whacky interactions between your mics. We'll discuss the kinds of interactions you can expect shortly, but when your mics are working well together, it's critical that they remain in their precise positions on the timeline. Of course, the moment you lock those drums together, whether there are four tracks or 11, you don't really have to think about it any longer. An edit on one track is an edit on them all.

As with any of our manipulation tools, you must consider the feel that you seek, as your aggression in this regard matters. An organic rock track edited to grid will yield a completely unique feeling to that same rock track left untouched. One is the sound of compliance. The other the sound of re-bellion. I personally never understood the whole corporate rock sound of the early *aughts*, and still don't. But these are the types of decisions that are made when you relinquish control of your Art to a large corporation that wishes to homogenize your product for purposes of predictability.

Anything that's electronic in nature will do well with quantization and editing to grid, but based on the relatively recent trends of complex poly-rhythms found in some programmed productions, there seems to be a backlash. These effects don't really take the track out of time, but they do provide the illusion of slowing down and speeding up. It's almost like breath-ing.

If all you want to do is edit large sections between takes, that's a rather easy process. It's when you adjust every kik and snare that things get a bit labor-intensive, and that kind of job requires some practice to do invisibly. The kiks and the snares are easy to move. It's the internal rhythms of the hats and cymbals that can get a bit squirrly. I don't typically prefer aggressive edit jobs on drums, but on those occasions when that's what I seek, I hire some-one with those particular skills to do the job. I would recommend you do the same. Yes, I realize you don't want to spend any money, neither do I. But it would take me many more hours to do a big edit job than someone who does it on a regular basis, and even the biggest edit jobs won't be prohibitively expensive.

All of that said, many of you will edit your own drum recording, which I also get. I do all sorts of things that I could hire someone else to do. Some-times it's just easier to do something yourself, and often it needs to be done in the here and the now. The best advice that I can give you for an invisible organic drum edit is to retain as much of the feel as you can. If you find some-thing distracting, fix it. Otherwise leave it alone.

Time Stretching

Many DAWs offer the ability to adjust timing discrepancies through time-stretching. As with all of our tools there are tolerances, and if you fall outside of those tolerances, you will introduce obvious artifacts. The good news is, you can always go to more traditional editing techniques if time-stretching isn't working out. You can also perform the part in better time.

I much prefer time-stretching to cut and slide techniques, but not eve-rything is a candidate for it. If you stretch something too far, it will get chipmunky quick. Keep in mind, even time-stretching requires you to phase lock your audio files, otherwise you could have some rather surprising re-sults.

I've used time-stretching to great effect on vocalists who tend to hold their notes too long. It may seem obnoxious for me to fix something like that as a mixer, and it probably is, but the singers don't seem to mind since it's far more musical in nature. If your goal is to become a great singer, forget about practicing your runs, it's your phrasing that sets you apart from the rest of the pack. I can find lots of singers who can perform amazing runs.

Show me a singer who understands how to phrase, and I'll show you one of the greats.

Sadly, time-stretching can only do so much for phrasing, but it's a great way to lightly fix timing issues on any instrument.

Here's my recommendation: Use comping and punching techniques to derive your feel and to get the part close, and use time-stretching techniques to fix the minor timing issues from your good-feeling parts. And if you want a programmed feel, then edit and quantize to grid.

You can practice your parts or you can practice your editing skills. The former will help you improve as a musician, the latter won't.

MIDI

These days most DAWs build software instruments into the platform, and we control these through MIDI. Typically, we interface with a MIDI controller such as a drum pad or a keyboard controller. Many DAWs include robust software instrument packs these days, which makes life really easy. For the most part this is all plug and play.

You have an enormous amount of control with MIDI instruments should you choose to exercise it. That said, it doesn't make a lot of sense to program a really dynamic MIDI part only to then compress it. There's also not a whole lot of point to compressing MIDI drums that all strike at 127, the top of the MIDI velocity scale.

You can program a MIDI part completely by hand if you like, but that would take an awful lot of time. It's probably easier to record the part as best you can and then manually alter the timings and the note durations.

Personally, I'll just play a part over and over again until I've got it really close. For starters, I go into record well before I'm ready to perform the part because I often want to capture my experimentation. Every now and then I play something completely by accident that's so dope I can't stand it, but if I'm unable to hear it back, that could very well be a one-time event lost to the ether.

There are all sorts of flavors that you can add with MIDI. There's portamento, which puts an automatic glissando between the notes of a monophonic synth part. There's also pitch bend and modulation which are sometimes programmed to provide expression variables. If you produce EDM, then you're surely familiar with the power of MIDI.

The EDM genre is insanely programmed and processed, and only you can determine how critical any of that is to your productions. I mean, if all you need is a little farfisa line, then find the patch and play the part. None of the rest matters. If you want to create a sonic movie in which there's all sorts of complicated motion, you have all the power you need to do it, all you really require is time.

External keyboards can be plugged into your direct inject inputs on your preamp to record the audio. It's not a terrible idea to capture the MIDI information at the same time. I mean, if your keyboardist can play amazingly, and you know the patch is precisely what you want, then there's not much point to that, I suppose. But if you have any doubts about the patch at all, then by all means, record the audio and the MIDI too.

Let me just say for the record, that I recognize the inherent disconnect between my insistence that you build a record with intent, and my suggestions that you record a DI or MIDI as backup in case you change your mind later. Much like Democracy, we must rely on certain norms, one of those being self-control and the other an ability to make a decision. Personally, I'm very good at making decisions. I'm not so great at ever truly committing to them. As a result, every save on a project is designed to provide me the ability to get back to any major stage of the project. And while that's just good saving habits, if I don't retain the discipline to move forward, then that could prove a time-consuming habit of second-guessing.

I can't save anyone from a lack of discipline, but one who lacks discipline can certainly employ strategies to minimize the ill effects of it. This all starts with knowing yourself. If recording something as backup is going to cause you to second-guess decisions down the road, then I would recommend you work at all times without a net. That is to say, record everything as you wish it to be, and forget about any kind of backup. Record your amps as you hear them. Commit to virtual amps by bouncing them down. Record your guitars with effects. Anything that you can do to force yourself to commit you should do. This way, to change your mind is such a pain in the ass, it makes more sense to just move forward.

Of course, if you're working in MIDI, you can change anything you like anytime you like, as it's all modular and programmable. I'm thinking if you have a difficult time committing to something, that would manifest itself in this medium.

The
Process

Recording can be the easiest thing in the world, or the most difficult. That's all up to you.

Most of you will record at home, or in a friend's home, or perhaps, even in a modest home studio, and the preponderance of my advice is tailored towards that reality. The best thing about recording at home? There's no pressure.

There's nothing wrong with pressure in and of itself. Some people absolutely require it. And as much as I insist you should get the pressure out of your way, that's not always possible nor desirable, even. But when you're making your Art at your house on your own time? The only pressure is that which you put upon yourself.

What will people think? Will I come off like a chump? Does it sound good? Am I good enough? Why isn't my music going viral? All of those are negative thoughts in which you are questioning your skills at a time when you should be doing and not thinking.

Of course, studio time comes with pressure. You have a clock, and you have a budget, and you must perform in an efficient manner in order to accomplish your goals. When you go on stage in front of an audience, that too comes with pressure, because if you play like crap, or if you don't engage, you'll lose the audience. In both cases, that's good pressure, because you're focused on the only thing that matters–how you perform.

As a producer, I use time management as a fulcrum to apply and relieve pressure from my Artists. When I feel like we're ahead, I take the pressure off so that we can experiment. When we're behind, I use that pressure to help push my Artists to perform.

There is an inherent advantage to hiring a recordist. You don't have to think about the recording technology at all. You don't have to think about the microphones, or their placement. You don't have to strategize over mic preamps or compressors. You don't have to concern yourself with recording levels or gain-staging. You can focus purely on the performance.

Although I can do most overdubs in my room at home, when it comes to tracking a full band or drums I hire a studio complete with engineer. As a producer, I need to focus fully on performance too. And while the personnel and the gear are important, when it comes to choosing a room, my first consideration is the room itself.

Why is that? Sound occurs in a space.

Source Room

The room is the number one reason that people have problems with recording. It's half of your recording. The instrument isn't captured in isolation. The instrument is performed and captured within a space, and the sound waves interact within that space. The louder the instrument, the more the space interacts with the sound.

I could play a whisper quiet Kalimba in a large studio without ever exciting the room. But the moment there's any kind of real sound pressure levels—like say from a very loud snare drum—the sound waves will bounce around that room and travel from one wall to the next and back again to cause our reverberation. But if the room is undersized, all of those sound waves can interact in negative ways as they crisscross the room and return to the mics. Which can cause problems if there isn't enough time differential between the initial sound and the early reflections that follow. As we will soon discuss at length, time and distance have a direct relationship with what your microphones pick up and how they interact.

Say you put a vocalist in a rather small closet baffled with carpeting on every surface. The high-end frequencies will be sucked up by the carpeting, but the low-mid and low-end frequencies won't dissipate. You see, carpet doesn't have enough density to stop low-end information from its travels. Which means those low-end sound waves will bounce around that little room and compound. The tone of 100 Hz to 500 Hz will surround the vocalist's head. And if it surrounds her head, it's surrounding the mic too. Which means the vocal will sound dark and boxy, both in the room and on the mic. Even a dynamic mic. Oh, and sorry, you can't use EQ to cut your way out of the problem, because the top end is already gone. By the time you cut the low mids, you've completely gutted the tone.

When you place a drum kit in an undersized room with parallel walls and eight-foot ceilings, your drums will be severely compromised. The cymbals will sound exceptionally harsh as the low parallel ceiling pushes the high-end wash back into the mics, then down to the floor and back up to the mics again. The snare will either sound thick and dark or papery and thin. The low end from the kik will overwhelm the room. You could very well have flutter in the corners, which sounds like rapid fire delay and which will return to the mics. The overall tone could be remarkably dark or unbearably bright, perhaps both. And you'll hear all those maladies just as readily in the room as you will on the mics. Even closely placed dynamic mics won't generally help you, because the reflections in a grossly undersized room could very well be louder than the direct tone of the drum itself.

This is not to say you need to gut your house for a proper buildout. It does, however, require you to be honest with yourself in regards to your limitations. Because if your recording space is undersized and lacking any real acoustic treatment, that will be problematic when it comes to recording drums.

If your expectation is to record big beautiful drums in your small spare bedroom, then you will likely be disappointed. You either have to find some money and go record the drums at a proper commercial studio, or you have to alter your expectations. Otherwise, you won't be happy with your record. I'm an expert at recording drums. I can't record big beautiful drums in a relatively untreated undersized room. How do you know if your room is undersized? Try recording drums in it.

You also probably have limited equipment. You may not even have two microphones of the same type. And if not, then how are you going to record these big beautiful drums exactly? With three dynamic mics? The rejection properties that make a dynamic mic a reasonable choice for close-miking a snare drum, are the same properties that make it a terrible option from distance. A dynamic requires more sound pressure levels to excite the capsule than a condenser or a ribbon. Besides, even if you have two condensers available, that might not actually be the better option. Half your problem is still the room.

Surely some of you are screaming *sample replacement* at me right now, and if sample replaced drums fit your production aesthetics, then by all means, replace away. Just be prepared to re-record your overheads too, because those will continue to reveal everything that's bad about your room, which will certainly overpower your samples when placed in balance. By the time you start asking your drummer to overdub the cymbals, you may as well just program the drums. That's no drum performance. So why put up the pretense?

Oh, and just to tell you, every recordist, producer, and musician has had the brilliant idea to record their drums separately one drum at a time. This would be the equivalent of recording each string of your guitar chords one at a time. And while we've all heard the stories about big acts with limitless budgets that have tried this, I can assure you, those acts long jumped the shark. You do stupid shit when you have no limitations. Nobody can meet the expectations of an infinite budget. And once released, the question is always the same: you couldn't have spent one more day on it?

There's just no way around it, if you want big beautiful organic drums, you need space. If you don't have adequate space available, and renting a studio isn't an option, then you need to go find an appropriate space for your drum recording.

I can think of three empty spaces within a few miles of me, and I live in a relatively small city these days. Two of them are former churches. And then there are bars with stages that would allow me to record drums during the day. They might even have some microphones that I could rent with the space. If that's not enough, surely your network of musicians in town can loan you some microphones.

You do network with local musicians, right?

Of course, an overly large space can be just as problematic as an undersized one. I was recently in an enormous unfinished church to film *How to Record a Vocal That'll Make a Grown Man Weep with Mixerman and Earnhardt*, and the room was far too large to tame realistically. I swear there had to be six seconds of decay time from that room. And while most empty spaces are going to require some baffling, I would have had to construct a veritable room of baffles and moving blankets in order to contain that space. Make no mistake, any space, large or small, that comes back into your close mics needs to be contained and controlled somehow. In some instances, appropriate containment could be prohibitive.

The moment I accepted the fact that what I hear in the room is what I hear on the mic was the moment that my recording life got considerably easier. I stopped pretending like the space didn't matter.

Source Instrument

Not to overstate the obvious, but an inert instrument doesn't make a sound without a performer. And a player can't perform music without her instrument. So the player and her instrument become inexorably attached and, therefore, make up the other half of the Source.

There are those that will tell you all that matters is the player, because somehow a great player can make even a poor specimen of an instrument sound great. Really? How does a great guitar player deal with overt buzzes, severe intonation issues, and sticky action? She finds another guitar, that's how.

Of course, there could be occasions in which that problematic instrument is somehow the perfect instrument for the job. It's also possible that a great player could figure out how to work around limitations presented by the instrument. This might even produce some interesting musical results. Perhaps you have a Rhodes in which certain keys stick or distort. If you can create a part which avoids those notes, then that could very well prove an acceptable solution. Or perhaps you could use just the distorted notes to your benefit. Creativity is always an option for getting yourself out of a jam.

While it's true that a broken instrument can be problematic, so can the wrong instrument. A mandolin won't sound like an acoustic guitar. A mandolin has double strings, is much smaller in size and much higher in register. Why would I say something so ridiculously obvious? How about this? A small acoustic guitar with dead strings won't sound anything like a big guitar with new ones. Yet, the first thing most of us will do to fix that is to change out the mic. And while we can agree that a large acoustic guitar with bright new strings is closer in its genetic makeup to a small acoustic guitar with dead strings than it is to a mandolin–that doesn't make the guitars interchangeable.

If all that you have is the small acoustic with dead strings you will be inclined to use your tools to mangle your way to big guitar glory, but if the instrument doesn't have the necessary attributes to produce that tone, neither your mic nor its placement will bring it to submission. You can derive proximity with how close you place the mic. You can pull more aggression by choosing a dynamic rather than a condenser. It's even possible that the small acoustic guitar with dead strings works perfectly for your production. None of that changes the fact that your acoustic guitar sounds like it's small and has dead strings.

Surely there will be occasions when your miking technique can produce unexpected results. They're rare, though. You just can't just mic-place your way to a tone with physical characteristics that don't exist. You can, perhaps, mangle it into its own unique thing. But at the end of the day, if what you wanted was a big bright acoustic guitar, that's what is required. I might suggest you borrow one. Perhaps even make a trade.

Drums with dead heads and rattles can sound amazing on the right record, but not when you seek big beautiful open-toned drums. A Fender P Bass has a beautiful deep tone, which is absolutely useless if I want the honky midrange that I'll get from a Hofner. A Strat into a Rectifier will give me some nice crunch guitars, but if I seek the sound of a Les Paul into a Marshall I'm wasting my time.

The room may be half the recording, but if your vision and the basic nature of your instruments are out of alignment, then one of them needs to change. More often than not, it makes more sense to change out the instrument for something that more closely resembles your vision.

Source Player

As a producer, I think of everything in terms of my Source. I pick the room based on its ambient attributes. Any and all subpar instruments are either fixed, tuned, or replaced before we record rather than through electronic manipulation. But what of the player? I mean, isn't that mostly you?

There's no getting around the fact that in many, if not most cases, you will be the player, and if not you, then one of your band mates. And so the players are often predetermined. You could all be brilliant. You could all be shit or anywhere in between. Regardless, the personnel are baked in. The good news is the quality of your players really doesn't matter, so long as you have great songs and you're able to combine your musical strengths in an effective manner. I've said it before, I'll say it again. Your Art is made with the resources you have available to you. If you use those resources in an undeniably compelling way, you will get a reaction to your record.

Now, if you hire sidemen to perform parts that are outside of your abilities, then you might do well to hire people who are exceptional. You should go out of your way to find all of the exceptional musicians in your proximity. Of course, if there's a shortage of quality musicians, you may have to expand your search.

There are also all sorts of A-list musicians who you could easily find, reach, and hire for your record. But those kinds of situations could very well require you to leave the part entirely up to their tastes. You're just as likely to get something brilliant as you are unusable.

You can do a remote session with a player through video chat or if you're willing to spend a few bucks through a live streaming service. Either of these would provide you with more input and control. But the closer to superstar status a player is, the less likely you'll have any kind of input into what they send back to you from their remote location. It's not that an A-lister will necessarily refuse input. It's that the logistics of distance makes communication difficult, at best. This often results in settling.

Of course, if the player is to be featured and the arrangement decisions are subservient to their performance, then you would do well to stay out of the way of their genius. But a part? That typically requires some direction.

Great players tend to have an evenness of tone and control over their balances, such that you don't need to do anything beyond put up a microphone in the appropriate room. The capture is pure. Which is great. If you're in the top two percent of players in the world and you have some space available to record, then you have that going for you. If you're with the other 98 percent of us, then purity of capture is irrelevant.

What makes you amazing, whether as a musician or songwriter, is your voice. It's what makes you unique. This is true of every Artist, whether musician, writer, painter, or photographer—you have a voice, and that voice is expressed through your Art. You need to discover and understand that voice. How is it that you speak with your instrument and thereby your Art that is yours and yours alone?

Something attracted you to music, and you practice it, and you require it, and you perform it. So, there must be a reason why this happened, because no one in her right mind would purposely *choose* music as her vocation unless there was literally no other option. So, if there's no doubt as to your destiny as a musician or an Artist, then the question simply becomes: what makes you unique?

Most of you won't be able to answer that question. Those of you who can, may not be able to verbalize it yet. It's not necessarily conscious at first, but it needs to be. What makes your voice unique is what attracts people to you as an Artist. And when you notice what attracts people to you as an Artist, you must capitalize upon it.

We already discussed the importance of confidence in musicianship, and I can promise you, to understand what makes you unique as an Artist, is to understand yourself. Once you understand yourself—once you have some sense of awareness, that's honest, and deep, and all your own—you will gain the confidence you seek. You'll also have an audience. Why? Because there will be no ambiguity.

So, what does any of this have to do with the source?

Everything. You're the source.

The Whole Source

Any time you're compromised in tonal options due to your available source, whether it's the source room, the source player, or the source instrument, then either you need to alter the source or change the plan. You don't just stick with a bad plan. You adjust the plan based on the reality.

Most of us don't have the tools or the space to be a purist. Nor do we need them. You just need to work within the limitations that you have, and creativity is your best weapon for that. So, it's okay to try and record your drums in an undersized room, but make that room work for you rather than against you.

The whole point of this book is to get the technical out of the way, and I suppose I should have known this would force me into more technical explanations because there's just no way around it—recording is a technical process. But it's also an artistic process when thought of in terms of your production. Either the tonality of the part works for your production or it doesn't. And the moment it doesn't, that's the time to pause and consider what you can do creatively to fix the problem.

There is no such thing as "fix it in the mix" anymore, because the DAW saves where you're at, so you don't need to leave balance decisions to a separate process. The mix can be made at the same time as the arrangement. That means constantly checking things in context, which means putting what you have in balance so as to figure out what's missing. When your early production decisions are flawed, then everything that comes afterward is flawed too. You're going to move forward with your record if the drums didn't come out right? Because you can get creative and work around them? I suppose you can. You can also use that creativity to pull them into alignment with your vision before you move forward.

You can't trust your early decisions if you're prone to bad early decisions. If you record drums that you abhor because they're totally wrong for your song and production, but then decide to keep them just the same, the only lesson you'll learn is not to trust your early decisions. Once you come to that conclusion your confidence will plummet, and you will be forced to learn the lesson that every professional record maker eventually learns—get it right at the time of the recording. Otherwise, you will always second-guess yourself. Trust takes time to build, even with yourself.

None of this is about purity. You can use as many tools as you like to mangle a tone. But if your mangling efforts merely result in something that can only be described as usable, then you will compromise your artistic aesthetics in the process. And for what? Your time?

The biggest reason that recording is so difficult is that people believe their tools will solve their recording problems. *If only I had this mic, or this preamp, I could make that snare really phat. If only I had this plugin or that. If only I had these converters, or those monitors.*

Sure, all of those things can help, possibly. What the fuck does that have to do with the record you're making right now?

There is no microphone with a capsule so skewed that it could capture the sound of a parrot from an elephant. There is no amount of mangling that could make an elephant sound like a parrot.

You have a song. You know how the song makes you feel. You know how you want the song to make you feel. The moment you record something that makes you feel the wrong way? Dump the part and try again. This may slow down the process somewhat, especially on your earliest records, but in the long run, you will force yourself to learn all the right lessons and develop all the right habits too.

Stereo Miking

The most challenging instrument, by far, is drums, if only because we tend to surround them with mics, and when you put mics in close proximity, they can interact. But before we start to talk about how to record drums, even in a less than ideal space, we need to discuss how those mics interact and learn what it sounds like. And since most people like to record their drums in stereo, it would make sense to first address stereo miking techniques. I'd like to start with a recommendation:

Avoid stereo miking.

Oh, I can hear the gasps from here.

First, you suggest my room is shit and not to bother recording drums in there, and now you're gonna tell you me not to mic things in stereo? What the fuck kind of book is this?

The kind that keeps you from getting into trouble. Isn't that what all Survival Guides are for?

The issues that make drums difficult, are the same ones that make recording stereo difficult. Unless you have a pair of Ribbons, LDCs, or SDCs of the same design type, and two of the same mic preamps to go with them, then you really don't have the appropriate equipment to record stereo.

Which means that many, if not most of you reading this, don't have the gear necessary to record a solid stereo image in the first place. Guess what? Neither do I. Which is why I go to a studio to record drums, where there's a space that I can control, the equipment that I need, and a guy who understands how to record in stereo. And yeah, I already know how to record in stereo. But do you? Stereo recording is fraught with problems.

I can sense the agita from here. Yes, *of course* I'm going to explain stereo miking techniques to you despite my advice that you shouldn't. You have what you have and what you have is going to change. Therefore, we must assume you'll be in a position to record in proper stereo sometime in the future. In the interim, we must address how you hear.

In the next section we will perform some listening exercises that will require you to sit in front of your DAW. It will also require a polarity inversion plugin, and for some completely inexplicable reason, there are some DAWs that don't offer this. Which is baffling, but worry not, we have ways around this. You can download a freeware plugin for polarity inversion, which I downloaded and tried for myself. While it's a far more complicated device than we need for the purposes of these exercises, it will, indeed, invert phase for you. Once you get the plugin installed and open, you will see two virtual switches labeled "Phase ø." That's the switch you'll want to use for the upcoming exercises.

Search "Stereo Tool V3 Flux" from your browser to get the download link.

Polarity

I've already discussed with you the pitfalls of *faux* stereo recording an acoustic guitar, which is a relatively compact instrument that sits on the performer's lap. If you'll recall, two mics placed in close proximity to a shifting source will interact negatively. The result is the sound of an acoustic guitar that swirls uncomfortably around your head. That malady is the result of a phase coherency issue which has everything to do with a time differential. Where it comes to sound, time and distance are one and the same.

Before we get fully into microphone interaction, you must first understand what it means to invert polarity and, in particular, you need to understand what inverted polarity sounds like. This requires sitting in front of your monitors right in the middle of the stereo field. If your monitors aren't set up such that they are perfectly equidistant from your seated position, that must be fixed first and foremost because these exercises require that you can hear the imaging clearly. Further, daisy-chained computer monitors in which the left speaker receives input and then sends the signal to the right will not supply sufficient width. If all you have available are headphones, then you should probably use those.

Open up a clean session and then bring in a mono kik drum. It can be a MIDI kik or an audio file of a kik, but it must be mono for the purposes of this, and there can't be any reverbs or effects that would cause it to appear stereo. Now go to your stereo output channel and insert a stereo plugin that inverts polarity (sometimes erroneously called phase reverse). Once the plugin has been inserted on your stereo output channel, click on the ø symbol on the left side. This will invert the polarity on that side. Listen to your kik drum.

Weird huh? Notice how that kik is no longer in the center, but rather comes from the sides? Do you hear how the low end has been significantly attenuated? That's no bueno.

So what's going on here? If you take a look at the graphical representation of a waveform, you'll notice a horizontal line that bisects that waveform.

We call that the o line or the null line, as it's the momentary point in the waveform oscillation in which there is no sound. Quite simply, when the waveform is above the null line your woofers are pushing out, and when the waveform is below the line, your woofers are pulling in.

When your mono kik drum is panned to the center, it is sending equal amounts of that kik drum to the left and right. Both monitors push the exact same signal at the exact same level, which causes us to hear that kik in the middle of the stereo field. When you invert the polarity on the left side of that mono kik drum, you are literally flipping the waveform on the left such that it's doing the exact opposite of the right. In the case of the mono kik drum, the left woofer is now pulling in as the right woofer is pushing out in a precisely equal and opposite manner. This results in some low-end cancellation and a lack of center image because those woofers are no longer working in tandem to put the kik drum in the middle.

A/B this a few times, and then bypass the plugin for the next exercise.

Now I'd like you to import a stereo audio file into your DAW. It can be anything. Your favorite record. Your latest production, even. We call this program material. Play it. Sounds nice huh? Now engage that left ø button on the stereo output channel again.

Whoa! Can you locate the center of the image? Did you notice the obvious dip in low-end response? Can you feel the music almost wrapping around your head? Now disengage the left ø button. Once again you have a defined center image and your low end has returned. We like that. Now click the right ø button. It's the same issue. You now have an undefined center that seemingly wraps around your head. Only it's not quite as obvious as it was with the kik drum, is it? Before I explain why that is, we need to perform another exercise.

Now I want you to reset the polarity to normal on your stereo bus, open up two audio channels and import (or record) two unique guitar parts (or keyboard parts), preferably ones that work musically together, and pan them hard left and hard right. The musical nature of the parts can be identical. It's the recordings that must be unique such that the parts can be heard distinctly from the left and the right. Reverse polarity on the left side. Now put it back. Reverse polarity on the right side. Now put it back.

There's no obvious difference is there? That's because those guitars panned hard left and right are completely independent of one another. Inverting polarity on the left guitar causes the left woofer to pull first rather than push. But because it's wholly independent of the right guitar in terms of the recording, it doesn't interact with the audio on the other side. They have no relationship to one another beyond a musical one.

You see, the pure side information isn't affected by the inversion, which is why inverting polarity on your program material isn't quite as obvious as inverting polarity on the mono kik drum. That side information makes it less obvious for someone who is hearing this for the first time.

Let's mute those guitars and return to our stereo program material. Invert one side and listen once again. The low-end attenuation could be significant, it could be subtle. But that skewed center image? You want to become allergic to this sound.

I would recommend you perform this A/B in headphones too. It's not as easy to pick off in headphones, is it? The interaction has been reduced considerably because the left and the right sides are isolated from each other. We combine the signals in our head, and so there is less obvious interaction. The center image skews, but it no longer wraps around your head.

Believe it or not, for anyone who is unfamiliar with this sound, the skewed center image from the program material, along with the attenuated low-end frequency response, can actually be easy to miss. In fact, many of us have had someone sit down and demonstrate this for us repeatedly until we could readily hear it for ourselves, and you need to do the same for yourself. I would recommend you return to your stereo program material and A/B until you can instantly hear the inverted signal. This doesn't need to be performed blind. You don't have to worry about expectation bias. Once you can hear it, you can hear it.

This is the same interaction that occurs when you reverse the wires on one speaker. In fact, you will start to notice that your friends sometimes have their stereo speakers wired out of polarity, and it will drive you crazy to hear the audio shift as you walk through their living room. You'll probably even fix the problem for them. All you need to do is flip the wires at the terminal of one speaker and that will put them in polarity again.

You will often hear people refer to polarity as phase. There are 360 degrees of phase. When we invert polarity, we invert the phase by 180 degrees which is precisely the middle point of 360 degrees. Polarity is binary. Either the polarity is normal or inverted by 180 degrees. One or the other. Which is why we can press a button to fix the problem or to break it again. It's when we introduce a time differential that we start to get into degrees of phase, and that's when things get considerably more complicated.

Time Differential

In order to create a stereo image of an identical signal there must be a time differential. Let's load a mono guitar track into your DAW and make a duplicate of the guitar and its channel. Pan the two identical guitar signals hard left and hard right. So long as the faders are at unity, you will hear one guitar—the only guitar there is—and it will appear in the middle. It will not appear to come out of the left and the right speakers independently. This would be no different from putting that guitar on one channel with the pan knob in the center. Either way, the same signal is pushing the cones in an identical manner which causes that signal to appear in the middle. We would need a time differential between those signals to throw them to the sides as if they were independent of one another.

Let's insert a sample delay plugin onto the duplicate guitar channel. If you don't have a sample delay, any old delay will do, but it needs to be mono, and you need to reset all the parameters. There should be no filters, no feedback, no LFO, no delay time, no level boost, no nothing. Even with the delay plugin engaged, your guitar and the duplicate must appear solidly in the middle before moving forward. Got it? Good. Now, set the delay to 23 ms, then listen. Voila! The guitars appear from the sides rather than in the center.

That might actually seem like a handy dandy little trick to make a mono guitar stereo, but this is just another example of *faux* stereo. While a 23 ms time differential is enough to throw the identical signal to the sides, it's not enough to prevent some measure of cancellation from occurring when heard in mono. This can be problematic.

This is where the arguments get fierce online, because many young record-makers wonder why the fuck they should give a shit about mono. I wondered exactly the same thing over 25 years ago. I mean, everybody had stereo by the time the mid-eighties rolled around. So why would mono matter?

For starters, anytime you find yourself well outside of the stereo image, you could be hearing an acoustically mono signal, which will cause some cancellation to occur between those two guitar parts as they travel to your position. This will manifest as a dip in overall level, and that dip in level can shift when walking around the room. But does cancellation really matter? As with anything in this craft, it kind of depends. Total cancellation surely does.

Why Mono Might Matter

For our next exercise we need to bypass the sample delay on the duplicate guitar in order to remove our time differential entirely, but make sure the guitar channels remain panned hard to the sides. We also need to invert the polarity of the duplicate guitar channel, but for this experiment, that has to be done on the channel itself. First, remove the polarity inversion plugin from the stereo bus entirely, and insert a polarity inversion plugin on the duplicate guitar channel. Invert the duplicate guitar. Listen.

Much like the mono kik drum that we started with, your guitar image will now appear skewed, and your low end somewhat attenuated. Now let's pan both of those guitar channels to the center and listen again. You will hear absolutely nothing. Gone. Nada.

Where'd they go?

When we invert a guitar against a duplicate of itself, the original guitar pushes and pulls the speakers as the duplicate pulls and pushes them in precisely the opposite manner. You can't push and pull a woofer in exactly the same way at the same time. Therefore the signals cancel completely.

This is called null. And like polarity, it's binary. Either the two files null, proving they are identical, or they don't, proving they aren't. Two files that are close but not exact, when inverted and summed, will produce a smattering of sound. That smattering tells you only one thing. The files are not exact.

Why am I telling you all this? Because the validity of a null test is the biggest myth around, and I want you to be aware of this, because you will read about people performing null tests as if they can derive information beyond a binary exactitude. They can't.

Okay, with our guitars still cancelling completely, I want you to raise the level of your original guitar at the fader ever so slightly, and then continue to raise it. You'll notice the guitar reappear, and as you raise the fader, that guitar will continually emit more level. The moment the two guitars have a volume differential, we begin to hear the guitar again. It's not a lot of level at first, but it's there, as is cancellation. It's just that now one of the files is a little louder and so we're hearing the differential in level between them.

Let's bring the guitars to unity such that the guitars cancel completely again, and then pan them hard to the sides. Once again, we have a skewed image and attenuated low-end response because there is a polarity inversion on one of those guitars. Guess what happens when we hear that in a mono playback situation? Why they'll cancel completely, of course, just as they did when we put them together in the middle. And while I could buy the argument that a little cancellation probably doesn't matter all that much, particularly on a relatively unimportant part, *total* cancellation in mono most certainly matters.

I requested a rough mix from a band I was talking to recently, and I was told that the mono roughs hadn't been made yet.

Mono roughs?

Of course, I asked why on earth I would want a mono rough. The answer? Because the guitars disappear when played off a smartphone. This I needed to hear for myself.

Apparently, the guitar player couldn't abide by an asymmetrical image, nor did he wish to perform the part twice, and his solution was to copy the guitar track, pan them to opposite sides, and reverse the polarity of one of the identical guitar channels. Just as we did a moment ago.

Whereas in my room I could clearly hear the two guitars were out of polarity due to the skewed center image, it was when I played the stereo rough from my phone that the guitars disappeared completely. Why? Apparently, my iPhone is mono. And even if it weren't, the speakers on the phone are so close together, the two guitars would cancel in the air before they could even be heard. So, when you read the argument that mono doesn't matter. It can matter.

When it comes to mixing music, I can't and don't consider every fucked up listening situation. I certainly don't worry about people who choose to use just one earbud. If I did, I'd mix everything mono. I don't concern myself with people who have their speakers inverted. And I can't do anything about people who place their left and right speakers in immediate proximity to one another, thereby producing an essentially acoustic mono signal. And then there's the phone.

What I *can* do is protect my balances from changing due to those times when the music appears mono, whether acoustic or electronic in nature. In this case, the guitars cancelled completely. If that's not a problem, I don't know what is.

Now, had there been a 23 ms time delay on one side, the guitars wouldn't have cancelled out completely because the time differential would have prevented it. Make no mistake, there is still some measure of cancellation, just not total cancellation. Does it really matter?

Probably not.

You know, if you have a mono string pad, and it's bugging you that it's not stereo and coming from the sides, then to duplicate and delay a side by 23 ms isn't going to prevent you from a Killer Record. No one is going to stop listening to your music because the strings dipped in level a little bit in mono. In fact, only engineers and others reading this book will know you even did it. And guess what? We've all done it, including me. And it most certainly didn't kill my career.

That said, I do find it perplexing that so many people will jump through hoops to avoid recording a second part. A performed double will produce a far more stable stereo image, and in most cases it will take less time than to duplicate and delay. Even if you're somehow "mixing," if you discover you need a double, you might as well just record it right then and there.

Everyone stumbles upon the Haas effect (yeah, it even has a name). But I have to tell you, 23 ms is an enormous time differential when it comes to musical timing, and that's a problem on anything that's at all rhythmic in nature. It's also kind of a problem on vocals, and where your creativity starts in regards to stereo manipulation, it should also end when it comes to your vocal. Beyond that, sure, use the Haas stereo effect if you like.

Thing is, now that you know what it sounds like you probably won't.

Stereo Miking Techniques

You may be wondering at this point, what does any of this polarity crap have to do with microphones? Well, you know that sound of the skewed stereo image from your program material? That sound I told you to become allergic to? Your two microphones can, and will, interact in a similar manner, and we call that a phase coherency issue. Unfortunately, your polarity inversion button can't always fix it. That's because when we deal with phase, we deal in degrees.

The good news is now you know what a 180 degree phase issue sounds like, and you know its sonic markers. You even know how to fix it—just invert the polarity of one signal. But now we need to talk about sound and time and how that relates to microphones so that we can learn to deal with the lesser degrees of phase coherency.

As you probably recall from physics class, sound travels relatively slowly, particularly in comparison to light. This is obvious from large distances, especially during a storm where the thunder clap will sound many seconds after the lightning. In fact, we can estimate approximately how far that lightning is by the length of the delay. Every five seconds of delay between the flash and the clap is equal to about a mile of distance.

Fortunately, we deal in much shorter distances in the studio, and setting aside variances for temperature and humidity, it takes sound approximately 1 ms to travel every foot. 1 ms is 1/1000th of a second, which is a very small unit of time, but when it comes to microphone interaction, that can result in big problems.

Let's say you put two mics of the identical make and model two feet over a crash cymbal. One a foot to the right and the other a foot to the left of it. Those two mics will receive similar information when you strike that crash. Assuming the mics are truly equidistant and we have adequate space, there will be no time differential between what those two mics capture. The left mic will pick up the sound at the exact same time as the right mic. If your levels are perfectly even, and your channels panned to the sides, that crash cymbal will sound in the center of the image, with some slight ambient information possible on the sides.

If you raise the right microphone six inches higher than the left (half a foot), now that cymbal crash is reaching the right microphone approximately a half a millisecond later than the left. This will cause the mics to interact negatively throughout the duration of that washing cymbal, and you will notice the cymbal wrap around your head. The reason? That little bit of extra

197

distance on the right mic results in a time differential, which means the mics are not time aligned, which also means they are not phase coherent.

Once you get microphones more than a few feet apart, phase coherency is no longer a problem, because if you have a sufficient time differential between them they react more independently. And while the rule of thumb is three feet, you very well may need more distance, and you may get away with less distance. But you can only determine that by listening.

When you place two microphones three feet apart on a drum kit such that the left microphone is over the floor tom, and the right is over the snare drum, those mics are likely placed far enough away from each other that they are picking up completely different direct signals. The left mic hears the direct strike of the snare, the right mic picks up a more ambient strike of that snare 3 ms later. The right mic hears the direct strike of the floor tom, the left mic picks up a more ambient floor tom strike 3 ms later. So, now you have a better shot at phase coherency, because the mic placements provide enough time differential to produce a stereo image. Notice, I said better shot.

We call this the Spaced Pair technique, and it's often used with Large Diaphragm Condensers which tend to be big and bulky, and which can be difficult to get close enough together for the far simpler X-Y technique. The problem with the spaced pair over drums, is you can't always get the mics more than three feet apart and that isn't necessarily enough distance. As a result it can take a little bit of fiddling to adequately eradicate phase coherency issues between the two mics.

Now, the most effective way to test for phase coherency between mics is to engage a polarity inversion on one of the overhead mics. Do you remember what it sounded like when the program material wrapped around your head? This is what you're listening for. If you hit the ø button and the center image of the cymbals becomes skewed and your low end attenuates, your mics were already coherent. If you hit the phase button and your center image becomes focused and you gain low end in the process, then you had a phase coherency issue, and you just fixed it. And if you can't seem to choose one over the other and both seem to have their own unique problems? The two mics are only slightly out of coherency. Which means they need to be time aligned.

This is really the crux of phase coherency. Time. And the way to fix time between microphones is to adjust their distance from the source until they're in alignment, which you must ultimately adjust by ear. You can make the mics look as perfect as you like, all that matters is what they sound like together.

But what if you've already recorded your mics? Or what if someone else recorded them? Fortunately, we deal with time in our DAW too. All you need to do in order to bring two microphones into phase coherency is to slide one of the audio files ever so slightly in time. And I do mean ever so slightly. We're talking samples here.

You can fix the issue by eye. All you need to do is match the waveforms. To do this you zoom way in on the two waveforms, and slide one of them until the waves go above and below that null line in tandem. This is by no means precise, since those waveforms aren't identical. They are similar, though, and once you've made a visual inspection you can fine-tune by ear.

If that sounds like a pain in the ass, I suppose it is. Fortunately, there are time alignment plugins that will automatically evaluate the two signals, measure the problematic time differential, and delay one side by that differential in order to bring them into coherency. Pretty slick, huh? Maybe, maybe not.

This is where things get really squirrely. You see, those two overhead mics don't just interact with each other. They interact with every mic on the kit, including the kik mics, the snare mics, the tom mics, the hat mic, and possibly even the room mics! And you might have only four mics in total on your drums, regardless of how many mics you have, you need to get all of them working well together and phase coherent with each other, and that will be next to impossible using time/phase alignment tools. As soon as you fix one thing, you just broke three others. So, if you have lots of mics around a drum kit, phase coherency really needs to be accomplished at the time of recording through microphone placement and adjustment, and you need to consider all of the mics and how they relate to one another sonically.

Phase coherency isn't just a problem with stereo miking. It can be an issue between two mics on a single mono source too. Let's say you put a dynamic inside the kik, and a speaker mic outside of it. The internal mic captures the attack and the body of the drum, and the speaker captures the subs. Typically there's only about a foot between the two mics. Which means they're going to interact, and the nature of that interaction has much to do with relative level between the signals.

Remember when we caused two identical guitar signals to cancel out completely, only for the sound to return as we increased the level of one? Relative levels alter the phase interaction between two signals. In the case of the guitars, they were identical, and so the change in cancellation was linear. When it comes to microphones, they are less than identical, and the frequency cancellation is dynamic.

Therefore, you can't necessarily fix the issue merely by inverting polarity on one mic, because as you alter your levels, you'll change both the level and nature of the cancellation. This often makes time alignment a better option than polarity reversal.

I qualified that last statement, because although cancellation occurs between those mics, you might actually like it. In other words, it's not a requirement to time-align all mics. I mean, when I was mixing on analog consoles, I really didn't have the option to time align microphones. All I had available was the phase reversal button. I suppose I could have used a delay, but those were usually reserved as effects.

You may even prefer your kik drum with one of those mics inverted. In fact, this will usually manifest as a change in low-end response, with one inversion placing the kik drum seemingly above the bass, and the other below the bass. You can shape that low end and control the cancellation with your relative balance between the two mics. This can be a bit of a dance, and you'll want to send those two channels to a bus for processing. Once you have that kik drum working, lock those levels down, and adjust everything from the bus.

Now, if you asked me just a few years ago, I'd tell you to use time alignment as a last resort. But now? As a musician? If you'd like to place two mics in close proximity to one another, you definitely should get an auto align tool of some sort. I've taught you what you're listening for, and that's the important part. All the time alignment does is apply a delay, which is the same as nudging the audio, and it'll get you very close in short order. I say, if you're only dealing with two mics, there's nothing wrong with time alignment. But if you have more than two mics in proximity, get it right at the time of recording.

That was a lot. I'm exhausted just explaining it all. The most important takeaway from this lesson is a sonic understanding of what phase coherency issues sound like, and hopefully we've achieved that.

X-Y

The simplest and most foolproof way to capture a stereo image is with a stereo mic in which the capsules are placed one on top of the other in an X-Y configuration. In some cases the capsules can be rotated in order to widen or narrow the image of your capture. There are stereo LDCs, SDCs, and Ribbons. The beauty of a stereo mic, is that you aren't required to use both capsules. So, a stereo mic isn't a waste of money, because you can lean on it for more than just stereo capture. And if you're ever in the market for a mic, and you're the kind of person that just loves to record stereo, then you would be a good candidate for a stereo mic.

The next simplest way to record in stereo is with SDCs, also in an X-Y configuration, which places the capsules adjacent to one another. This really only works with SDCs which are typically narrow mics, more like a pencil than an anvil.

This is what an SDC X-Y configuration looks like:

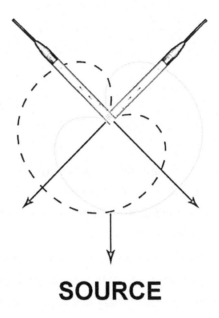

SOURCE

X-Y Diagram

The two capsules can face each other at a 90° angle, or they can cross as pictured. Either way, in an X-Y configuration, the capsules are placed such that they are the exact same distance from the source, which means they will be phase coherent. The two heart-shapes represent the cardioid pick-up pattern for each mic.

You can employ the X-Y technique with a pair of LDCs or Ribbons, but you will need some equipment, starting with a microphone bar which spreads the mics apart. Two LDCs can get rather heavy, so you'll also need a robust mic stand with a counterweight so that you can mount the two mics on to the one stand without the whole configuration tipping over. That said, the bulkier the mics, the more difficult they are to mount, even with a microphone spreader.

The X-Y technique pretty much requires you to use the same model mic. If you use two different mics, you could get some rather strange results, as they will not capture the same overall frequency response.

I left dynamics off that list, mostly because it's a little weird to use two dynamic mics to capture a stereo image from distance, given how they generally react, but you experiment away with that. You might have better results with a single dynamic overhead mic. It certainly won't have any fidelity, but if you're in a punk band or an Indie rock band, it could be just the kind of trashy tone you seek. You can also place the dynamic in close proximity to the cymbal, although, if you place it too close, you could also capture outrageous levels of low end on your crash. Cool!

It's certainly not a requirement to present your drums across the entire sound field. The kik and the snare are almost always placed in the center in modern productions, and if all you have is one cymbal, then you can pan it in order to give the mild illusion of a stereo space.

There are other stereo miking configurations—Blumlein, mid-side, and ORTF. I rarely used any of them as a recordist, so I can promise you they aren't a requirement. If you'd like to learn more about those techniques, I encourage you to pick up *Zen and the Art of Recording*.

What's most important is that you now know what you're listening for where it comes to microphones interacting. Which means you're probably in decent shape to start recording stereo. That doesn't change my recommendation. Avoid stereo miking.

Drums

When you really think about it, a kik is a kik and a snare is a snare, and although kik and snare tones can be remarkably disparate, their functions are far less so. They don't have to sound amazing in isolation. They need to sound right within the production. They also don't have to be featured. Not every track calls for a prominently placed kik and snare drum, although that is surely the usual.

In my world, the drums are recorded first along with bass, mostly because they provide the rhythmic and the low-end foundation of the track. I much prefer to start from the bottom of my track and build up.

Every now and then, an Artist will bring me an acoustic guitar/vocal demo in the hopes that it can form the foundation of a full production. I suppose there are times that I might consider overdubbing drums to something like this, but I do all that I can to avoid it, especially if the demo was performed without a click track. Recording drums on top of a free-form acoustic performance is a shit show every time.

Even with a click, this can be a difficult prospect, because most drummers are far better at dictating the feel and tempo than they are at following it. In other words the band follows the drummer, not the click. So it'd have to be a remarkably compelling performance for me to even consider overdubbing drums to it, and if it's so amazing, why would I change anything about it? I'd rather just record another version of the song entirely. Besides, not all productions require a band. If the guitar/vocal is compelling as it is, then why add anything at all?

If you're an Artist or a musician, or a singer-songwriter, then drums are probably optional. Which gives you a ton of latitude in which to get creative. You can program your drums. You can forgo them completely. You can derive your rhythm from percussion. You can employ loops. You can do anything you like when you're not beholden to band personnel.

All of that said, if you're in a band and you have a drummer, and you'd like to keep your drummer, then you need to record drums. If you need to record drums, then you'll want to know how to mic them up. And since most of you will be recording drums at home, regardless of my advice in this regard, then we should probably go over some creative strategies to do so in less-than-ideal circumstances.

Drums in an Undersized Room

The fact of the matter is, we don't always seek big beautiful drums. Sometimes we just need drums, and you may even find that your room is adequate for the kinds of drums you require. So long as your expectations are in alignment with your situation—you're good. If the drum part is relatively simple and the kit is small, there's no reason why you can't produce something totally usable, if not radically cool, from nearly any space. The smaller the kit—that is to say, the less pieces in the kit—the better shot you have at recording something usable.

This should be no surprise. Toms ring. Snares rattle. Cymbals splash. The more pieces, the more interaction there is among the pieces. A kik, a snare, and a cymbal is way easier to record than two kiks, two snares, five toms, three roto toms, a hat, a ride, eight crashes, a bell tree, and a shaker taped to a stick. This is especially so in a compromised room.

This is where things get a little tricky when it comes to an instrument as complicated and as varied as drums. What you can do with three mics isn't what you can do with eight mics. And no, you don't need eight mics around a small kit in an undersized room, but it sure is helpful to have options.

Really, if you could capture the whole kit in perfect balance with just two mics, that would be the optimal setup. Unfortunately, if you place those mics too far away, the drums lose their immediacy. If you employ them as overheads, you have no proximity effect and therefore a lack of low end information.

I'm sure if you gave me a day with a good room and a drummer who can play in balance, I could find a mic placement configuration that picked up the kit with just the right blend of immediacy and ambience. Maybe. It also puts the engineering ahead of the music, although I'm not sure that can be avoided on drums, at least not initially.

We all operate within limitations. If you have but three mics to record your drums, then you need to strategize based on your source and the properties of your available mics. All you really can do is make a plan, place the mics, listen, and adjust.

Even under the best of circumstances, there is some measure of hit or miss when it comes to recording. I have no qualms about ripping down my overhead mics if I'm not hearing what I want, but that hasn't happened ever since I took Ken Scott's advice to stop fucking around and just use my favorite ribbons on the overheads all the time.

I like ribbons on drums. I like ribbons on just about everything. The longer I record, the more I love ribbons. I finally realized why in an aha moment writing this book. The top note of a violin sounds out at 3.1 kHz.

In terms of notes, we don't go much higher than the top note of a violin. Yet, in terms of frequency, that's not all that high, since 3 kHz falls within the bottom third of our audible frequency range.

Well! That means the preponderance of harmonic information falls below 3 kHz. And ribbon microphones have a steep rolloff at around 16 kHz. So, they're not bright, and clearly don't need to be bright, given where the fundamental harmonic information resides.

Look, I'm not suggesting you should record everything with ribbons. I'm not even suggesting that I should. But they do shine on instruments with an abundance of high-frequency information—like cymbals and high-gain electric guitars and horns for that matter. The ribbons naturally attenuate the most grating frequencies, but you can always bring those frequencies back in again with an EQ boost. Frequencies above 16 kHz merely drop off. They aren't eradicated. So long as the frequencies exist, they can be boosted.

Let's try another listening experiment. Open your DAW again, load your favorite record onto a stereo channel, and insert a High-Pass Filter onto that channel. Set the HPF to about 4 kHz. What do you hear? Do you hear any harmonic information? Slide the HPF down the frequency spectrum as you listen. At what frequency point do you begin to hear harmony? I just did this myself, and the harmonic information on my track didn't start to appear until about 1 kHz!

Frankly, I think the biggest mistake that young learning musicians make with their recordings is that they try to make things too bright. There's a reason to boost the high frequencies at times, as it does bring out the overtones of a part, which can open things up. But that doesn't mean you have to put a high-end sizzle on everything. Now that we all recognize where the meat of the harmonic frequency information lives, perhaps it should give us all pause in how aggressive we are with top-end boosts.

The predominant information in the upper frequencies comes from harmonics, percussion, and cymbals. And it's the cymbals that carry the least important information in your production. In fact, most people place their cymbals way too loud. Yes, I understand how great a cymbal wash placed above shredding guitars can be. And if your goal is to agitate, then it totally makes sense to place cymbals loud in your drum balance. But if they're compromised to begin with because your ceiling pushed the early reflections right back into the mics, you might want to consider other ways to bring in that high-end rhythmic information. Or maybe you should simplify the cymbal part. But if the cymbals are a problem, then you need to figure out how to deal with them at the time of the recording.

Of course, if you're starting with drums, it can be difficult to tell where they fall short. Evaluating drums in isolation takes some practice, and without any low end from the bass, and harmonic information from the other instruments, there's nothing to counteract them. This is true even if recorded in an appropriate space. It just requires a little practice is all.

Your best defense for an undersized room is to play softly. I know that this sounds like a really bad option because everyone is convinced that you need to play drums as hard as humanly possible. But that can, and will, choke the tone. The biggest drums I ever recorded were performed with a light touch.

For whatever reason, I was setting up to record a band many years ago, and I decided to put a 70-year-old ribbon on the kik drum, something I almost never do. The producer loved it so much that he insisted we use it without even hearing it. Which was fine by me, I put it there. But that kind of ribbon can't take the SPLs from a driving kik, which meant the drummer had to be mindful. The poor guy was so worried about the ribbon mic, that he literally tapped his drums. He revealed this to me just after he picked his slack jaw off the floor upon playback. As he put it, they were the biggest drums he'd ever recorded. That whole scene still makes me laugh. Most drummers would have complained before we took the first take.

This is in no way a suggestion that all drums sound best played softly. For starters, that can be difficult to pull off, as it's far more difficult to maintain a dynamic consistency playing soft. But if your room is introducing problems, and you can lighten up your touch without destroying your feel, that will yield far more useful results than if you simply bash it out.

Your second best defense for an undersized room is genre. For whatever reason, the more Indie the Indie Rock, the rattier the drum tone needs to be. It almost seems a requirement to record drums in a room two times too small, if only for purposes of cred.

Kik

When you want a phat kik, and you do, then a speaker mic can be a good addition. If you don't have any speakers lying around, find some. Amp shops will have cones strewn about. Musician friends will have speakers. You'll even find old speakers on Craigslist. The woofers can be in the original cabinet or not. They can even have a tear in them, although that might introduce some distortion. Good! Low end and distortion go together like chocolate and peanut butter. Yum.

Many people like to thread a dynamic through the sound hole of the kik, but it can often sound like a basketball that way. There are some dynamic mics that sound better than others for this application, including some mics that are designed specifically for the inside of a kik drum.

I personally prefer a condenser placed just outside the kik drum as it picks up the low-end thud that comes from the body of the drum. Others of you might prefer the dynamic, because it picks up more of the attack. If you do put a condenser outside of the kik, avoid the sound hole. That is, unless you really love the sound of wind hitting the capsule of your expensive condenser mic.

Condenser mics outside of your kik drum will pick up considerable levels of cymbal information, and adding compression is only going to make matters worse. To deal with this, you may want to place that mic under a tunnel. Typically, I just set up two chairs on either side of the mic, and drape a blanket so that it blocks the sound of the cymbals from the mic. Others prefer to build tunnels out of less absorbent materials.

Dampening and tuning are critical to the tone of the kik drum. If the drum is tuned too low, the head will be floppy and you lose all semblance of tone. If the drum is pitched too high, you lose your low end, at which point a speaker mic is even more desirable. Old heads can sound awesome for the right record, as they can sound like nothing more than a thud. New heads will have more attack, and more overall brilliance.

A pillow or a blanket can be placed inside the kik drum for purposes of dampening. The amount of dampening you apply to the beater head will have a significant impact on the tone of it, as will the makeup of the beater itself. A kik drum without a hole has a much thuddier sound, and will manifest in an almost circuslike manner without sufficient dampening on the inside. You can always remove the resonant head to insert a pillow, but once you take a head off, it's never quite the same after that, so you may want to apply your dampening to the outside of the heads, or get new heads.

Snare

There is no doubt, that condenser mics sound way more natural on a snare drum, because condensers have a fast transient response. That isn't really debatable, and if you have a condenser that you can use for the snare, and you want to try it, I highly encourage it. What you need to check for is whether that condenser is also picking up an overbearing level of cymbal and hat information, which very well could prove problematic later. You can use a condenser on a drummer who plays with remarkable balance, like Jim Keltner or Matt Chamberlain, both of whom I've recorded. But for most band drummers with limited studio experience, a condenser on the top of a snare drum is a tough call. Many drummers hit the cymbals and hi hats far too aggressively, which puts them out of balance with the skins. So, as much as I may not love a dynamic mic on the snare drum, more often than not, that's what ends up there.

The big issue with a dynamic mic on the top snare head is that it requires proximity to the head, which results in a rather dark tone. Much of the brightness from a snare comes from the shell and the bottom head, and so, snare drums miked with a dynamic often sound better with a bottom mic too. An SDC is preferable for this application. A dynamic will do if that's all that you have, but it won't generally open up the tone as effectively as an SDC will.

Be sure to reverse polarity on the bottom mic or your snare will sound papery thin. When the drummer strikes the top head it pushes the top skin away from the top mic and the bottom head towards the bottom mic, which means the top capsule is moving in the opposite direction of the bottom capsule. This results in low-end cancellation. A polarity inversion on the bottom mic will reveal the missing low-end information. So will a polarity inversion on the top mic, but then that mic will be out of phase with the overhead(s). Remember, all of your mics need to work together.

I've never had much luck in miking the shell of the snare drum, but it wouldn't stop me from trying again in less-than-ideal circumstances. Once I'm in a wholly compromised recording situation, I'll try anything, even if it hasn't worked in the past. Besides, there are engineers that swear by miking the shell, so someone figured out how to make it work.

It's likely that you'll want to brighten that top snare mic, especially if you don't have a bottom mic. It's best to introduce top-end EQ at the time of recording or you could have a surprise later. Once you apply EQ and compression to that top mic, you'll bring up the level of the hat, which could sound louder on the mic than the snare itself. It's always good to solo the snare as your drummer plays the kit so as to determine how much brass you're picking up.

There are a number of ways to combat an overbearing hat in your top snare mic. The best solution is to change out the hats for something smaller and thicker, but that requires availability. Tape on the hi-hat and the cymbals will attenuate the top-end sizzle nicely. The drummer could adjust how hard she hits the hat relative to the snare, but that's a tough adjustment to make five minutes before a take.

You might try to place a small square placard of cardboard as an obstacle between the snare mic and the hat. This will prevent some of that high-end frequency information from directly reaching your snare mic. You can attach the placard to a boom stand.

Toms

Toms are really a major pain in the ass. For starters, many drummers place their cymbals with the minimum amount of clearance possible. This can make threading a microphone impossible. If you can't get a mic to a tom, aside from abandoning the close mics, you'll have to raise the cymbals.

You might be wondering about miking the resonant heads on the bottom of the toms. This is rarely an effective placement, as there is almost no attack and the bottom head is rarely actually in tune. In general, I find the bottom heads unusable.

Due to their rejection properties, dynamic mics are usually the preferred choice for toms within the context of an entire kit. Placing a dynamic close to the skin will reduce the level of cymbal leakage and increase the low-end information.

Gates can be inserted on the individual drum channels in order to remove unwanted cymbal information that bleeds into the close mics. You don't ever want to record with a gate as they are prone to mistriggers, and anything you can gate as you record, can be processed just as effectively on playback.

For some reason, there seem to be a great many people who use gating techniques as a matter of course on drums, mostly because they believe this is how the "pros" do it. In reality, well-recorded drums are not in need of gating.

Toms emit a sympathetic ring as the drummer plays, and if that ring is overbearing, or if there is an excessive amount of cymbal leakage, the drums could be well served by riding the offending information down between strikes. The more toms there are on a kit, the more likely this will be a necessity. That said, when you eradicate all of the ring from the toms, you remove much of the tone of the drums themselves.

Rather than to gate, I prefer to edit out the offending information from the toms, but that can sound somewhat unnatural, as there is often cymbal information during and immediately after a tom fill. To combat this, you can make duplicates of your toms in their natural state and blend them in to taste with the stripped toms. You won't need all that much level out of your unstripped toms. This is just a quick way of automating the tom hits without actually using automation. You can use the range setting on your gate to produce the same results, and you can use the hysteresis setting to help with mistriggers, but if a gate is proving problematic, you now have another way to deal with the issue.

You can also gate your kik and your snare, but that, too, can sound exceptionally unnatural. Honestly, the drums have to be really fucked up before I start pulling out gates. I think I'd sooner sample replace them.

Sample Replace

If your kik, snare, or toms just aren't working, you can sample replace them. Not to overstate the obvious, but sample replacement means to replace with samples. The problem is that samples sound programmed, which can sound somewhat offensive when blended into organic drums. Besides, it's so *aughts*. As with everything, it will surely return to style.

Some DAWs include functionality that will search out your drum hits and convert them to a MIDI file. There will be occasional mistriggers which can be repaired manually, but once your MIDI file is right, you can use any of your available MIDI instruments or samplers to supplement or replace the offending drum tones. I personally prefer to supplement than to replace as a mixer, but the recording and the production dictate the best choice.

There are third-party sample replacement programs if your DAW doesn't offer this functionality. And you could always replace every drum hit by hand, but that would be extremely labor-intensive and inefficient. Surely your time has *some* value.

You can sample replace your skins, but you can't effectively sample replace your cymbals, which means you'll have some measure of the drums in your overheads blended with your samples. If you find that problematic, then I suppose you'll just have to overdub the cymbal information too. Fun times!

I'd sooner program drums than to record them in such a manner that they require sample replacement. But then as John Steinbeck alluded, "the best laid plans of mice and men often go awry."

Drum Tuning

The most significant improvement to your drum tone is achieved through proper tuning and dampening. The more open the tone, the more critical the tuning. Your close mics will amplify tuning artifacts, such as beating or resonant pings, especially when placed in proximity to a skin. And while mic placement can help with these sorts of maladies, you will lose proximity if you don't deal with them at the source.

If you're a drummer, it's just as critical that you practice tuning your drums as it is to practice playing them. In fact, I would even recommend that you take lessons on tuning your drums until you have a full command of it. That alone will improve your drum recordings tremendously. Surely, there are all sorts of instructional videos for this on YouTube.

Dampening gels, rings, paper towel, tampons, and some tape, can all be used to dampen a drum. The more dampening you apply, the less tone you'll derive, and the deeper the drum will sound. A wallet on the snare drum will make it dead and phat, to the point it could have almost as much low end as the kik drum.

Programmed Drums

I mixed a track with programmed drums once that were so realistic I almost couldn't tell. That was the last time that happened.

I mixed a project recently that had programmed drums with overdubbed cymbals on what was essentially a pop track with hard rock aesthetics. And while the drums certainly didn't sound organic, they didn't sound out of place either. Given the size and scope of the production, and given the genre of the track, they worked. But they most certainly didn't sound like organic drums.

If your production calls for organic drums, and you know it, then you should record organic drums. Somehow. Someway. If that's just not an option, then base your production conceptually around programmed drums. But make no mistake, you really can't make programmed drums sound organic.

Really, if you're an Artist, and you have no band, it doesn't make sense to even bother with organic drums. Certainly not at the early stages. Besides, technology drives all music trends, and at the moment that puts music production in the home and in the computer. As a result, programmed tracks are the current trend.

And why not? My DAW comes with an enormous library of software instruments, thousands upon thousands of loops of any instrument or genre you can imagine, (all of which will conform automatically to my tempo), professional grade plugins for processing, scoring, editing, and mixing, all for $200. Can they make it any easier?

As a teen, I didn't have one tenth of the power available that we all have at our fingertips today. My Apple II+ had all of 64 *Kilobytes* of RAM. A commercial studio was prohibitively expensive. My high school job paid me $3.35 per hour, and my first synth cost me $1600. That's 477 hours just to get the power of one synthesizer with no way to even record it. Fortunately, I also had a paper route.

Working with programmed drums is 10,000 times easier than working with real drums. I'm not sure why that would matter. We choose our drums like we choose anything–based on how they make us feel. Surely you can do whatever you like, but just as there is some music that needs to be performed as a group, there is some music that begs to be organic.

I love loops, but they do have their pitfalls. Any loop that you purchase in a package, or that comes in your DAW is available to everyone else. Which means any loop that you employ could very well pop up in another production. If that production happens to be a hit, then you appear to be the copycat. That said, I'm not sure it really matters, at least not when it comes to drum loops. I mixed a ton of hip-hop in the early part of my career, and young producers all used the same P-Funk loops on their productions. Clearly, the beat doesn't generally define the song.

You should probably be careful about the more melodic loops, as they are far more recognizable than a drum loop. Even an identifiable drum beat doesn't generally define the song. But a harmonic or semi-melodic part can, and will, be noticed.

Many loops come with variants, and sometimes I'll just chop up the different variants and move the bits around to create entirely new loops. Sometimes, I'll pinch the basic vibe of the loop with MIDI. There's a lot of room to get creative with how you implement loops.

When I construct a track from the ground up, I fire randomly through my thousands of drum loops until I find something that catches my fancy or fits the vibe, and then I do it again. And again. And I keep selecting loops until something pushes me forward from there. I have no intention of using them all, but if I'm starting from absolute scratch, it's usually because I'm not sure how I'm feeling.

As much as we want to build our track with intent, we don't want to eradicate kismet or fate from the process. The most difficult place to work from is a blank screen. You can get the party started just by hearing something, anything. At some point, inspiration strikes, and you're on the path to a record. Sometimes you'll come up with pure shit. Welcome to the club. You don't get to the great stuff without wading through the shit in the process. That's like a metaphor for life.

Bass

Bass loves distortion, which might help to explain why so many bass players prefer to use an amp over a DI signal. An amp distorts the tone, even if only slightly. That said, I typically go out of my way to distort the bass for purposes of clarity, although it's useful for purposes of edge too.

Bass distortion brings out the upper harmonics of the instrument without overt brightness, which can be particularly useful in dense tracks. The distortion allows us to bring out the clarity of the note motion without making the bass the loudest part in the mix. Don't get me wrong, I'm all for a loud bass, but the denser the track, the less space available, and the distortion allows you to keep the bass robust as you retain audibility.

A boost in the upper midrange will certainly bring out clarity, but can also make the bass stringy and thin in the process. And if you allow the upper midrange from a busy bass part to dominate the middle, you may be forced to place the vocal louder than you might otherwise.

How you treat your bass in terms of audibility and placement in balance has everything to do with the overall makeup of the arrangement. The denser the track, the more difficult it is to place the bass and to fill the low end without consuming the production with it. In a dense track, your bass treatment becomes a constant battle between low-end push and top-end clarity. In sparse productions, you can get away with almost no top end, and no distortion.

That said, a synth bass that's made up entirely of subs can all but disappear in some smaller consumer systems. There might not even be top-end information available to boost, at which point you would do well to introduce some distortion to the tone. The slightest addition of distortion can do wonders for the audibility, even in full-range systems.

Frankly, some of the third party amps and distortion plugins that we have today are almost preferable to an amp. That doesn't stop me from recording an amp when it's available, but I often much prefer to mangle the DI signal with either a virtual amp or a saturation plugin. Sometimes I even use the amp signal and the DI signal through a virtual amp, which I blend together. Whatever makes it great.

The DI signal will be ever so slightly ahead of the amplified signal which will put them out of phase with each other. You would do well to time-align them, but before you do, try to invert polarity on one of the signals. A polarity inversion in combination with your balances can push the bass down into the sub-frequencies.

Normally, the bass lives above the kik drum, but not always, and much of it has to do with personal taste. But if the low-end blossom from the kik is down below 40 Hz, then you'll surely want that bass to appear above the kik in terms of frequency. If you find it difficult to balance the two, then you need to pick a winner. Which part drives the rhythm of the song? The kik drum or the bass? That should help with the decision.

If you wish to combine a DI signal with an amp, you'll want to bus them together and compress them as one part. To compress each independently and then combine them could cause odd cancellation. You want the low end of that bass to remain rock solid. When you have bass notes sticking out, and others disappearing, you greatly weaken the impact of the track. So long as the bass is doing more than holding space, it should be strong and audible.

Don't be shy about compression when it comes to bass guitar. It's not a bad idea to push a low-end EQ boost into your compressor almost as a tone control. The EQ pushes the low end. The compressor responds to and attenuates that low end, which will congeal the part and reduce its dynamics. You can really make that low end sing when you push those frequencies into a compressor. An EQ after the compressor is useful to fine-tune the tone.

Synth bass also loves distortion, as evidenced by the buzz bass that's featured in the dubstep genre. You can add distortion right on the synth module, or you can use your favorite saturation plugin.

Acoustic Bass

Standup basses are not perfectly stationary instruments, and neither are the players. Like any low-end instrument, they like space. They also prefer wood floors as far as I'm concerned.

If you're in an undersized carpeted room, it's probably best to eradicate the tone of the room as best you can. Most upright bass players attach a pickup, which can be used to reduce any maladies introduced by the room. And if the room tone is unusable, then I really don't see what choice you have other than to use the DI exclusively.

One of my favorite ways to mic a standup bass is to stick an SDC between two pieces of foam and wedge it between the bridge and the body of the bass. This way, the mic is picking up plenty of strings and low-end body, and the bass player can swing about with no ill effects.

If you have the room, there's nothing quite like an LDC in front of that instrument. There are two f holes which allow the low end to escape the large cavity. It's probably best not to mic up the f holes directly. They could get a little windy.

Really high-quality acoustic basses are ridiculously expensive instruments and typically end up in the hands of orchestral players. The better the bass, the more even the tone across the notes. Unfortunately, more standup basses lack this feature than have it. The best way to deal with an uneven tone is compression. If the bass sounds great in the room then you can back the mic off and use acoustical compression to your advantage. Or you can compress the bass in your DAW, but keep in mind that also brings up the tone of the room. This is where the DI comes in handy.

Electric Keyboards

Electric keyboards like Rhodes or Wurlitzer are bland and mushy and tend to live in the lower midrange. When played in the upper midrange, they're somewhat peaky in nature, yet don't cut through a production all that well. In general, they're relatively undefined, all of which might explain why they're so often plugged into an amplifier. They are in desperate need of some compression and presence, and that's precisely what an amplifier will bring to the party.

Even a clean amp is often better than none at all. Any added distortion can be overt or subtle, but make no mistake, electric keyboards benefit from some measure of distortion. Not only will distortion help the keyboard cut, it toughens it up. How tough you want it depends on the genre and taste.

If you can use the real thing, that's great, but they do go out of tune, so don't feel bad about using a keyboard sample as they're rather convincing in tone. If you run your electric keyboard sample through an amp or saturation distortion, it would be difficult for anyone to tell.

It's not a requirement to introduce distortion, and if your Rhodes or Wurlitzer is a featured instrument placed forward in the balance of the production, it can be presented clean and warm if you like it that way. It just can't withstand any competition for space.

You can compress the snot out of a real Rhodes or Wurlitzer to great effect, and that will cause it to take up more space in your production as it starts to get dense, but you'll have an easier time placing it in the balance too. It's all a tradeoff.

Some Rhodes models sit upon a rather large sideways cabinet with two speakers on each side for purposes of a stereo tremolo effect. Set to its extreme, the tremolo will auto-pan the Rhodes wide between the speakers. A stereo tremolo or an auto-panner will reproduce this effect quite nicely.

Wurlitzers, on the other hand, often include a vibrato control. A mild tremolo blended in with the dry signal will mimic vibrato.

Electric keyboards are somewhat vanilla without some kind of motion or distortion, although delays can help. In fact, keyboards in general like a delay tail, as do the keyboardists who play them, as they smooth out the choppy nature of the instrument. Sustain pedals help with that too, but electric keyboards can get even mushier with sustain, and so the delay can really help matters.

Electric Guitar

There is a wide variance in tone when it comes to electric guitar. A Gibson Les Paul Jr, which employs humbucker pickups, produces an entirely unique tone from a Stratocaster, which doesn't sound like a Telecaster, which is not the same as an Epiphone, which is not like a Gibson SG (a solid body that was designed to compete against the Stratocaster in the early sixties). Yeah. They all sound like electric guitars. They also have their own tonal shape, which manifests as a feeling.

I frequently find myself on sessions with many guitars and loads of amplifiers, and that certainly provides me with a wide array of tonal options. It also makes things take a bit longer as we seek the right texture for the production.

The pickups will also affect the output level of the guitar. A humbucker, for instance, has considerably more output level than the single coil pickup you'll find on a Strat. Humbuckers are also less likely to introduce hum, hence the name. Not that hum matters anymore in the studio. There are plugin packages that will remove noise from your amps, and they don't seem to destroy the tone in the process. Of course, they're not cheap.

On the one hand, I find it disturbing to ignore the hum rather than to deal with it at the time of recording. On the other hand, now I don't have to waste time dicking around trying to eradicate a guitar hum. And why would I when I can so easily remove it with a plugin? Unless you're attempting to record a vintage amp, you likely won't have to deal with guitar hum. Of course, it's only a matter of time before "add hum" becomes an option on a virtual amp package.

Intonation can be problematic on some guitars, which will cause tuning issues at certain frets. In other words, you could have your open strings perfectly in tune, and still have chords that sound out. Your intonation can be optimized by a professional guitar tech, but as with anything, some techs are better than others. That said, if your guitar has intonation problems, it's best addressed at the guitar.

There are now polyphonic tuning modules which can help you out in a pinch, but they aren't a replacement for a properly intonated guitar. There is way too much interaction between the strings to avoid obvious artifacts, and this is not a tool that you should rely upon.

I had a mix session last year in which the guitarist was on the minor chord while everyone else in the band was on the major, and while I don't mind a good #9 chord, this was not the ideal circumstance for that particular color tone. The polyphonic tuner allowed me to adjust the third from minor to major. In the context of a somewhat busy rock production with ratty distorted guitars, the artifacts weren't noticeable. Even if they were, the artifacts would surely be preferable to the rub.

Many singer-songwriters use a capo, which they clamp across the fretboard in order to raise the guitar to a higher open key. Capos are super useful in a live setting, because the performer can easily transpose between keys for purposes of barre chords. They also raise the tonality of your guitar, which doesn't tend to record as well.

Clearly, if a capo is required to adequately perform the part, then a capo you shall use. But any time you can avoid using a capo for purposes of recording, you should. The guitar will be better intonated, and will resonate in the manner for which it was designed. At all times, I'd much rather a guitarist drop her tuning than to raise it.

Drop-tuning means you drop the low string. The most common drop-tuning is probably D, which can be preferred to the natural tuning given how high on the neck you'll play in that key. Drop C is the lowest I've been able to successfully record a guitar and it's not easy. The string gets exceptionally floppy, and the intonation of the guitar is suspect at best. In fact, it may require you to tune certain chords individually and to punch them in. You'll also want to tune the guitar between every take, because dropping that E string down four steps takes it way out of its optimal tension. That said, sometimes the rich and dark deepness of the 64 Hz C on guitars, and 32 Hz C on the bass, is totally worth it.

Guitar players often implement pedals, given their convenience in a live setting. There is nothing wrong with recording a guitar with pedals, so long as they're providing the tone that you seek. And surely, if you have a delay pedal that you adore, and it's not something you can recreate easily in the DAW, then go ahead and record it with delay.

Of course, you're stuck with it when you do that. But if you're playing your guitar through your pedal board, and you have an eighth note delay coming from your pedals, and you're able to play the part well with the delay, and it all sounds great to you—now you want to stop everything and go back to something less inspiring? You should spend your precious time making a plugin sound like that pedal? What was that saying again? Oh yeah! If it ain't broke, don't fuck with it.

A delay adds a rhythmic element to your part, which will affect how you perform it. Could you imagine the Edge laying down a dry guitar part? He plays off those delays. It wouldn't work for him to play it dry. Therefore, it doesn't make much sense to record without the delays. And if you're concerned that you don't know how much delay to put into the balance, then err on the side of too much. Where it comes to music production, it's almost always better to be bold. Besides, if you want a safety net, record the DI. Then you can re-amp it and run it through a delay plugin later.

The Amplifier

There are a great many engineers who like to use two mics on an electric guitar amp. I've never quite understood why. There's always some measure of cancellation that occurs, which we already know is dynamic based on how we balance the two mics. Frankly, I find it a completely unnecessary pain in the ass. That said, at least the cabinet is stationary.

Anytime you put two mics on a source you are complicating your life. And for what? So you can have that perfect guitar tone? That comes from your hands. Seriously, if you have bad tone, you need more practice, not more mics. Better to focus on the part and how you play it.

Two mics go to two tracks, which means they must remain tied together for any kind of editing and bussed together for any processing. Maybe that's not a big deal, but I find it's far simpler to deal with one track when it comes to guitar. As a third-party mixer, I dump the second mic 99 percent of the time. Seriously. It's just so easy to convince yourself that the second mic on that deafening guitar amp is making a difference, when just a touch of EQ is often all you need. Keep it simple.

I really abhor dynamic mics on guitar cabs. Don't get me wrong, they're not a bad choice for high-gain guitars given their generally pronounced midrange. My problem with them has to with how difficult they are to place. Even a centimeter change in position can cause a remarkable variance in the tone. And when you're dealing with a blaring amplifier, you have a limited time frame with which to find that placement before you need to clear your head for a spell. Which is why I use a ribbon mic on guitar amps. Not only do ribbons knock down the top-end sizzle, which pushes them into the mid-range, but they're far more forgiving in terms of placement. Keep in mind, only certain ribbons can handle the blistering SPLs of a cranked guitar amp.

An LDC is also a great choice for electric guitars, but the high-gain tones can get a bit sizzly in nature. This can be dealt with through placement. The center of the cone will be exceptionally bright. As you move the mic to the sides of the cone, you will start to lose top-end brilliance. You can derive and attenuate your low end by how close to the cone you place the mic. Between the amps controls and the placement, you have tremendous control over the EQ of your guitar capture without ever inserting a plugin.

Where you place the cabinet will make a big difference in the tone too. If you place your amp on carpeting, the tone will be darker and less ambient than if you place that amp on a wood floor. And if you place the amp on a chair, there will be considerably less low end in the capture.

Some guitar players turn down their tone and volume controls the moment they stop playing. This may be a good habit live, it's a terrible habit in the studio. To combat this, I typically ask the guitarist to set all of their guitar controls to full and adjust the tone from other places. If for some reason we need to use the tone controls on the guitar, then I mark the location of those knobs with some tape.

If you'd like to find the most accurate mic placement without going deaf in the process, you can use the line noise from the amp to assist with that. The trick is to get the tone of the line noise in front of the cabinet to match the line noise you hear in your headphones. With the guitar safely in its case, turn the amp up to a level beyond reason, make sure you can hear your mic clearly in your headphones, and maneuver the mic in front of the cabinet until the tone of that hiss sounds the same in headphones and out. This method will assist you in locating an accurate placement for the mic. After that, you need only adjust what's coming from the amplifier.

Now, if you want a really big guitar tone, I would advise against stacking your overdriven guitars with multiple takes. They chorus, which obfuscates the tuning and airbrushes the tone. That's a perfectly fine treatment if the guitars are used for texture. But if you want big, in-your-face rock guitars, the best way to do that is with one guitar placed prominently on each side of your production. You can even put an acoustic guitar through an amp opposite your high-gain electric. Believe it or not, it can be difficult to tell they're not both electric guitars. In fact, I often record a much darker electric crunch guitar on one side for purposes of texture.

Guitar amps tend to like robust levels, and although most guitarists set their amps too loud, it's considerably better than setting the amp too low. I understand that neighbors don't often take kindly to really loud guitars. As a result, you may be required to turn your amp down to keep the peace. The good news is that the room will be less of a factor at low volumes. The bad news is that high gain guitars sound best when they push some air.

If you want to derive some texture with your electric guitars and add some dimension to your production, then you will need some diversity of tone. The good news is there are now virtual amplifiers that sound downright convincing.

The Virtual Amp

Guitar purists everywhere freak out anytime anyone suggests using virtual guitar amps. And I can understand why. For years they were absolutely atrocious. As with everything in life, things change.

If you're a guitar player, and you don't like virtual amps or haven't found a package you like, then you should record with a real amp. Some guitarists don't like how virtual amps react. Others don't believe they sound authentic. I get this. And you should use your analog amp(s) all the time if that's the case. But let's not pretend that amp plugins aren't a great tool for a young guitarist who finds herself short on amplifiers and microphones to boot.

The great thing about virtual guitar amplifiers is that you have access to just about any tone you seek. The bad thing about virtual guitar amps is the same as the good thing. Too many options require discipline.

If you're able to pick a tone and stick with it, then you should be in good shape. But if you constantly change the tone, all because you can? That would be the opposite of building a track with intent. Find the guitar tone that causes you to feel the right way, then lock her down. If all those options are overwhelming to you, then fire through the presets until you find something close. Tweak from there.

After a while you will start to find go-to patches for certain situations. Eventually you find your rectifier tone, and your crunch tone, and your breakup tone, and your buzz tone, and your clean noodle guitar tone, and before you know it, you're tweaking those tones and saving them as custom defaults. So they become like modules that you can mix and match.

Rather than look at tools such as virtual amplifiers and reverb units, loops, and synthesizers as technical devices that you need to learn how to manipulate and program, view them as modules that you can mix and match based on what happens to work best.

Surely some of you will take umbrage at that suggestion. *Break my Art down to modules?*

Yes. How is that any different from music?

I can promise you, over the course of thirty years of making records, this concept will manifest itself naturally and automatically, and there's nothing that you can do to prevent it. Nor would you want to try. Music, and the recording of it is all about patterns.

Patterns

Pardon the digression, but this is an important concept that I need to address, and this is as good a time as any.

I–V–vi–IV   I–V–♭VII–IV

I–vi–IV–V   I–IV–V–IV

I–V–vi–iii–IV–I–IV–V   I–vi–ii–V–I

Those are all common chord progressions that can be found in thousands if not hundreds of thousands of songs. They're also patterns.

Surely, you've heard of court vision. An expert basketball coach who operates at a high level with decades of experience can see the entire court all at once. She can see how a play is developing, and she knows what every player is doing, and why they're doing it, on both sides of the ball as it's happening. Meanwhile, you or I see the girl with the ball. The ability to see everything at once? That kind of vision has everything to do with recognizing and processing patterns.

If you've ever gotten really good at something, like a video game or a card game or any kind of sport, then you understand patterns. Of course, if you ever took a music lesson, you're also familiar with patterns. You started learning them on your very first lesson.

What's the first thing you learn when you take a piano lesson? Scales. What's the first thing you learn when you take a guitar lesson? Scales and chords. What's the first thing you learn when you take a drum lesson? Paradiddles

Patterns. Patterns. And more patterns.

The first patterns in any new activity emerge quickly. As you progress, simple patterns combine to make larger pattern modules that help provide you with a wider view. As you continue to practice, new patterns emerge, which make even more composite patterns, which become a series of *aha* milestones along the way to mastering a skill.

We learn patterns through repetition. And although there are some people who seem to possess an almost unworldly natural talent that accelerates the learning curve, repetition is still a requirement. You don't become great at anything without repetition. That includes music and recording too.

This is why I'm so insistent that you build your record from the ground up with intent, and that you stick to that discipline throughout your early records. It will force you to discover the most important patterns, that is to say, the musical patterns, because then you will think in terms of your music and not in terms of your recording.

You can become good at something rather quickly. All the other levels take time. Just when you think there are no more levels you hit a new one. Eventually, you become so good at something, that it doesn't even look difficult anymore because it's not. But there's only one way to get to there. Practice.

There's a reason why it takes 10,000 hours to become a master at something. It takes that kind of time to sufficiently familiarize yourself with the patterns. As someone with probably around 60,000 hours of recording, mixing, and producing experience, and tens of thousands of hours of writing experience, I can tell you, the discovery of patterns will never cease. But you have to be able to see those patterns, and that takes time and repetition. Lots and lots of repetition. There's just no way around that. Because it's not your ability to solve problems that gives you an edge as an expert. It's your ability to quickly recognize solutions that makes you valuable. A newbie could solve any production problem that I could, given enough time. But then that just amounts to practice, and that would be the point.

Patterns allow our brain to break down a lot of information into modules. For instance: An arrangement comprises six musical functions–bass, harmony, rhythm, melody, countermelody, and response. Frequency can be thought of in four major bandwidths—low end, lower midrange, upper midrange, and high end. Panning decisions become nearly binary—a part either goes in the center or on the sides. A four-piece horn section or a quartet of strings provides harmonic movement as a single unit. A drum kit with two kiks, two snares, five toms, a hi-hat and ten cymbals makes up one drum part, which fits perfectly into a stereo image. Layers of keyboards create a single textured part. Stacks of harmonies blend to become one chorus of singers. Five percussion instruments make up a percussion section. There are four microphone types with their own unique general characteristics—

dynamic, LDC, SDC, and ribbons. Reverbs can be broken down to four types—plate, room, hall, and gated. Distortion is applied for edge, obfuscation, clarity, or sustain. Compressors shape tone, control dynamic range, and control low-end response. Contrast is effective for manipulating emotions, and forward movement. Certain chords call for certain resolutions. Song forms are basically comprised of some combination of the following sections: verse, chorus, pre-chorus, post-chorus, intro, outro, solo, and bridge. Patterns upon patterns upon patterns.

And I don't have to sit and think for a long time to type out that list. I mean, you'll have to take my word on this, but those patterns literally just flew out of my fingers because I have been through them so many times, and because record-making seems so simple to me now. And why not? Every production breaks down to just three critical elements:

The song, the arrangement, and the performances.

And where it comes to evaluating the overall effectiveness of those three elements, I need only answer in the affirmative to three questions.

Are the song and the production in alignment?
Does the track make me move the way that I should?
Do I find it difficult to stop singing the song?

If the answer to all three of those questions is *yes*, then I've made a Killer Record. The same goes for you. But I'd be remiss were I not to point out, those questions get awfully difficult to answer if you don't absolutely adore the song. Read them again with that in mind.

All of this, the patterns and the pertinent questions themselves is why I urge simplicity. It's why I suggest simplifying mic techniques and arrangement techniques down to their core. An acoustic guitar requires one mic. An electric amplifier requires one mic. A bass guitar amplifier requires one mic.

A piano requires one mic. And sure you could record everything in stereo if you like, but that will have no bearing on your success other than to retard it. Because you're trying to do too much with what is likely your biggest weakness. And surely some of you will argue that you must address your biggest weakness, to which I would say, we already are—by simplifying things down to their core. To simplify things isn't merely an exercise. It's a path to success.

It's easy to imagine that experts employ all kinds of complicated recording techniques as they get better at their job. The opposite is true. I don't overthink anything on the recording side. In fact, I try not to think about it at all. And there's no doubt, that I can think far less about recording things because I'm so familiar with them. But if I go out of my way to simplify a process that I'm so familiar with, then why on earth wouldn't you?

And yes, a big session with lots of mics in a big room, that complicates matters tremendously, and it requires space and equipment and experience, which is why even I hire a studio and an engineer for those times. Not because I don't have the skillset to record in that environment. But rather because, as the producer, if I'm allowed to focus on the performance, the arrangement, and the needs of my Artists, then everything comes out better.

I'm not one to finish a record based on the clock. If the record isn't great, the record isn't done. But there is a budget, both in terms of money and in time, and we can't pretend they don't act as limiting factors. The fact of the matter is, you can only spend so much time on a piece of Art before it's dead. And believe me, you can kill Art with love.

When it comes to mixing, I suggest mixers mix fast—as fast as possible—because fresh decisions are good decisions, and the longer it takes to mix the track, the less fresh you are. The same can be said about producing your record and even writing your song. Surely, there are amazing records that took longer than they should have, but those would be exceptions. Certainly there are Artists who must grind out every detail in the most painful manner possible—also the exception. Most great Art comes out of us like an unexpected vomit of creativity.

Over-thinking, over-processing, over-arranging, over-producing, over-singing, over-playing—these are all maladies that weaken a production. But what happens when we exchange under for over? Under-thinking, under-processing, under-arranging, under-producing, under-singing, and under-playing? None of those even exist. I've never heard anyone ever utter these sorts of criticisms in regards to a musical production. The only "under" term I've ever heard is *under*dub, and that's the process of removing superfluous information due to *over*-production!

There's no doubt about it. It's way easier to do too much than it is to do too little. Therefore, the discipline comes in keeping things simple, not the other way around. Let me say that again in another way. The discipline lies in doing less, not more.

And now back to our regularly scheduled program.

Acoustic Guitar

If drums are the most challenging instrument to record—and they are—then acoustic guitar isn't far behind, if only because it's human nature to complicate matters.

Honestly, I couldn't possibly even instruct you on how to record a stereo acoustic guitar with two close microphones, because it's not something I would do.

I had a conversation with an acoustic guitarist recently who insisted he had to record his acoustic stereo because it's the only instrument in the production. Apparently, he's like a champion at fingerpicking guitar. Which is cool, and I can understand why he might want stereo imaging for something like that, but the image doesn't have to be derived at the guitar. Were I to record a stereo acoustic guitar, I'd put one mic on the guitar itself and two in the room. And I would carefully place those mics by ear to maximize the imaging and balance the overall ambiance. But it'd have to be a room with some reflectivity, and the desired intimacy would dictate how much reflectivity I seek in the capture.

Once you get into capturing a single instrument in stereo, everything gets more complicated than it needs to and requires more space too. And you know, for someone who is going to deliver a solo performance, it can make sense to take a little time to find the right room, and to spend a little money to capture your instrument with some depth and imaging. By the time you're done playing your record, your record is pretty much done.

Mono Acoustic Guitar

You really need to consider what function your acoustic guitar part is serving before you mic the thing. We've already established that the guitar itself needs to match the purpose and that it's not generally the kind of instrument you can mangle into submission. There's no way around it, if the guitar is designed to be out front in the production, then you need the right guitar.

As we've already discussed, acoustic players tend to move. Even slight shift to the left or the right can dramatically alter the tonality of the guitar which can be problematic when punching in. Even if you implement compiling techniques, tonality shifts can be difficult to deal with. So it's not a bad idea to get your acoustic player comfortable, and place marks at her feet. This way your player can easily locate her position, and you will reduce the instances of problematic tonal shifts.

If you want an exceptionally aggressive midrange tone from your acoustic guitar, a dynamic will probably do the trick. This is particularly useful on arpeggiated parts and lead lines, especially on rock tracks. It's not a natural sound, and full chords can get a bit thick, which might be a feature. Or you could re-voice the chords, and avoid the bottom strings or avoid the top ones for that matter. This tone also does well with distortion. You can apply some saturation, or run a pickup to an amplifier, which can supply both distortion and midrange presence. Either way, you get a nice aggressive guitar tone that'll cut though just about any production.

Of course, more often than not you'll want a natural sound from your acoustic guitar, in which case either an LDC or an SDC will work well. The sound hole emits the low-end information and the fretboard the top-end brilliance, so really, it's just a matter of capturing a balance between the low end and the top end through your placement. This can only be done by ear.

While it's true that any microphone will pick up a performance with absolute fidelity, the tone that we capture is certainly affected by placement. Clearly, you can't just jam a mic into the sound hole of an acoustic guitar and hope to capture anything useful for most productions. It may not even sound like an acoustic guitar. That said, not all mic placement results are predictable, and if you ever place a microphone purely by ear without any care as to its final destination, you'll find they can land in some rather interesting locations. Like microphones can end up on the floor facing the wrong way and shit. At which point you're left wondering if you have any clue at all how any of this works.

Most people prefer to put the mic right on the guitar for the immediacy of the tone, but if you're struggling to find a placement that's in balance, you can always back the mic off, even if that means collecting some ambient room information. The distance provides you with "acoustical compression," which, when combined with the ambiance makes the guitar appear softer in nature. This is especially effective if you want mostly harmonic information without the percussiveness of the transients that drive the rhythm.

Acoustic Guitar / Vocal

As much as placing two mics on a shifting player and her instrument is a bad combination, there are times that it's unavoidable.

Some people sing better when they play. As much as I understand the desire for isolation and control, ultimately people react to a performance. I'd rather have an amazing performance than a perfect recording, and if that

233

means putting a guitar in the singer's hands, then so be it. I've recorded many acoustic guitars with vocal at the same time, and there are a number of ways to approach it.

First, there's the one-mic capture, which requires the player to perform with some modicum of balance in conjunction with the mic placement; otherwise, you could have too much guitar and not enough vocal, or vice versa.

An LDC is probably your best option for a one-mic capture. But if you want any kind of immediacy out of the vocal, then you'll want to significantly cheat that mic toward your mouth, and allow the guitar to be picked up almost incidentally. You could even try a figure-8 pattern to get some immediacy out of the guitar.

When it comes to this kind of capture, there's no way around the engineering required, but it's really all about placement, and once you have it, you can perform without thinking about it.

There's no doubt, if you can capture the guitar and the vocal with a single mic, you will manage to avoid any and all phase coherency issues. You also have a guitar and a vocal on one track, which means they live together in the middle. You'd better have those balances right.

A pickup on the acoustic guitar can be useful, but most acoustic guitar pickups tend to produce a distorted plucky tone that's not all that pleasing in nature. Even the good ones tend to introduce these sorts of artifacts. And while that kind of tone can be useful at times, most guitar/vocal productions are designed to draw the listener in. I find a pickup to be more of a repellant. That said, the pickup can be used to assist with balance. An LDC placed on your singer will capture some of the natural acoustic guitar tone, and the pickup signal can then be introduced for purposes of immediacy. You will likely need to time-align the pickup with the mic.

You can also employ two mics, with one mic on the mouth of the singer and the other mic on the guitar, which goes against all of my recommendations in terms of simplifying things. But this is the one situation in which you really can't be too concerned with phase coherency. I get very nervous when

I have to ask a performer to remain still at a time they're trying to emote. I'd rather just live with the swirl.

I've mixed and recorded a number of acoustic vocal tracks for Ben Harper. There's one track in particular, "Widow of A Living Man," that has come up in audio forum discussions. It was recorded with a mic on the vocal and a mic on the guitar, and you can hear all sorts of comb filtering and tonal shifting on that track.

Ben, at times, can literally whip his head in excitement as he sings, which is what causes the phase issues. Were he to stay perfectly stationary, you wouldn't notice a thing in the recording, but then, how is that a performance? Technical considerations should always take a back seat to performance.

I often prefer to soft-pan the acoustic guitar in these situations as it offers some slight stereo imaging. This results in the vocal shifting to the side on occasion, as he whips his head to howl off mic.

I did have a choice. I could have used the pickup with the vocal mic and dumped the acoustic mic to alleviate the phase coherency issues. But the pickup wasn't inviting, and I made the determination that I'd rather have phase coherency issues than a plucky distorted acoustic guitar. Sometimes you have to pick your poison.

A dynamic mic on the vocal can be helpful, in that it will reject much of the guitar information, but that will only make matters worse if you don't stay on the mic.

Piano

Pianos are big broad instruments that cover the full harmonic range. And when you present a piano across the stereo field, whether it's a grand piano or an upright, they can take up a ton of space in your production.

There's no shortage of pianos in the world, and chances are you know someone or some organization that houses one. Grand pianos are the bigger variety, of course, and require more space, which bodes well for recording them. But a good upright can sound great, and could be preferred in some instances.

Tuning is often an issue with pianos, and tuners—as in the people who tune pianos—aren't cheap. It could actually be cheaper to hire a studio for a few hours and record on their piano than to hire a tuner.

Despite the enormous size of a grand piano, in a concert setting, it appears as a mono source instrument in which the hall provides the stereo imaging. Yet, when it comes to modern records, we often stretch it across the stereo field as if our head is stuck in the end of the piano. Myself included. Because we love that.

I'm all for stereo pianos on piano-driven productions. But if the piano part is subservient, or merely bringing in some flavor, it may make more sense to record it in mono.

The closer you place the mics to the hammers, the more aggressive the tone. The hammers are useful for rock records as they allow the piano to cut through big distorted guitars, or Latin records which are super rhythmic in nature. The further you pull those mics off the piano, the mellower the tone, and the more the room comes into play.

Stereo miking a piano is no different from stereo miking drums. You need to get those mics playing nice with each other. The easiest way is an XY configuration (or a stereo mic really), but now that you understand what a phase coherency issue sounds like, you can space them out if you like. If you're having a difficult time getting the mics to play well with each other, you can always use a time-align tool.

LDCs and SDCs are typically the first choice for piano. Dynamics won't pull a natural tone, but they can be quite useful on piano for many genres. In fact, my favorite piano tone comes from placing a dynamic mic right above one of the sound holes, which is then smashed into a steady state with a limiter. Any time you put a piano into a steady state, it becomes dense with harmonics. I'll warn you now though, this treatment will eat up a surprising amount of space.

Uprights can be recorded from the top of the piano, or you can remove the soundboard covers and mic from there. A stereo upright requires a mic on each side of the player, and you could very well also pick up fingernails on the keys. This may or may not be desirable. If you find the performance noises distracting, then try a dynamic mic. You can either close the mic into the top of the piano or place it on the back.

If you want a super wide piano, you do it the same way as with guitars. Record it mono and double it. This is especially great on arpeggiated parts, or big chords, as then the piano parts come out of the sides in a pinpoint manner. If you put enough saturation on a piano, it can sound much like an overdriven guitar.

Piano / Vocal

A piano/vocal is a bit easier to deal with than an acoustic guitar/vocal. For starters, a piano is perfectly stationary. They can also be closed up with the microphone inside, and this goes a long way towards isolation. A dynamic mic on the vocal and a dynamic in the piano, and you're good to go!

Of course, I could certainly understand why you'd want the piano stereo for this sort of production. Really, all you need to do is place two microphones in the piano, half-stick the lid, and cover the gaps with blankets. Just be sure those mics are locked down well. Heavy moving blankets are useful for purposes of isolation.

Uprights often open up on the top, and you can stick your mics inside. It might even make sense to leave the lid open, given the limited size of the cavity. As with anything, you'll have to listen to make that determination.

A dynamic on the vocal seems to make the most sense, since it will reject much of the piano information as you sing. That said, if you have decent isolation from the piano, you might be inclined to try out an LDC. Make sure you apply some compression to the vocal at the time of the recording; otherwise, you could have some surprises later. The compression will bring up the bleed of the piano.

If you isolate the piano well, you can always overdub your vocal again later, but then that kind of defeats the point. The main reason to play as you sing is to help with your singing. Not your playing.

Organs

There is nothing quite like a Hammond B3 organ with a Leslie. This could very well require you to visit a studio that has a B3 available, but it's probably worth the expense. The Leslie cabinet was an aftermarket build, and Mr. Hammond was horrified by the cabinets because they introduced distortion. Yeah. And if you turn up the preamp, they can get downright nasty with distortion if you want them to. That's a good thing.

Leslies come in all sorts of configurations and sizes as do Hammond organs. The most common Leslie has spinning horns on the top and a spinning drum on the bottom. The spinning provides motion to the tone. If you put a mic on each side of the spinning horns and pan them left and right, you will capture a solid stereo image. The spinning bottom drum delivers the low-end information, and you can put a mic down there too if you like. The bottom mic can be quite useful to mellow out the tone, but often just results in mud.

You can mic the horns with any kind of mic. Ribbons and LDCs will be the most common choice among engineers. If you're recording a Leslie at home, dynamic mics will work in a pinch, but will likely produce an unusually aggressive tone.

The Leslie has two speeds, fast and slow, which can be controlled by a foot switch. Some B3s have a hand switch, which makes it difficult to operate on your own. Really, you can't expect your average keyboard player to make a B3 sing. These beasts require quite a bit of practice to perform in a convincing manner. That said, not all B3 parts call for an expert player. That really depends on the nature of the part and the production.

B3 organs have drawbars which introduce harmonic information, This allows tremendous control over the tone. B3's also have presets, and two tiers of keyboards with their own set of drawbars. This allows a player to smoothly switch between tones.

Some Hammond B3s come with pedals, which will produce some awesomely deep low end. But they can sound very churchy. Go figure. Others come with a spring reverb. They're fun instruments, and if you're making a roots rock ballad, or a southern rock album, they're virtually a staple.

Where it comes to Hammond B3, I much prefer the real thing, but organ samples in general tend to be reasonably convincing. Organs do well with distortion whether overt or subtle.

Synths

Synths are diverse and can perform just about any function in an arrangement and serve nearly any tone in a production. They can cover the full spectrum of the audible frequency range and beyond. They can be stereo or mono. For the most part, you can completely program and manipulate patches from the synth module itself, including distortion, motion, and reflectivity from internal reverbs and delays. There is nothing that a synth can't cover in a production.

Many synth pads and patches are automatically stereo in nature, but they're also a rather weak stereo, and they tend to really muck up the middle, particularly if you start to layer them.

In order to find the perfect tone, many programmers layer their parts. MIDI performances can be duplicated in order to create identical layers, and so long as the patches you use are wholly independent, you won't have issues with cancellation. Layers not only provide texture, they offer you control over tonality.

If you have too many layers all mucking up the middle, you'll have a difficult time balancing them, so it's important to use placement to your advantage. There is no rule that says all of those layers need to be attached. You can pan them to their own places in the stereo field if you like. This will allow you to take up space without eating it in the process.

Delays are often a staple on synth patches, particularly lead lines which can get a bit choppy without a tail of some sort. Distortion is also useful, and you might choose to derive your distortion from a plugin rather than the module. For whatever reason, synth distortion often amounts to nothing more than the addition of white noise, which isn't particularly useful distortion.

Percussion

Percussive instruments like space, although they don't necessarily require it, and you can always add more later. But if you want your percussion to sound organic, then canned reverbs aren't optimal. At which point, a large wood room might be nice. That said, I've mixed and produced plenty of records with bone-dry percussion, and canned verb is commonplace, especially in the programed genres.

If you're recording percussion one instrument at a time, just set up an LDC in your most appropriate space and be done with it. Condensers react well to transients due to their fast response times. If you want proximity, put the LDC close. If you want more ambiance pull it away. Do you see how simple recording can be?

It's really easy to place your percussion too loud in the balance. Whereas you want to push some air to judge the low end of your balance, the top end is best judged at relatively low levels. Not whisper quiet, mind you, but at a level in which you can comfortably have a conversation over the music. At lower levels, your percussion will be considerably more apparent, and you need to find a compromise that works between a variety of monitoring levels.

You have lots of latitude where it comes to your stereo presentation of percussion. You can close mic congas with dynamic mics facing the skins and spread them hard left and right. Or you can put a single LDC over the congas and collect a mono capture. You could even set up two SDCs in an XY configuration if you want some stereo imaging.

A djembe offers a conga-like slap from the top skin, but produces a beautiful low-end bloom from the bottom of the drum. You can put a condenser on the top and on the bottom. Just make sure that you're not getting wind as a result of the bottom placement. The top and bottom mics should be distant enough to prevent phase coherency issues, but because the bottom mic is facing a top skin, much like a snare drum, the bottom mic will likely require a polarity inversion to get the full bloom of the bottom end.

I should probably just warn you, egg shakers will effectively dull guitars. Maracas and a shekere fall into a far lower frequency range, which makes them more suitable for rock productions. And for whatever reason, you can generally place a tambourine as loud as you like—even too loud.

Cajons can also produce a really great low end out of the back hole, but many of them have snares and that really fucks up the whole kik drum aspect. In other words, if you want your cajon to sound like a drum kit, you're better off without the internal snares. You can always overlay another cajon with snares. It seems like everyone wants to turn their cajon into a drum kit for some reason, and I get it. I want that too.

There are literally thousands of percussion instruments. In most cases, I could set up one LDC in a good room with a good percussion player and use mic placement in order to derive my desired levels of ambience from the capture. Anytime you need more immediacy out of your skins, you can place one mic close and another in the room. You can also just set up a pair of SDCs in an X-Y, which will allow the percussion player to dictate where a part sounds in the stereo field. However, this can be problematic if not planned out, especially for control freaks.

Unless the percussion is an integral and featured part of a production, I often record it last. Tambourines and shakers can bleed from headphones, and a purposeful musical drop implemented later could reveal the headphone bleed. It's not the end of the world when this happens, but it can be prevented with some forethought.

Some percussion is so integral to the genre and the production that it must be recorded early with everything else. A Latin record without the percussion would be as difficult to evaluate as a hard rock record without crunch guitars. It would be impossible to tell where you're at in the production, as those internal percussion rhythms are critical to how the tracks make you feel and move.

Horns

Given an outside section of players, you either need to work out the parts in advance with MIDI and teach the players their parts, or you have to make charts. Winging it is certainly an option with many horn players, but they won't wish to just hang with you all day without pay, so a little prep work goes a long way.

Horn sections work best if everyone plays together. I know that circumstance could prevent you from recording them that way, but the instruments just don't interact quite the same when overdubbed separately. Whatever. It is what it is. But don't expect to overdub three players individually and achieve a convincing section. I'd just as soon use MIDI horns than to record one player at a time. Perhaps even a combination of both.

If you can record three players at once, it's not the worst idea in the world to record everyone on one mic. It does require some discipline from your players. For starters, you need to physically adjust their position to get the blend right. And the players not only need to stay on their mark, they need to blow in tune and with some consistency as a group.

Typically, I'll put a mic in front of each player, but that requires a room with sufficient space and equipment. Ribbons are great for knocking down the strident nature of most horns, but if you don't have those available then a condenser should work. Condensers are often the first choice on woodwinds. You could get away with dynamics, but they could lose some fidelity on pianissimo sections.

Woodwinds emit most of their sound through the finger holes, although one or two notes may sound though the bell. You'll want to place the mic towards the fingers with a distance of one or two feet so it captures the totality of the instrument. And if you stick a mic directly in front of the blowhole of a flute, you could get some rather windy results. It's best to mic the flute either from above or on the fingers. As with everything, you place your mic, then you listen and adjust based on what you hear.

In many ways, miking an instrument can be an exercise in common sense. If you understand how and where the source emits sound, then you can better strategize as to where to capture that sound. Most players will understand how and where their instrument emits sound, but even if they don't, determining the best spot for a mic is as easy as listening to the instrument itself.

Unless you're recording an established section of horn players, tuning is often an issue. The players really need to be able to hear each other to keep in tune as a section. Many horn players will pull out one of their In-Ears, or slide one of their headphones to the back of the head. Others will prefer to keep both ears on, in which case you need to be sure they have enough of themselves in their headphones.

Voice leading is an important skill set to have when it comes to working out horn parts. If you find it difficult to come up with four parts that work well together, that's because it *is* difficult. Like anything else, it just requires practice. It's also totally worth the time it takes to learn voice leading. There are many musical rules when writing four-part harmonies, most of them rather obvious when you hear them—like no parallel fifths—but understanding those rules makes it easier and faster to deal with problems.

Four-part arrangements are considerably more challenging to write than three. A good horn section should be able to help with that, even if it's outside of your wheelhouse. In fact, if you've never written for horns, you might do well to work directly with a horn player. Or work out your horn parts in MIDI first. Just keep in mind, when it comes to horns, the note ranges can vary based on the skill of the player. Most trumpet players can't play above the high E, but that is by no means the full range of the instrument.

If you're making an organic funk or rock record, then it makes sense to use real horns. Canned horns laid over an organic band can sound almost offensive in nature. You'd be better off using some other instrumentation than to use horn samples in that situation. A synth can produce a similar timbre to horns without trying to sound organic.

I'm not sure what it is exactly about the addition of sampled horns to an organic production, but it doesn't generally work well. If you're fully electronic, you can get away with the addition of organic instrumentation. No worries there. You can even get away with mixing and matching organic with inorganic tones, so long as you establish it early. But if the rhythm section is fully organic, you could completely destroy any semblance of authenticity with the introduction of canned horns–canned anything really. It's similar to hiding an embarrassing part low within the balances. All that does is make the offending part more obvious.

Horn sections often perform countermelodic and response parts. These sorts of parts don't have to be performed by horns. A guitar player could perform horn parts. A synthesizer can perform horn parts. Vocals could perform a horn part. And what makes a horn section rich is the diversity in timbre in combination with their register. You can create that with any combination of instruments you like. What's important is how the parts combine to function in the arrangement.

Recording a horn section all at once requires preparation, space, and equipment. You're also recording four people, which usually means paying them, and if you're compensating players, then it doesn't make a whole lot of sense not to hire a studio too.

Horns are exceptional for adding drama to a production either through musical response interjections or countermelodies. They can also be used to fill in harmonic information. And if you want to learn how to arrange for horns, the best way to do that is to listen to lots of music with horns and imitate.

Strings

String samples are generally more forgiving than horn samples in terms of authenticity of tone, but that really depends on the nature of the part. A section of strings playing long drawn-out chordal arrangements sounds relatively convincing. An expressive solo gypsy violin? Not so much. Not without a really good sample to start, and the ability to express yourself with a keyboard and a modulation wheel.

There are just some things you can't rightly pull off with samples without some skills in programming and a basic understanding of how the instrument is expressed. If this is outside of your wheelhouse, you may need to choose some other more forgiving instrumentation. It's difficult to mimic the expression of an organic instrument with a keyboard sample.

Pizzicato string samples sound authentic, and work as samples. Cellos are more authentic than violins, but all of this is dependent on your sample library. The good news is many of the more expensive sample libraries offer subscriptions now.

I've mixed a great many records in my career in which the strings were arranged by self-admitted hacks, and I gotta say, they don't usually come out all that great. Of course, I've also mixed tracks with string arrangements delivered by top professionals, which also didn't come out that great. This usually occurs when the strings are written in an orchestral manner, almost as an afterthought to the production.

A string quartet that can play in balance requires only two condensers. You could put a mic on each player if you like, but that really shouldn't be necessary. Doubling a quartet will give you a fuller sound, but the chorusing that occurs isn't all that natural and can get downright phasey. That said, it's way more expensive to record eight players, and so most of us double track the quartet despite the underwhelming results.

Horn players are generally far better at winging parts than most string players. Horns also tend to be a more common instrumentation in modern records, and so they are more likely to perform in band settings than string players. You might have an easier time with strings in the South, due to the popularity of bluegrass, but fiddle players don't tend to sit and play as a group.

Anything beyond a quartet requires a studio, an arranger (who often acts as the Leader), and a recordist, preferably one who has recorded strings before. This makes strings an expensive proposition. Even a small string section can be prohibitive, as many string players must be paid through the musicians union. You might be able to put together a section without the union, but that will often provide you with a crew of scrubs. Programmed strings seem the better option in general. And just as with horns, it's often the part that matters more so than the actual instrumentation.

Vocals

The vocal is money. It carries the melody and the lyric, which means it carries the entire song. Everything else in the production—harmony, rhythm, countermelodies, response, and bass—is there to support the vocal. For some of you, the vocal session is the only time you'll require a mic.

By far, the most commonly used microphone for vocals is the LDC. They're big sensitive mics that capture the full range of the frequency spectrum. They also look impressive in front of a singer, which can have the added benefit of boosting the singer's confidence, even if you're the singer. But an LDC is not automatically the best choice, and not all LDCs sound great on all singers.

As a producer and recordist, it's not uncommon for me to shoot out several mics at a time until I find a mic that shines. But as an Artist or a singer, you really only need one great mic, the one in which you generally sound best.

If you perform live, then you probably already have a dynamic. I've used dynamic mics for vocals on plenty of records. Some of you may even sound best on a dynamic mic, in which case, that's what you should use. But at some point, you might want to investigate a good condenser. And not just any condenser, but rather, the best condenser for your voice.

How do you find that? You could go on the Internet and ask random strangers of varying experience levels what the best microphone is for your vocals, all based on a description of your voice. Which is kind of weird, because I couldn't predict the best mic for you, even if you were to sing right in front of me. How could anyone suggest a mic based on your own skewed description of your voice? *Um, hi first time poster here! I sound like a cross between Bono and Bruce Springsteen. What's the best mic for me?*

Pffft.

If I were a young Artist, and I was willing to pony up some money for a microphone, I would first rent out one or possibly even a few local studios in the hopes of finding the best mic for my voice.

It's always good if you can get in the room with someone experienced, but unless you've worked with this person and know their tastes, you need to trust yourself first and foremost. It's the subjectivity of recording and music that makes it so difficult. We don't all hear the same, and my platinum records or someone else's Grammy may indicate success, but they do not guarantee musical alignment. You also know how you want your vocals to sound, and if you like what you hear as you sing on a particular mic, then that's the best mic for you, regardless of what anyone else thinks.

As a producer, I'm always interested in what the singer prefers and will defer to her wishes in all but the rarest of instances. All I care about is the performance, and if she's in a good space and happy with the mic, then I have a better shot of her delivering an inspired performance.

Should you decide to audition mics at your local studios, it's best to be completely up front as to your intentions. Be sure to tell the manager that you seek the counsel of the engineer and that you're willing to pay for the hour or two of studio time required. Most studios will rent their room for less than $50 an hour, and the home studios might charge as little as $25 per hour. Even a large commercial facility will be inclined to give you a decent price on some time if it means time with a potential client. To lay out a $100 for the opportunity to try out a bunch of mics seems a less expensive venture than to purchase a mic blind only to sell it a month later. Good LDCs can cost anywhere from $500 to thousands of dollars. Some vintage mics bring in tens of thousands of dollars.

It's important to note, you can't really evaluate how you sound on one vintage mic and then assume that's how you'll sound on another vintage mic of the same model. Environment and maintenance over the course of decades will result in a significant variation in tone between identical models. Some mics have been modified or cleaned, others have never been touched. So, if you're somehow convinced you need a vintage mic, you have to sing on the actual mic you wish to purchase. This may require flying to the mic.

Most vintage mics are overpriced and, unless money is no object, you would do well to stay away from them. I'm not suggesting that I don't like vintage mics. Nor am I saying that new mics are better. I'm saying that vintage mics are subject to supply and demand, and it doesn't make sense to spend all of $500 on room treatment to house your $5,000 vintage microphone.

I'll admit, there are quite a few crappy new stock microphone lines on the market today, some that have captured the imagination of home-recording enthusiasts, which has everything to do with price point. But there are also some boutique lines of microphones that sound absolutely stunning across the board. It can take many years for a new microphone brand to overcome perception issues, so just because you haven't heard of a particular line of microphones doesn't mean anything in terms of quality. In other words, ignore the hype or lack thereof, and choose your mic based solely on how the tone of it makes you feel about your vocals.

When it comes time to compare mics at the studio, you need to get some variables out of the way. First of all, you should bring a stereo track to sing against, preferably your own recording and production. Secondly, make sure that your engineer uses the same variety of preamp for each of the mics. Finally, ask her to record it. This way you can listen to the results for yourself.

Now, as much as you are on a quest to investigate condensers, it is possible that you will sound best on a dynamic, and you would do well to include some of those in your shootout. You might even want to bring your current mic to see how it stacks up.

Dynamics will shine on singers with an obvious glut in their midrange. I'll warn you now though, dynamics can be a major pain in the ass on vocalists who sometimes get excited and forget about proximity for a moment. Even slight shifts on a dynamic microphone will manifest as obvious tonal shifts within the production.

Mic placement is a big deal when it comes to vocals, but you wouldn't know it to watch most engineers as they will routinely put the mic directly in front of the vocalist's mouth. It's really not an unreasonable place to start. Unfortunately, it becomes nothing more than a default, because singers and producers often get weird if the mic isn't directly in front of them.

A pop filter is also usual, although, if you place the mic well, you don't need one of those either. That said, I use a pop filter regardless of the placement. For starters, I can set the filter up as a target for the singer, which allows me some latitude with mic placement. But the main purpose is to prevent plosives caused by the rush of air from the b's and the p's. In fact, I use a specialized SPL filter, which is designed to protect ribbon mics. And although it does slightly change the tone picked up by the mic, I'll take that if it means no plosives ever.

Proximity will help you derive some low end from the vocalist, it will also result in more ess and more plosives, which is just another reason why you might want to place the capsule out of the direct line of the singer's mouth. The esses are super directional and are the first signal that your capsule picks up. The best way to fix it is to raise or lower the mic. This keeps the ess from a direct hit on the capsule. It also prevents the errant plosive.

When you lower the mic it will derive more low end from the chest cavity. This can be overbearing on a male vocalist in his lower register, but quite useful on female vocalists who tend to get whiney in their higher register. Don't take offense to that. Violins are whiney too. That adjective has to do with frequency not gender.

Copious amounts of compression are usual on a modern vocal. Music must compete with all sorts of external noise in the real world, and an overly dynamic vocal will disappear from audibility. That's no good. The right analog compressor can help a vocal tremendously, but poorly designed analog compressors will introduce obvious artifacts almost immediately, which are best avoided. While there is nothing wrong with audible compression, if the artifacts are obvious regardless of your settings, then you can't rightly control them.

Don't be afraid to move the meter on your compressor. There are some analog compressors that you can hit very hard without any obvious artifacts. There are others that will introduce woolliness and distortion. That's not something to be afraid of, but rather something to use to your advantage when it suits you.

There are times that I will produce a vocal with copious and obvious compression. There are other times that I want the compression completely invisible. Much of that has to do with the genre or song, although trends might have some influence. Obvious vocal compression was all the rage in the mid-nineties. Currently, it's the obvious tuning artifacts and distortion that are popular. Like everything, that will change.

When you've been through enough trends, you treat them for what they are. Or at least you should. They are moments in time where technology is used in an unintended manner to produce a fresh new effect. Once one Artist uses it, then everyone has got to use it. That makes trendiness a useful module to implement in your productions. Following a production trend is a great way to bring in something modern and familiar to your production, especially if your record falls outside of what is trending musically.

The precise nature of the desired vocal tone is often dictated by the genre and placement within the track. You can dip an aggressive vocal into a production and have it cut through like a knife. You can also put a big warm vocal boldly over the track, but that requires space in your arrangement and a low end that can support it, otherwise, you'll dwarf the track. People don't dance to a little pitter patter of rhythm in the background behind a stupidly loud vocal.

You have two competing forces that operate in tandem to provide a listener enjoyment–rhythm and melody. The only way to get them to work together is to give them both their due. Your rhythmic elements cause the listener to move, and your melodic elements cause her to sing. And if you have no rhythmic structure in your production? Then you have the rubato melodic meanderings of a poet. A melody doesn't even exist without a rhythmic structure.

There's no way around it, you want the listener to move appropriately to the track and you want them to sing. If you get the balance wrong between the track and the vocal, you will kill one of those reactions. That said, I think that you're far better off placing a vocal too loud than trying to duck it into a track.

If you want to keep the vocal loud and the track strong, then your vocal must sit perfectly in the mix from top to bottom. Compressors and limiters are the first step toward accomplishing this—vocal rides through automation are the second. The more aggressive you are with the compressor, the less vocal rides you'll need to automate. Aggressive compression on a vocal brings out breaths, sibilance, lip smacks, foot shuffling, rustling, and any other noise the mic happened to pick up during the recording process. Sometimes all that noise is perfectly acceptable—desirable, even—in which case you can be as aggressive as you like with your compressors. Should you choose to implement a few compressors in series, you will also reduce the need for automation.

The bottom line is, the vocal is what sells the song, and you don't do yourself any favors by making it difficult to hear. Place it loud and proud in your production and keep it focused with compression and automation. And if you leave lots of space in the middle for it, you'll derive strength from the sides too.

When it comes to reverb on the vocal, I choose the space based on the level of intimacy I seek. Trends also come into play, but in general, if the production and the song are intimate, I'll keep the vocal that way. I've mixed many records in which the vocal is bone dry.

Where it comes to selecting your reverb module, it's best if you can narrow down your options by category: hall, room, plate, outdoor, or gated verb. Then by size: small, medium, large. From there, you can scroll through your presets, at which point you'll either find an appropriate verb or choose a different category and size.

A little goes a long way with reverb, and the tendency is often to add too much. Sometimes a bold reverb treatment is absolutely called for, but you start to lose clarity when you bury the vocal in reverb. I mean, that's one of the functions of reverb, to obfuscate, which is the opposite of clarity. Once again we get into a territory of taste, but I find it's best to err on the side of too little reverb than too much. But then, I rarely seek to obfuscate. As a mixer and producer, I'll take your weakest part and feature it if you let me.

Aside from your general intimacy, you can choose your verb based on what it's filling in terms of frequency. A bright track or a bright vocal might like a dark verb. A bright reverb could set off the vocal nicely on a dark track.

You can also use a reverb to thicken the vocal. A tiny bit of almost imperceptible short room can help set a vocal nicely into the track. Notice I said imperceptible, not inaudible. You place it so that it's not perceived as space, but when it goes away, you notice it's gone.

Delays on vocals are easier to deal with than reverbs because they give you a tail and you can place them bold in your balance without taking up an inordinate amount of space.

Stereo Vocals

Once a week it seems a post comes up online from someone asking for advice on recording a vocal with two mics for purposes of a stereo vocal. The funny thing is, based on the hundreds of comments encouraging this sort of technique, you'd think that recording a vocal in stereo was the most common thing around. Yet, when you listen to known records, one after another for hours, production after production presents a mono vocal dead in the center.

I understand creativity. I get pushing boundaries. I'm all for inventiveness. But there's a reason why, for the past 50 years of stereo, 99.99 percent of the vocals from popular records are placed dead in the center. The vocal is the song.

So, how do we reconcile the nonexistence of a stereo vocal on major releases with a forum full of people who do it on regular occasion?

Record-making requires listening, and not just to what you're doing, but to what everyone else has done before you. At this point, nearly anything that you come up with in regards to recording has been done a million times before you even thought of it. That doesn't mean you shouldn't try your creative ideas. You should. But if stereo vocals never caught on, it's probably because everyone who thought of it before us realized it doesn't work all that great.

Much like an acoustic guitar, a singer is not perfectly stationary. As such, unless your singer is physically restrained in a vice, that vocal will shift within the stereo field, causing weird and dynamic phase issues. And while this kind of interaction can occur on an acoustic-guitar vocal recording, we merely accept it for the benefit to the performance.

You can do anything you like with your Art. But if you want to be successful with your music, you might want to avoid phase-shifting issues on the one part that contains the entirety of the song. There are plenty of other places to get creative. Engineering trickery on the vocal isn't one of them.

Background Vocals

The same pitfalls that exist when writing parts for horns and strings apply to vocal harmonies. They all follow the same rules. The most important rule being to never cross lines.

If the harmony starts off above the melody, that harmony has to stay above the melody, otherwise, you've crossed lines. Once you cross lines, the function of the parts switch, and that's a musical mistake that requires a technical fix.

Say we have a male singer performing a harmony for a female lead vocalist. The male harmony starts out a third below the melody, balanced a few dB under the female lead. Halfway through the phrase, the male part goes above the female melody. Not only do we now perceive that male vocalist as performing the melody (which he's not), he's 3 dB too low to boot. That's a big problem.

The melody gets a line, the harmony gets a line, and every subsequent harmony gets a line and those lines never shall cross. None of them. And while you can get away with crossing internal harmonies, if you cross a harmony with a melody, the harmony becomes the melody. That is how the listener will perceive it.

You should also avoid unison moments in your voice leading. Harmonies that land on the unison are weak. There are times that it can work, and there are other times when it's the best solution to get yourself out of a corner. There might even be times that you do it on purpose, but in general momentary unison notes aren't the greatest.

Believe it or not, crossing lines is rather unnatural, and difficult to do. In fact, many of us, myself included, write and perform our background parts on the fly. So, your parts don't necessarily have to be worked out in advance. Just keep in mind, it's far more difficult to voice lead for four parts than it is for three, and the melody is one of the parts. The first harmony is easy. The second harmony too. It's when you get to your third harmony that you might find you've harmonized yourself into a corner.

Harmonies are typically placed below the lead in the balance, although you can push them all the way to even with the lead vocal if that's what you prefer. But once the harmonies are louder than the lead, then you have a problem. Your melody becomes ambiguous, and the listener confused.

Stacking harmonies as overdubs one at a time with doubles, triples and quadruples has a sound to it, as does a group choir. Unfortunately, they aren't interchangeable. The best way to bring the feeling of a choir into your production is to go to a church and record a choir. If that's not an option then you can create the illusion of a choir by placing several singers around a condenser set to omnidirectional, and then track them all performing together one vocal line at a time. You can then double track them. You can even quintuple track them if you like, it all depends on how big you want that choir. There is a point, however, where chorusing turns into phasing, and that will bust the illusion of a choir.

You can record your stacked background vocals one at a time, and you can record them super tight or super loose—that's all a matter of style. The loose backgrounds will certainly feel more carefree in nature and the tight ones more controlled, and your production would seem to dictate which is best.

When you want your backgrounds super tight, it's good to work in small sections. You need to learn what you did on take one in order to match it on take two. You also need to hear that first take well in your monitor mix in order to effectively double it. You can pull an ear off your headphones and cup your hand against your jaw with fingers to your ear, which will sound as if you're singing directly into your own ear. This can make it far easier to sing in tune.

I have to say, it doesn't make sense to inject a whole lot of personality into a stacked background part. Vibrato is a little weird when you have lots

255

of parts, and if you keep the background stacks relatively plain, it leaves a lot more room for your lead vocalist to riff. In general, vibrato as a technique has gone out of favor, mostly because it's no longer necessary to obfuscate tuning. Whatever. I say good riddance. Nothing makes me reach for the skip button more readily than overt vibrato.

Be mindful in regards to how aggressively you tune your background vocals because they can get a little phasey and weird when you do. If strange phasing artifacts on your backgrounds don't bother you, then carry on. But if you want those vocals to sound relatively natural, then you'll have to get the preponderance of them in tune as you record. This just requires attention to detail.

The more vocals you stack the less intimate the track. If you want an intimate harmony, just record one person per part. Four-part harmony is clearly less intimate than one-part harmony, but it's the doubling that breaks the illusion of intimacy. The moment you double, the party just got too big.

Background vocals love chorus *efx*, phasers, ensembles, exciters–anything with motion or mild distortion. That's not to say you should apply these sorts of *efx* to all background vocals, but if you're having a little trouble pulling clarity from them, the addition of upper harmonic distortion will help, and it doesn't even need to be overt.

Any Other Instrument

By now, there should be no instrument that you can't figure out how to best record, even one that you've never seen before. All you need to do is ask yourself some questions.

> Where does the sound come from? Does the sound come from more than one place? If so, do I need more than one mic to capture it properly?

Is the instrument stationary or shifting? Will more than one mic cause me phase coherency issues? Is there any way around that? Would it be best captured with some proximity effect? Would it be best captured from distance?

Does the instrument react well to space? How much space do I need to record it effectively?

Does my production call for a natural tone or an aggressive one? What frequency range does it cover? What musical function does it serve?

Once you have the answer to those questions, you'll know exactly what to do.

That would be for the win, my friends.

The
Outro

Artistically, I'd rather work with a great band than a mediocre one. Sadly, if the mediocre band is good at marketing, they're likely the better bet.

There's no doubt, if you're the kind of player that stands head and shoulders above the rest, people will notice you and find you and you will have fans. For everyone else? You need to find your lane, you need to find it fast, and you need to have your shit together on the business side of things. That's asking a lot from a crowd that chose music over business.

After releasing five books with a publisher, I made the decision to run an Indiegogo Campaign in order to fund, and subsequently self-publish, this book. Why did I choose to forego my publisher? Because I have a fanbase willing to purchase the book in advance, and because I can fully distribute my product without them. Essentially, Amazon has turned the publisher into a middle man. That's quite the trick.

Sure, I'd love to be with a big publisher selling millions of books, but this is not the kind of book for that. For this product, for this market, for the fanbase that I have now, it only makes sense for me to put this book out myself. But this is just the first step in my plan. It's only a matter of time before publishers seek out writers based purely on their independent sales numbers. As a consequence, publishers will no longer be the filter they once were. That's been true for record labels for some time now.

The days of seeking a label deal from your garage are over. Why should a corporation take a chance on you without any evidence that people react to your music? A Distributor can see how many Facebook fans you have, and can see how many Twitter followers you have, and if there aren't a whole shitload of fans visible, then you're not in a position for a label deal. You wouldn't want one anyway.

If you think that paying for a service to pump up your social media numbers is going to bring you over the edge, forget it. That's the Major Label game now, and you don't have enough money to play it. Sure, you can tweak your SEO and post regular updates, and set up an email schedule and that's all important to your business. But at the end of the day, your fans have to find you, and that requires a reaction of some sort.

It's more critical than ever for you to own your product these days, and the same technology that has devalued music has also given us the opportunity to reach fans from any position. The stigma of independence is gone. Most successful musicians and Artists are independent at this point. Of course, my definition of *successful* has nothing to do with wealth. Eighty percent of us couldn't cover a month of bills with our savings. At this point, if you can sustain yourself financially with your music, then you're successful, if for no other reason than it puts you in a position to scale. All that any of us really wants is an opportunity to get ahead.

The Business

I live in Asheville, NC these days. It's a city with a population of nearly 100,000 and an unusually high *per capita* of musicians who call it home. There are scores of studios here, including one of note, yet there is no semblance of a music industry.

I can tell you, it's not easy for musicians in the current climate because venues are also businesses, and they don't want to pay bands who don't bring a crowd with them. And you can understand their argument. If you're not able to attract an audience, then why should you be paid? Of course, the real question should probably be why should you be booked? But then the answer is because the venues have to fill their schedule with three bands seven nights a week. Multiply that by enough venues, and there's not enough population to support the number of shows. And tourists are usually tired after a long day, and don't want to go catch an act they know nothing about at 11:00 at night.

To make matters worse, musicians aren't great at organizing. They tend to have a libertarian streak to them despite a liberal bent, and as a group, they don't take kindly to collective bargaining. Which means there is little to no joint negotiation. And don't go to the city for help. Most cities would sooner piss on you, even ones that revere their musicians.

Asheville invested millions in music, and despite my pleas for them to invest directly into the music community, they chose to invest in advertising to tourists. Much of that has to do with county and city laws that bind them, but let's be real, those can be changed. I could have made a record for every Artist in this city for what they paid outside ad agencies. Come to Asheville! Music town USA! Meanwhile, musicians are paid $50 each per night because eight more venues opened up. No worries. There's also tips! Criminal.

I won't pretend this isn't complicated, and I don't mean to go down this rabbit hole, because this book is meant to be an uplifting experience. As frustrating as things still are, musicians stand to win this battle in the long run. But you need to treat it like a business, and if you think that you can rely solely on the local economy, you probably can't. You need to expand your fan base, first regionally, and then nationally. And yes, I understand that you want a viral hit, but that's considerably easier to do if you've built up a base first.

Surely, you can attract people to listen to you online, but the predominant income stream for musicians and Artists currently comes from their live shows. That would make your online activities promotional in nature. A loss leader, as it were. And since it's tough to get paid well for your show, you also need to sell product, and that starts with your CDs.

The Product

I get many requests from Indie bands who want me to quote them a rate for mixing their full-length album. I don't even offer a quote anymore. I mean, if a band is crying poor on their introductory note to me, then I'm certainly not going to bother to negotiate against myself. But if you want to make me an offer? I'll certainly consider it.

I've been accepting offers like this for several years now, and the first thing that I do is listen to some roughs, and if I like the music, then I'll consider an offer. But I rarely take the gig because the large majority of bids come in around $100 for a track. That's at least six hours of my time probably as much as ten (because I don't slough off mixes regardless of what I'm paid for them), which would bring my perceived value to what? $10 per hour? That's what I was paid as a staff engineer to record The Pharcyde album in 1992. I could get paid more than $10 an hour at Starbucks.

I understand that musicians are poor, and the entire business is in flux, so I don't take too much offense to my brand being distilled down to barista levels of pay, but it does make me wonder. Why record a full-length album if you can barely afford to make a single?

From a business perspective, you're far better off to put out three EPs over the course of the year than an entire album every two, which is exactly what happens when you make a full-length album, because it requires so much of your resources that it takes that long to recover. I mean, you recorded ten songs.

The name of the game today is to release content with absolute regularity. You can't have periods of inactivity because you'll lose your audience and all momentum too. The key is to get people into the habit of visiting you.

If the goal is to make money making music, and you wish to build your fan base and your audience, then you have to treat your music project like a business. And as a business, you have to be visible at all times. If not, you're forgotten.

It's no accident that Coca-Cola, a brand that has been on top for the better part of 100 years, advertises everywhere. If they don't, other companies will begin to eat into their market share, which means less shelf space for Coke products, which will result in a contraction rather than continued expansion. So, it's worth it for them to spend ungodly amounts of money to maintain their position, otherwise someone will take it from them.

If a company as well-established as Coca-Cola needs to stay visible, then clearly we do too. Unfortunately, we don't have the resources to invest in ubiquitous everlasting advertising campaigns. Nor can we just buy up the competition. We have to do it by attracting rabid fans who engage and spread the word.

As far as I'm concerned, there's really only one viable business plan for content creators that wish to make a living as such. Get famous. Capitalize. Unfortunately, that usually doesn't happen overnight, even if it appears that way to the outside observer. Often, a rapid climb to fame—even moderate fame—obscures all the work that was required to get to that position in the first place. Other times it's dumb luck or good timing. Either way, there's no way around it—as independent content providers, we must develop rabid fans.

In other words, as much as your plan may include going viral, you still must be willing and able to go through the grind of building your business one fan at a time until you've reached some mass. That will put you in a far better position to generate something viral, because you have a large enough fan base from which to expand. Your fans are just waiting for something dope that they can share with all their friends.

Frankly, if your first product goes viral, that's not necessarily a good thing. Believe me, you'll take a viral hit anytime you can get one, but if it comes too early, you won't be in a position to capitalize upon it. There are far worse problems to have, but in the long run it will be easier if you're in a position to scale. This requires you to maintain your existing fan base through a regular stream of content. The full-length album no longer seems to fulfill that requirement.

If you put out a ten-song album at the beginning of the year, what happens for the rest of the year? Singles? But your current fans have probably already listened to the whole album, and a single release is nothing more than old news. And sure, you can put out a new video three times a year, but you could release a new record with a video too.

Given the realities of how things work today, I think it makes far more sense to put out three songs at a time as often as you can. It might even make sense to only put out singles. This way you offer your fans a constant stream of new music rather than merely repackaging previously released material into a video.

Regular and consistent releases provide you with several benefits: You get the opportunity to determine what music resonates. You break up your costs and time into smaller more affordable budgets. And you get a higher return on your investment. Fans will pay $10 for your three-song CD just as readily as they will your full-length album. Around these parts, CDs are the currency of musicians. It's an important part of the business plan.

All of that said, there are also many good reasons to record an LP, and this should not be taken as a full-throated argument against the medium. It can make way more sense for a touring band to put out an album. But then, a touring band likely also has the resources to make the product, which only further illustrates my point. If you have to go out of your way to beg, borrow, and steal in order to make an album, perhaps you should consider an EP instead.

There's no doubt about it, you need to keep your audience engaged through the regular release of product. It's how your fans feel connected to you. I've avoided this reality myself for far too long.

Making a Connection

In this age in which we've all become a part of our own private *Truman Show*, it's more important than ever to make a direct connection with your fans. It's not good enough to email spam masquerading as updates and announcements. Your fans want to know about you. They want an experience.

As you might expect, I have an email list, and the day I began my Indiegogo Campaign, I sent out an email telling my list of fans about the new book. The result? Crickets.

Oh sure, I had some initial support, but it wasn't what I'd hoped. I recognize that many people prefer to procrastinate, but I set the campaign for a two-week turnaround specifically to combat that reality. Unfortunately, the reaction to my first email was poor at best.

Well, I pretty much had a private little freak out on the second day of my campaign, because just as some prefer to wait until the end, others often jump right in. Unfortunately, there just weren't enough early adopters for me to have any chance of reaching goal. A few dry heaves later, I had an epiphany. This needed to be personal.

So, I wrote to my list, and shared with them my realization and asked them to tell me their stories. This is a business in which we must listen, after all, and if people are going to listen to me, then I need to listen to them. After years of writing and sharing my own stories, it was time to read the stories of my fans.

The response was amazing. The first day I received well over 100 emails, and I read and replied to every one of them. Not only did this give me the opportunity to learn who my fans were–it opened up sales too.

I'm not a big believer in pummeling people with emails that amount to spam, but I had a two-week window in which to run a successful campaign, and many thousands of dollars to go until goal. So, I composed another email, touting the response, and I asked my fans to send me even more stories. The results of which were another 100 emails from fans who wanted to share their history.

I sent an email out every other day, sometimes every day, and I wrote and shared my experiences about running a fundraising campaign, and I wrote and shared portions of the book to attract more sales. Then I hopped on Facebook and made it personal there too. I asked all of my friends and fans if they could help me—to share my campaign and to share their stories too. Facebook rewards interaction, so I made sure to *Like* and reply to every post in order to make it visible to all of my followers. While it was no doubt obnoxious to have to sit there all day and reply to any and every response in order for my post to show in the Notifications of others, there is no doubt that it was effective.

Whereas I started my Mixerman career as an anonymous donor, with a definitive wall between myself and my fans, now I must make a personal connection with each and every one of those fans. How times have changed.

My fans are no different from your fans. My book is my Art. Your record is yours. And so it is critical that you connect with your fans personally, before and after shows, on Social Media, and through your emails. It's not enough to make people aware of your new products, you must make them a part of the product somehow, which will give them a reason to share your Art with their friends.

Surely, there comes a point when there are too many fans for you to maintain direct connections beyond the most rabid of them. At which point you'll have no choice but to limit access. If you have a million fans, you can't rightly read, let alone respond to, 10,000 comments to your latest Tweet. But in this day and age, in which reality television has infiltrated our politics, you still need to make it personal somehow. Those that can figure out how will be the most successful among us. For the now, anyway. Everything changes.

The good news is, I'm at a point in my life where I want to be out front and center, and I'm fully comfortable with having a personal relationship with the people who support my efforts. So I extend to you the same offer that I made to those on my email list. Tell me your story. Let me know who you are. Share with me your accomplishments and your dreams. And go ahead and tell me what you thought of the book. All you have to do is send me a note to mixerman@mixerman.net.

Bringing It Home

As a young lad I would have killed to have the processing power that you have in your DAW. Looking back, I'm kind of glad I didn't.

Why? Because we're prone to do too much.

When you're new to something, and you don't know anything at all, it is impossible to discern what you need and what you don't. You could have 30 plugins in your DAW. For all you know, you need them all on every channel. You don't.

If you're programming your music, chances are it's not all that dynamic, which means you won't really need much compression. You can program the precise velocity of your parts in MIDI, but in most electronic productions everything hits at full at all times. While it's true that compressors can help to shape tone, they aren't all that effective when there's no dynamic range to contain. Surely, parallel compression can be used to accentuate the initial transients, but if you just slap compressors on everything as a matter of course regardless of the actual dynamic, then you're skipping the most important step. Listening.

Now, it might sound silly for me to suggest that you need to listen, but believe it or not, it's a lost discipline. Perhaps the constant onslaught of media has resulted in an ability to tune everything out. Which is a good skill set to have these days. You still need to listen.

Much like everything important about record-making, this too is about life. We have lost our ability to listen as a society. We talk over one another. We don't consider perspective beyond our own. We've become openly tribalistic. We are more concerned with socializing than learning. We argue rather than debate. We shun the well-founded advice of experts in favor of forging new ground. Meet the new ground, same as the old ground.

I have no illusion that I can somehow diagnose and cure our societal ills, but they do seem to break down to one core problem. We don't listen.

We spent a decent chunk of the previous chapter on listening exercises. It would seem almost ridiculous to perform listening exercises from a book if it weren't more ridiculous not to, considering the subject matter. At its fundamental core, our job as musicians and record-makers is to listen. You can't expect to be heard if you don't bother to listen.

Every day I read a thread on an audio Group in which both the question and the comments leave me wondering whether anyone ever actually listens to records. Like, how do you make records if you don't at least listen to and mimic successful records? And yes, I understand there comes a time where you must forge your own thing, at which point it can be good to ignore what others have done before you. But that only happens after you've established a foundation.

You can shun what everyone did before you, but you're not coming up with anything new. You're building on what came before you, using the same notes, and the same rhythms, and you're creating it with the same gear and the same basic techniques as everyone else. That still leaves tremendous room to create something unique and familiar at the same time. But if you want to understand what makes records great? That requires that you sit down and evaluate great records.

I've given you a method in this Guide, one in which you simplify the technical process and build your record musically with intent. It's a method to get you started, As you learn recording, as you advance, you will naturally start to operate outside of those restrictions.

I made a recording yesterday in which I ignored almost all of my own advice in this book. I even used two mics to create a stereo image of an acoustic guitar. Why? Because it worked in this one particular case. And the only way that I know that it worked is because I listened to it. You make your decisions based on what you hear and what you feel, and nothing else.

There's just no way around it. If you want to make a Killer Record, you need to reference Killer Records. Lots of them.

Referencing

Whereas referencing *music* is a great way to learn about music, referencing *sound* is great way to confuse the living shit out of yourself. The reason? There is no consistency in sound. Were I to select 20 records from the past 50 years across the genre spectrum, their sonic makeup would be all over the map.

Technology pushes the sonic trends. In the seventies and early eighties, records were pressed to vinyl, and you couldn't push the low end aggressively without the needle jumping out of the groove. In the mid-eighties CDs took over, but it wasn't until the mid-nineties that mixers like myself started to really push the low end. The late-nineties until the mid-tens were all about loudness. And today the low-end curves are off the charts as streaming sites now reward the delivery of dynamic tracks over loud ones. A reasonable dynamic range leaves us more space for the low end.

I always find it fascinating when someone claims a record from the eighties as their best sonic reference. The EQ curves from that time were atrocious, and many of those records were remastered in the *aughts* to be loud. As a result, not only do they have insufficient low end, they're often loud to boot. This reference translates how? I listen to records from my youth and wonder where's the beef?

Consumer playback systems typically boost the low end considerably. Beats headphones push them beyond reasonable limits, and these days the boombox has been replaced by a brick that acts like a subwoofer. Yet, despite this, young producers push the low end almost beyond reason.

Don't get me wrong. I love it. I'm right there with anyone and everyone that wants copious amounts of low-end information in their production. Clearly, people can't get enough of it.

I say it all the time. Low end is what separates the men from the boys in this business. To mix with a robust low end that's in control and doesn't completely overwhelm your production takes some practice. If you've mixed anything at all, then you're probably familiar, because most of us push too much low end when we start out. Which brings up a salient and important question: how the hell do you avoid pushing too much low end, if the expectation is ostensibly a production with too much low end?

It's all about control.

You can push the low end in your balances, so long as you contain it. Low end sings when it's contained, and it consumes when it's overly dynamic. So, you can push as much low end as you like, so long as you have the space for it, and so long as you keep it under control.

There's no way around it, you just can't compare the EQ curve of an old record to a new one. You can reference the song and the arrangement based on how the track makes you feel. But sonics? Even if you were to limit your references to just the past three years, there will be a stunning variance in tone that makes it difficult to figure out what's acceptable. The reality is, any and all of it is acceptable.

For starters, the instrumentation and the key will both have a significant influence on the overall EQ curve of any given production. Drop-C is an outrageously dark key in which the bottom note of the guitar is C2 which sounds at 65 Hz, and the bottom note of the bass is C1 at 33 Hz. That's really low. You just aren't going to get a light bright record out of a drop C presentation. So, if you're referencing tracks in Drop C against tracks in the key of A, you're going to come away with the impression that your record is dark.

It *is* dark. You recorded it in drop C. That would be the reason to record in that key.

Genre will also have a great influence on the overall EQ curve of a record. An R&B track can't rightly be compared to a rock production. The rock track is heavy in midrange and often light in the low end. Conversely, the R&B

track is typically light in the midrange and heavy in the low end. As a result, the rock record will sound small in comparison.

Were you to go out of your way to find tracks that are similar in nature, the sound of them still can't be compared. Even the feelings they evoke can't be compared. Every record is unique in the feelings it causes, and our mood often dictates what we want to hear. If your record sounds good, it feels good, and if it feels good, it sounds good. That evaluation must be made in the isolation of the record at hand.

Rather than to concern yourself with whether your record sounds good in comparison to other records, you need only consider whether the record makes you move and sing in the appropriate and intended manner. If you can't get yourself to react to your own record, then you have no earthly shot at getting anyone else to react to your record.

The best way that I know to momentarily shatter my own confidence in regards to how a record sounds is to start referencing how other tracks sound. And I do it. We all do it, and I'm telling you, the only good that comes from it is a day or two off. Once I put myself through that frustration, I'm clearly exhausted, and I'm ultimately forced to seek some distance.

We evaluate sound because we deal with sound. The punters don't care about sound; they only listen to the music. You would do well to do the same, and at all times.

Referencing a record for tempo, feel, arrangement, even process decisions, can provide you with some useful information that you can mimic on your own production. To reference the sound of your production as you near the end of the process will provide you with nothing useful. How could it? Despite the similarities, the sonic makeup of any given track will be as varied and unique as the crystalline shapes of snowflakes. My friends, comparing snowflakes is an exercise in futility.

Mastering and Mixing

It never ceases to amaze me how the same people who would offer me $100 to mix their track will pay a mastering engineer (ME) $100 to master it.

Whereas a mixer employs balance to cause a reaction, the ME merely shapes the EQ curve of the stereo mix and brings it to the appropriate level, as determined by you. The mixer deals with emotion. The ME touches up the sound. She doesn't have enough control to do much more. She can only adjust internal balances at the margins through the implementation of compressors, EQs, and limiters on the 2-track mix itself. All great mixes were great before the record ever went to an ME.

The world is full of frustrated MEs these days. Many were once mixers themselves who may have had trouble finding gigs. As a result there is a whole class of MEs that seek to fill in their schedules and stroke their own egos by offering stem mixing. Frankly, I find the concept wholly predatory in nature. In other words, stem mixing is a service best avoided.

Stems are basically stereo sub-mixes that make up your mix when combined at unity gain. The stems aren't for mixing. Stems are for movie directors and television broadcasters who need some modicum of control over the music. Film also has dialogue, Foley, and sound FX, all of which must work together. The stems provide the re-recording engineer control over the levels of your production for purposes of theirs. As important as your music is to you, for the director, it's just another part of the big picture, and they must be able to fully manipulate the parts.

Your stems depend on your instrumentation, but a typical Stems configuration would look something like this:

Bass L&R;	Guitars L&R
Drums and Perc L&R	Vocals L&R
Keys L&R	Background Vocals L&R

Many MEs now offer stem mixing as a mastering service. That sounds kind of weird already, doesn't it? In reality, it's neither mixing, nor mastering, because those two jobs can't be done concurrently. Mixing is an aggressive sport in which you seek to maximize the impact of dynamics and pull an emotional response from the listener by how you balance the arrangement. Mastering is a passive sport in which the goal is to limit dynamics for purposes of level, and tone shape for purposes of translation. You cannot operate from both an aggressive and passive stance at the same time. It doesn't work. It's not even possible.

The goal of stem mixing has only to do with balance and sound and nothing to do with pulling a reaction. How do I know this? Because the ME doesn't have enough control to view it any other way.

It's the height of arrogance for someone to suggest to you, that she can mix your record better than you, and with less control over the individual elements. No, she can't. Never. Won't happen, because it ignores emotional impact. Maybe she can balance the overall sound better than you, but that has nothing to do with a great mix.

If you suck at mixing, it's probably because you have an issue with your monitoring–typically the room. And if that's not the problem, then you're not taking frequency into account, or your productions are too dense, and we have addressed all of those maladies in this Guide. A good mix starts with your arrangement, and with a little practice on that front, your mixes will come together without the help of someone who believes music is about sound. Besides, if you're so terrible at mixing, then how is it you can even deliver decent sub-mixes? The whole concept is just remarkably disconnected from reality. It's a service that serves no one, least of all you. If someone offers you stem mixing, run.

The level of competition is actually a problem at this point, with young MEs looking to break into the business with $40 masters that you wouldn't play for your own mother. If you're just learning, it doesn't make a whole lot of sense to send your work to someone equally as green because you get no benefit from it. You would be far better off going to a well-regarded ME. At least then you get some knowledgeable consultation.

There are plenty of legitimate MEs in the world who can help to bring your record to the next level, especially if you have it mixed professionally. Unfortunately, the hack MEs outnumber the pros 1000 to one. You can find a successful ME with a hit-laden discography to master a record for $100 at this point. You want to pay the $40 guy, why? Because it's $60 less, of course, but if the results are unusable, then you wasted $40 to save $60. A $40 per track ME can literally render your record unlistenable. The problem is, there are no guarantees that someone won't butcher it equally as well for $100.

Given this, how do you choose an ME? I don't know that you do.

Look, if you're putting out records, and you're hiring professionals such as myself to produce and mix them, it only makes sense to have your record mastered. You're going to spend good money on a mixer only to skimp out at the end? But really, if you're just starting out, or if you merely want to focus-group a new song, I don't think it makes much sense to pay to have it mastered.

That said, you do need to get your record to level, or no one will be able to turn it up loud enough to hear it in their car. So, at this point–and I can't believe I'm about to write this–it would seem to make more sense to use an automated mastering service.

The problem with automated mastering is that there is no notes process. You can't just call up the bot and ask: *could you add a little top?* And you most certainly don't want to try and chase the algorithms of the automated mastering system with changes to your mix. So, you get what you get and that's what you get. But if the song is unproven, then what exactly is the point of having it mastered other than to give it some level? Because if you don't have it mastered, the production won't compare? What about the mix? I mean, that's where we derive the emotional impact. There just seems to be quite a bit of confusion in regards to what a mixer actually does.

As your mixer, I will spend an average of six to eight hours mixing your production. It could go days. It could go for an hour. There are many factors that go into how long a mix will take me, and the price isn't really one of those factors.

By the time I make my initial print of your mix, I'll know every nuance of your production, I'll know what parts come in where and why. I'll under-dub parts that aren't serving the production. I'll maximize the payoff. I'll automate the parts so that the balances push the listener forward through the song. I'll be able to explain every arrangement decision and every pan decision. I'll recognize where you may have gotten confused along the way and will have addressed those sorts of issues. And all of this will be based, not purely on what I think is best, but on what you reveal to me through your recording. Your decisions in recording the track will dictate my decisions in the mix. My goal throughout will be to maximize impact in order to cause a reaction from myself in the hopes of causing the same reaction from the listener.

After the initial print, we will go through a notes process in which you tell me the issues you're having with the mix. I'll listen to you, share my thoughts and offer you my consultation, and then I will implement your first set of Notes. We will go back and forth once or twice like this, which will include a negotiation and pushback from me, because I'm not there just to do what you want me to do. I'm there to provide my expertise, my consultation, and ultimately a mix.

Ideally, by the time we're through the second or third round of notes, I won't even be able to get through the song because I'll keep forgetting to listen to it as it causes me to react. Same with you.

That sounds downright valuable. Now, let's evaluate what the ME will do.

The ME will spend at most twenty minutes with your mix, she will apply some processing to the track–some EQ, perhaps some compression and probably some brickwall limiting for purposes of level. Somehow, that has equal value?

This idea that the ME is somehow as important as the mixer is nothing but a crock. And if you can't pay a mixer, ostensibly because it's too expensive, then why on earth would you pay an ME? The ME can't deliver you a mix. The ME can only master what you give her. And if you give the ME stems? Not only did you retard your own progress, you got ripped off to boot. Rather than to complete your record with intent, you will have passed it to someone whose only goal is to make you dependent upon them.

Until you have a fanbase, and until you're putting out records on a regular basis–until you're making money from your music–I wouldn't bother mastering your records. Just run your production through an online automated mastering service and be done with it. Or get yourself a good brickwall limiter and bring it to level yourself. That suggestion alone will cause people to pull their hair out. *You have to hire a mastering engineer!* No, you really don't. If you're going to hire anyone, hire a *bona fide* mixer.

Let me just be perfectly clear, because I'm sometimes paraphrased poorly on the Internet. My records are mastered by a professional mastering engineer. I'm a professional producer and a mixer, and I intimately understand the process. I hire people who hear like I do, and whose consultation I trust. I know what the mastering process does and, as a mixer, I automatically compensate for what will happen in that process. While the difference between what I deliver and what I get back from an ME is nothing short of subtle, it often feels like the biggest difference in the world. So, a great ME can bring a great mix up another level.

That said, unless you're paying to have your record mixed, you shouldn't pay to have it mastered either.

Producing

Let's face it. If you make your own record, you produce yourself, which is certainly what you should do at the early stages of your record-making career. The producer's mindset is not out of step with the musician's mind-set, so this is not any kind of issue where it comes to making a Killer Record. It'll just take longer. You can either pay in money or in time.

There will come a point, however, that it no longer makes sense for you to produce yourself, and there are a great many people who are confused as to what a producer does and what she can bring to your project. I can't vouch for all producers, but just as I did for mixing, I can explain to you how I ap-proach the job, which is based on my time spent recording and mixing for some of the great record producers of our time.

Once I decide that I'm interested in producing you, I'm going to learn everything I can about you musically, and what drives you artistically, which I'll determine through your existing recordings and our conversations. I'll evaluate your strengths and your weaknesses to determine the best course of action for your record. I'll listen to everything that you give me, and we will discuss your songs and make a decision as to which of those songs to record based on your goals and brand as an Artist. Not only will I adore the songs–a prerequisite–I will find you compelling as an Artist. I'll also have a clear vision for how to approach your record, in which I consider your genre in conjunction with the current music and production trends, and how you fit against that landscape. Which I will relay to you through rehearsals and ref-erences. Does it make more sense to follow current trends or reject them completely?

Should you accept that vision, and should you agree to the budget as presented, it's at that point that I will accept the gig. If you don't buy into my vision, then we've got nothing to make, and we will both be happy to have discovered this before we ever entered the studio.

Now, if you're a band, then I can help you make a successful record be-cause you desperately need leadership through the recording process. Without it, you'd be going four different directions or worse yet, two, which means there's two power couples in the band. Oh, joy! And everyone in the band is going to be cool with me taking the lead, overjoyed actually, because it prevents the band member that everyone least wants in charge of the record from running the show.

Once I express my vision, which I will have demonstrated to you in pre-production, we will then follow that vision as we make your record from top to bottom with intent. By the time we're finished the record, you will have a clearer understanding of yourself as an Artist because I will help you to make discoveries about yourself and about your music that you'd never even considered.

I'm going to run the sessions, and when the overbearing member of the band tries to take over, I will thwart those attempts. You're going to know at all times where we're at on your record because we don't move forward until things are right. And I'll use time as our fulcrum for pushing our session forward. I'll also be in charge of the funds, and we will accomplish your record on time and under budget.

At some point, you will turn to me and tell me that you absolutely have to sing your record, at which point my team will have you on the mic and performing within about five minutes' time.

Every record is tailor made for you, the Artist, because it's your record. It's not about me. I don't have a sound. It's about you—the Artist. That said, I'm not there to do your bidding. I'm there because I'm an expert at making records, and I get work by doing great work. So, it doesn't matter that you're paying me. You're not hiring me to make the record you think you want. You're hiring me based on the record we agreed to make, and unless it's mutually agreeable for that to change, that's the record that I'm going to deliver.

But they're paying you so you have to do whatever they say!

Yes and no. All of this is stated clearly up front, and the fact that I require some measure of veto power in order to produce your record isn't buried in the fine print. I can't push you to perform, and I can't help you discover yourself if you're running the show. By the time we start to make your record, we will have already established a bond of trust, because I won't even actually accept the job until I know we're on the same page, and it will be exceptionally clear that I'm not there to change you. My goal is not to turn you into something that you're not. I'm there to help you discover what makes you unique as an Artist or band, and to show you how to capitalize on it. But make no mistake, our success with the production has everything to do with mutual trust.

If I don't have your trust, and if you don't have mine, then we will fail on our mission, which is why I go out of my way to maintain our trust through-out the project. You will lose your trust in me if I constantly insist that you do things that make you uncomfortable, or that don't fit you as an Artist. If at any point you don't like what you're hearing, we're going to address that. For any production idea that makes you uncomfortable, I've got four other ideas behind it that will effectively solve the same problem. Besides, you can't just play it safe either. There must be some give and take.

There will come a point in your career where it's time to bring your rec-ords to the next level. When that time comes, you should interview producers that you feel would be a good fit for your music. And yeah, that means you might get a no. But you cannot get to a yes without flushing out the no's. Besides, a refusal could very well turn into a lead to another producer. Just like anything, finding a producer is a numbers game.

The Coda

I stated it up front; you have what you have and what you have is going to change, and as promised there has been no mention of specific recording gear models in the body of this Survival Guide. I'm very happy about that, because it really forced us to keep the focus on concept and strategy rather than on specific gear that you may or may not have available at the moment. That said, we haven't substantively addressed the other half of the equation– what you have is going to change.

There is no way around it, the deeper you get into your record-making career, the more gear you will acquire. If you're able to make money with your music, then your time becomes valuable and any gear that can save you time is also valuable. It doesn't take long before your acquisitions start to add up.

I mean, to own one dynamic mic, a ribbon, an LDC, and an SDC would be to own four microphones, right? Which means you need at least four preamps and converters, and then you might want some analog compressors, and plugin packages, and sample packages, and synth packages, etcetera. Before you know it, you have a room full of equipment. And why not? You're making money making music, and all because of this book!

Ahem.

The point is, you will buy gear. That can be a terrifying experience for many of you, especially when it comes to analog gear. Clearly, most plugin companies allow you to download a demo. This gives you ample time with the unit before you have to make a decision. But when it comes to everything else? That must be done either in your room, or in the studio, and on music in which you have a stake.

I bring this up because you will find all sorts of shootouts online in which you can compare audio files between microphones and mic preamps and converters, and while this sort of shootout may seem useful on the surface, it is not a reasonable way to evaluate gear. And believe me, I know that just about every manufacturer does this sort of thing, and I understand why they do it. That still doesn't make it an effective way for you to judge gear.

For starters, a mic preamp can't be judged based on one static level. One click of 5 dB on your mic pre gain can make an enormous tonal difference, and if you're not there to make that adjustment, then you have no idea how that mic or preamp actually react beyond one particular setting and outside of the purview of the source.

Unless you're in the room with the source, you have no way to make a value judgement. I mean, the mic that you feel sounds the worst online, could actually be the most accurate representation of the source. And if you're listening to the tone of a vocalist you've never recorded and in total isolation, you've removed the musical impact from the evaluation.

I said it before, I'll say it again. Frequency is the building block of music. Just as a painter deals with color, we deal with frequency as producers and musicians. But the color doesn't make the Art, it's just a means to an end. Likewise, the sound isn't the Art. The music is.

Even A/B tests in which you compare sounds in quick succession are useless. Although this does provide you with a basis of comparison between A and B, you are completely separating the emotional impact from the evaluation because music affects you over time. A short burst of the verse without the benefit of the chorus payoff doesn't provide us enough perspective in which to feel the emotional impact of the music.

It's actually difficult for most people to hear the difference between an MP3 and a full WAV mostly because the comparisons rarely include emotional impact. Were you to take your favorite record of all time and play the WAV file of that record from the top through the first chorus, immediately followed by playback of the MP3 of the identical record, the difference in how those playbacks make you feel will be obvious. There's a very good reason for this. You're listening to your favorite record, which means it's a record in which you have an established emotional response. In other words, you have a stake.

Granted, as Music Fan your name may not be on the record, but your favorite record will have importance to you and, as a result, you will immediately notice the degradation of a compressed playback format. When you play back the lo-res version of the track, the missing information from that MP3 becomes nothing short of obvious. When you listen to just the sound, the difference is subtle. And yes, I can hear the difference between a compressed format and a WAV purely based on sound, but then I've been doing this for a while.

Further problematic, if you aren't part of the team that's making the music, then you can't judge a work until it's done. It's not Art until it's finished. I can't rightly insist that your production doesn't move me if it's not done. It's a work in progress, and as such, you are the sole arbiter of what improves or detracts from it. You are the one with the vision. Once you finish your record, and once you put it out there, then the rest of us get the opportunity to react to it. That reaction will be based on how you touched us emotionally with your music—not based on the gear or the sound.

To judge a mic pre, or a converter, or a microphone, outside of the context of the music, is to judge all the wrong things. To judge them outside of the context of a performance is to also judge all the wrong things. Because no matter what gear you choose to use for your capture, if it's the kind of performance that leaves me gobsmacked, and it's the kind of song that hits me emotionally, then it's the kind of song I will want to play repeatedly until I'm just about sick of it. And if I have that reaction to your song as a consumer—even as a professional producer—I will never, not once, ever question what you used to record it.

The good news is, unless you're completely isolated, opportunities will arise in which you can try out gear that you don't normally have available to you. You may be at a studio, or at a friend's place, and while you're making music, you would do well to concentrate on the music. But when someone pulls out a piece of gear on a project in which you have a stake, that's the time to pass judgment.

The Review

Alright, so we've discussed the necessary mindset for making a Killer Record, we've talked about the supreme importance of the song, the arrangement, and the performances. We've discussed frequency, at length. We spent time on space, and we went over microphones, and the strategies involved to choose one over the other. We even became allergic to phase coherency together. We went through processing, compression, EQ, distortion, reverbs, delays, and motion. We thought about the source instrument, the source player, the source room, and how they dictate the quality of our capture. We learned that music causes a reaction and sound is merely a means to an end to deliver our music. But with all of that, I would be remiss were I not to put one last emphasis on the most important concept in this Guide. Your intent.

Where it comes to the listener, your process is almost irrelevant. There are things that engineers do, that I've never been able to make work for me. I can watch them do it, and I can listen to the results, and it still won't work for me. I mean, I almost never put two mics on a guitar cabinet, yet I have many friends who do with great results. My argument has nothing to do with whether any given technique is viable. They're all viable at some point. My arguments break down to keeping things as simple as possible on the engineering side so that you can keep your focus on the music.

At least, now, when you try to place two mics on a guitar amp, you'll understand that the mics are interacting, and you will be able to judge for yourself whether that improves or degrades from your capture. And the best part? You'll probably change your mind over time.

When I started out, I hated compression. I couldn't understand why anyone would compress their mix. I couldn't understand why there was a compressor on every channel of the desk. But once I started using compression and once I began to control the compression, I began to understand how much easier it made my life. And then as I started to employ compression more, not only did I find that I could fix problems, I noticed that I could make the record feel more aggressive too. Which meant I could manipulate emotions with my sonic decisions. And so, my choice of how to use my tools became less about fixing things, and more about presentation.

Aggressive compression in which the spitting, and breathing, and steady state congealing are plainly audible is just as legitimate a technique as inserting several compressors in series for purposes of inaudible compression. A wholly organic capture, in which real musicians set up in a room and play can be just as moving as an electronic dance track. Copious amounts of overt distortion is equally as good as a production in which there is no obvious distortion whatsoever. That doesn't mean the recording is clean, it just means the distortion isn't overt.

If I put a filtered radio effect on a vocal, it's because I want to distance the singer from the song for some reason. Perhaps the singer is performing from the perspective of a character, or maybe the subject matter is slightly off, or the vocal is compromised in a distracting manner. Whatever the reason, there *is a reason,* even if I don't know what that reason is at the time. Surely, many decisions are wholly innate, and sometimes it's not until I reflect upon those decisions that I understand the reasons for them. Make no mistake, there is always a reason.

The point is, it doesn't really matter how you choose to present your record, so long as you present it with intent. If you intend to distort the vocal, then that's good distortion. That said, even if you didn't intend to distort it, once you put the record out that way, that *becomes* your intention. Your finished record *is* your intent. That means there are no excuses. There is no, *it woulda come out better if;* there is no, *it coulda come out better if.* Once you put it out, that's your Artistic intent, and if you feel that you need to excuse it, then I would suggest you don't put the record out. It's not Art at that point. It's a demo.

I started out the book stating that it's better to do and not to think, and I stand behind that advice. You can't stop to justify every decision along the way. You will slow the process down to a crawl. This means you're going to have to trust yourself–even if you don't believe you deserve that trust. For some of you, the only way that you're going to become great at recording is to make every mistake that there is along the way. It sounds vaguely familiar. Hopefully, this book will prevent that.

Make no mistake, you will learn from every record you make, and you will continue to improve even 30 years in. Your musicianship alone will improve, which will have an effect on the records that you make, but we really don't have time to wait until your children have all grown to make your first Killer Record (unless they already are). You have the musical skills that you have, and you have the space that you have, and you have the equipment that you have, and somehow, someway, you need to figure out how to make a

Killer Record. That, my friends, starts and ends with the song. Do not forget that.

We have gone through an enormous volume of information, and we have barely scratched the surface of all that you will learn along this journey that is record-making. Believe me, it will be a journey. And perhaps, your first few records won't come out exactly as you hoped. Maybe your first twenty. But I promise you, if you follow my prescription here, and if you think of your record musically, and if you manage your expectations, and operate within your limitations through creativity, and if you make your decisions with intent? It won't be long before you put out your first Killer Record.

Send it to me when you do. mixerman@mixerman.net

Did you enjoy the book? Great! I need your review. Please go to the site where you purchased this Guide, and *please* tell others what you thought of it. But do it right now! Because if you don't, you'll forget, and then it will never be done because that's how life works. If you go to give me a review right this instant, then it will be done, and I will be able to write more books. If you want people to share about your music, then understand that I need you to tell people about this book.

MIXERMAN
Recommends

You can't record without some gear, and while a minimal setup is enough to get started, as you expand so too will your gear collection. Of course, if all that you currently record is your vocal, then you really only need one great mic. But once you seek to record other things, a variety of gear can prove downright useful.

People write to me all the time asking for gear recommendations, especially in regards to mics, preamps, and interfaces. And while I have an expansive basis of comparison where it comes to mics and preamps, I really have only had occasion to use one or two current interfaces. Most people will have a similarly limited basis of comparison, so asking for a recommendation for an interface is often an exercise in futility.

The same is true about DAWs. Ask anyone what their favorite DAW is, and they will answer with the one DAW they've used. And although you'll find some engineers familiar with more, that would be the exception to the rule. There are nearly 20 DAWs on the market right now, and I've personally used no more than four of them, and only two of them extensively. I personally believe that my DAW is the best DAW on the market, just like everyone else.

In other words, the interface and the DAW that I use are irrelevant. They serve my needs, which are likely different from your needs. But where it comes to microphones and plugins? I have a vast basis of comparison in this regard, and I would like to offer you my thoughts on a few lines that I think will make your life considerably easier.

As you may have noticed, I've taken great pains to keep all of my advice in this book relevant to the needs of musicians who record. As such, you can rest assured that I've taken the same careful consideration with my gear recommendations.

These are companies whose product lines I endorse that I think will benefit musicians just as readily as professional recordists. Not only are these products kind to your pocketbook, they are exceedingly simple to use with exceptionally satisfying results. In other words, they will help you to get the technical out of the way.

Lewitt Mics

There's just no way around the fact, that if you want to capture organic instruments for your records, you will need microphones, and often more than one. Unfortunately, you cannot judge a microphone based purely on price. Which makes it very difficult to pick without some basis of comparison. I can save you quite a bit of frustration in that regard. Buy a Lewitt.

Seriously, this is, without a doubt, the best line of mics I've ever used across the board. The mics are super clear, warm, responsive, and best of all, don't introduce the high-end sizzle or the wooly distortion that plagues some of the more popular home recordist mic lines.

I first discovered Lewitt mics back in 2012 when I was recording my audiobook for *The Daily Adventures of Mixerman*. My producer Aardy and I went to record Julian Bunetta at his studio for the part of Johnny Enigma. As was typical, Aardy and I brought our favorite mics with us. He insisted that we use his Lewitt.

Lewitt? What's a Lewitt?

Neither of us had ever even heard of a Lewitt. It was certainly a beautiful looking mic. And since it was already plugged in and Julian was ready to go, there wasn't much point to protest. Sure. Let's try the Lewitt.

Well! I'd never heard a mic with this kind of clarity. It was as if the mic wasn't even there. Like I was just listening to Julian as he sounded in the room. Aardy and I both began to pepper Julian with questions as we raided his mic locker. *Who is this company? How much are these mics? Where can we get them? Can we borrow them?*

I was so blown away by this mic, that I contacted the company the moment I got home. That's right, I sought them out.

Lewitt audio has been around since 2010. They are a microphone company from Austria, and the word is just now starting to really get out as to how special their mics are. This is especially true for the home recording market, mostly because the entire Lewitt line is priced so aggressively. But make no mistake, they are great mics despite the price, not because of it.

Just a few years ago, whenever I'd mention Lewitt mics to producer friends, I would get quizzical looks in return. Now I get knowing smiles. When someone posts online asking whether to buy microphone brand A or Lewitt B, poster after poster will simply reply with "the Lewitt," without equivocation. I mean, it has to be exceptionally difficult to break into the microphone market given the sheer brand power of stalwart mic companies. Some of them have been around for my entire lifetime and beyond. Make no mistake, Lewitt will join the stalwarts club, it's merely a matter of time.

Now, the thing about Lewitt mics that I love more than anything else is their clarity in conjunction with their warmth. That's not easy to do. Usually, you either have too much clarity or too much warmth, and with the Lewitt line you get both. Not just one or two mics in their line. Every mic of theirs that I've used, which is most of them. And because Lewitt mics don't introduce high-end distortion, you can apply top-end EQ without ill effects. This is similar to how ribbons react.

Now, for those of you who are still relatively new to recording, I would recommend you start with their inexpensive mics and work your way up to their more fancy ones. You can greatly enhance your mic collection without breaking the bank with their Beat Kit Pro 7 CO drum kit package, which provides you with seven great mics, for which the lowest possible advertised price is currently $1099 (prices subject to change). Seven mics! Let's just take a moment and go through them.

First, there's the DTP 640 REX which is a bullet mic with both a dynamic and a condenser capsule. It's like having two mics in one inside your kik drum. Good luck getting two mics perfectly time aligned inside a kik drum. Now you can. Of course, any mic with a pronounced low end and two capsule designs will be useful in all sorts of applications.

Then there's the three DTP 340 TT mics for your toms. These are super-cardioid dynamic mics, which means they have exceptional rejection properties, which can be useful in an undersized room. They also mount to the tom itself with clips, which I much prefer to stands as it allows the mic to move in perfect harmony with the shaking tom. Three clip-on mics means three less mic stands. Bonus.

The package also comes with the stellar LCT 340s. These are killer SDC microphones, folks. In fact, these two mics alone are worth the price of the entire bundle. Set them up in an X-Y pattern and you're good to go. And once you're done with drums, set them up on percussion, acoustic guitar, or even piano. Place them anywhere you'd use an SDC.

Then there's the MTP 440 DM, a dynamic which you can put on the top of your snare drum, and which will do an amazing job at rejecting the hi-hat information. Better than the usual snare mic that everyone seems to use. And once you're done with the drums, you can place it on your guitar amplifier too.

Here's the thing, and I can't stress this enough. I'm not recommending this as a starter kit that you will outgrow. It's not a kit to be replaced when you get better at recording. It's a kit that you will keep and add to over time. You'll use these mics to your advantage throughout your career. It doesn't much matter whether you've been recording for a day or for twenty years, this is a stupid good collection of mics for a ridiculous price, and you most certainly aren't limited to recording drums with them. Seven mics gives you lots of options.

I would also suggest you get yourself an LCT 240 PRO, which has a medium sized condenser capsule in what appears to be an LDC housing. This is a $150 mic at retail, and honestly, I don't really understand why CEO Roman Perschon doesn't double the price of it. I recorded an acoustic guitar with the 240 PRO the other day, and it's a great sounding mic. Normally, I'd tell you to shy away from the more inexpensive models of any given microphone line. In the case of Lewitt, that's where the recording musician should start.

The craziest part about the Lewitt line is their aggressively priced LCT 440 PURE sounds just as clear and as warm as their top-of-the-line LCT 940. The price difference between their mics has more to do with added features than their overall sonic quality.

For instance, the LCT 440 FLEX provides eight selectable polar patterns. The LCT 640 TS allows you to change your patterns after the fact. And I realize, for some of you who are just starting out, those features might prove a bit advanced. But there will come a time when you'll want some microphones with selectable patterns. As you improve at recording, it's possible you'll want to implement more advanced techniques as part of the creative process. The good news is, you can grow into that.

The LCT 940 is my go-to vocal mic as a producer, mostly because I've yet to find anyone who doesn't sound amazing on it. That has much to do with the mic's flexibility. Some people sound better on the warmer tube position, others sound better on the solid-state FET position, and still others somewhere in between. That's right, there's a variable control. I adore this mic. I adore all of their mics.

The bottom line is this: I want you to be successful, and there are microphones that are going to make your life more difficult, and there are mics that will make your life easier, and that would be the case with Lewitt mics. You want to get the technical out of your way? Start with mics that are clear as a bell and warm, to boot.

You can't go wrong with any Lewitt mic, and we can't predict the future, but if there is any line that is going to increase in value over time, it's this one. You know, you purchase some tools based purely on what they can offer you in the here and now. When it comes to mics? The great ones will increase in value over time. Quality microphones are an investment.

I cannot recommend this line enough. Lewitt-audio.com

Soundtoys

I may be a little late to the party when it comes to Soundtoys, but that doesn't make me any less of a fanboy. I first discovered the line when multi-talented cult film director, Peter Litvin, sent me his DAW session of "Gunz Up!" to mix for him. We both use the same DAW and his sessions are full of keyboard layering and in this case it made more sense for me to start where he left off. There was just one problem. Peter had a saturation distortion plugin called the Decapitator in his session that I didn't have. So, I did what anyone would. I downloaded it.

It didn't take me long to realize how special this plugin was. All of five seconds, really. I'd never heard a saturation plugin that was so perfectly aggressive and simultaneously musical as this one. In fact, I'm absolutely convinced it's responsible for the current trend of copious distortion on pop productions. And why not? Once Soundtoys finally made it easy to introduce musically aggressive distortion in the box, it would most certainly end up on all sorts of records.

The Decapitator works just as well subtly as it does overtly, as such, I often distort my kik drums with it. This allows me to give that kik some personality and punch. It's also one of the best bass amp plugins you'll find. Just add a little drive from the Decapitator, and your DI bass will absolutely come alive.

As you'll hear on the "Gunz Up!" track, Decapitator is great for distorted vocals. It's great for distorted anything, and there are times I'll even use it for purposes of gain on guitars in lieu of a virtual amp. With its multiple distortion flavors, its high-pass and low-pass filters, and its "thump" feature, you have plenty of variables to shape the tone of your distortion.

Were the Decapitator the only plugin Soundtoys offered, it would give them legend status in my mind. As it turns out, they have more.

The Soundtoys package also includes the Devil-Loc Deluxe and the Radiator, both of which can be used to great effect to fatten your drums and bass. To fatten anything really. The Devil-Loc provides aggressive over-compression in combination with a sick crunch tone. The Little Radiator is a model of the gritty Altec 1567a tube mixer for yet another beautiful flavor of saturation distortion. Between those three units and the ultra-colored Sie-Q with its drive knob, you have a beautiful array of distortion tones available to you. Distortion is your friend. I use them all.

I think that what I like best about the Soundtoys package is how remarkably easy their plugins are to use. There's nothing worse than to have to spend my valuable time just to figure out how to make the stupid plugin sound good. It should sound great the moment I insert it. This way, I can merely fine tune my parameters. That's a far easier process than to program a plugin from scratch.

Ask any professional audio forum what their favorite stereo delay is, and more than half the answers will be *Echoboy!* There's a very good reason for that. The moment you plug it in, everything gets better. I mean, I literally avoided stereo delays on vocals for the first two decades of my career because they are such a pain in the ass to program and the presets were generally useless. I don't have time for that, and I never have. Now that I have a module that provides me with instant results, I use stereo delays. Go figure. Of course, you'll want to dig deep into parameters, as you will come across a long list of tonal options. This will allow you to put together some stunning stereo delay effects with little effort and professional results.

Sometimes you may want a dark grainy delay, in which case you can insert the Primal Tap, or the Little Primal Tap into your session. These units basically allow you to multiply your delay time by as much as eight, which will divide the sample rate by same. This results in a wonderfully low-fi tone useful as a tail and taps alike. I can tell you, the Primal Tap sounds remarkably like the original Prime Time M93 delay from the seventies. I know, because I own two of the original units. And no I don't use them. Why would I? Not only does the Primal Tap sound like my analog units, it works for longer than twenty minutes at a time! Isn't technology wonderful? For Sale: 2 semi-working Prime Time M93 Delays.

The Soundtoys line also comes with a number of plugins useful for deriving motion, starting with the Pan Man. As a young hip-hop mixer I often struggled with where to place certain parts in the sound field. It wasn't unusual for me to put certain parts through an auto-panner. Oftentimes, it was the best way for me to provide a relatively mono track some stereo imaging.

There are many ways to set a panner. A part can trigger the panner starting on the left and move to the right. A part could pan back and forth steadily and smoothly. A part can ping pong back and forth. All of these options are available with Pan Man. And while it's true that you can program panning effects by hand in your DAW, that can be an exceptionally time consuming affair. I'd rather use the Pan Man.

There's also the FilterFreak, which is a resonant filter like you'd find on a vintage Moog keyboard, only you can apply it to anything. Between the FilterFreak and the included FilterFreak 2 with its dual filters, EDM producers can introduce all sorts of interesting sweeps and rhythmic effects to their production. More often than not, however, I use the FilterFreak to fix and mangle parts into submission, especially kik drums. You can deliver to me the most awful kik drum you can muster, and I can mangle it into something useful, if not downright great, with the FilterFreak.

Next up is Crystallizer, which has to be the most interesting effects unit I've ever used. It allows you to combine pitch shifting functionality with echoes to generate super-creative motion effects.

Rounding out their motion plugins we have the MicroShift which will add width. The Little Alter Boy which can deliver amazing robotic effects.

The Tremolator, useful for introducing motion to guitar and keyboard parts. Last but certainly not least, the Phase Mistress, which can introduce phase sweeps locked to tempo. Too cool.

The best part of all? You can pick up the entire Soundtoys line for $500. Half that price if you're a student. And sure, you can purchase them a la carte. But it will be considerably cheaper to pick up the entire Soundtoys line. I mean, really. That's 19 plugins for $500, which comes to a little over $26 per plugin for a line that offers amazingly useful and easy to use tools for the home recording musician and the professional producer alike.

You should choose your tools based on simple criterion: will it make my life easier? In the case of Soundtoys?

Without question. Soundtoys.com

Slate Digital

I've been a fan of Slate's plugins for as long as I can remember, and I know Steven personally and he's a good egg. I even have his 46-inch Raven MTX touch screen controller in my room. At the end of the day, he has the most useful plugin models around.

For starters, his Virtual Tape Machine is the only plugin ever made that actually sounds like tape. I'm not going to tell you it's exact. It's not. But he sure has come close. Certainly closer than anyone else by far. The same is true of his compressor models and his EQ models, of which he has numerous useful flavors, and he has a number of saturation plugins that offer great distortion properties too.

I first discovered Slate's line when I tried the VCC, which is meant to offer slight distortion to mimic what a summing box does. It's super subtle, but it will offer you some of the benefits of an analog reproduction chain.

Slate also offers a brickwall limiter/compressor unit called the FG-X, which is super transparent, and can help you to bring your productions to a good level. You certainly don't need to hire an ME if all you want to do is make the track a little louder. Just add a little FG-X brickwall limiting and be done with it. That's what I do.

Then there's the Eiosis E2 Deesser. You know how I told you that I'm a nut about esses? It shouldn't surprise you to know there are very few de-essers on the market that I haven't used. None of them are as good as plugin designer Fabrice Gabriel's Eiosis, and it's been my go to de-esser since the day it came out. You can be super aggressive with this de-esser and it will be remarkably forgiving. It even has settings for background vocals among other things.

Now, here's the dirty little secret about DAWs. Many of them don't come with the greatest processing plugins. Stock plugins can be nothing short of hit or miss. Some only come with one compressor, and it's usually digital in nature. Those are very tough compressors to use as they have no personality and really offer no tonal benefit. EQs are often bland and lacking personality. And I understand that you don't want to spend a zillion dollars purchasing plugins, but if the ones that come with your DAW are holding you back (and in most DAWs they are), then it doesn't make sense to keep using them. The good news is, you can get every one of Steven Slate's plugins for $20 a month to start. And if you decide you love them, you can commit to a full year, and pay just $15 per month. So, you don't have to pony up a ton of money to spend some time with this plugin package. And if you like them, which you will, then you can keep your subscription for as long as you like.

Personally, I love subscriptions for everyone involved. It keeps the cash-flow steady for the company, which allows them to constantly update their products and innovate new ones without charging you for updates. You get less flash sales in your inbox. And if you go on tour, you can just shut off your subscription until you're back to making your next record.

So, if you haven't spent any time with the Slate line, I recommend that you sign up for a subscription. It's a no-brainer. SlateDigital.com

In this 2021 version: The Gear chapter is entirely new. The Mastering chapter has significant updates. The rest of the book has been trimmed, revised, recast, amended, and fluffed to match the realities of mixing today.

My goal wasn't to rewrite the book, it was to bring it current to the times, which was a far deeper revision then I'd anticipated. And although I'm quite sure that I write much betterer today, I feel there was a certain charm to the original that shall remain.

For those of you who enjoyed the original versions, this is the book you love with the relevance you require. For everyone else, I present to you my most popular work, to date—*Zen and the Art of Mixing 2021.*

I need your review!

Reviews bring visibility to my book, which is critical to its success. This allows me to write more books. It doesn't have to be a long review. In fact, you can just rate it if you like. Or you can describe how you feel about the book in just a word or two or three. The QR code below will take you directly to the Amazon Reviews page for *Musician's Survival Guide to a Killer Record*. If you go there right now, it'll be done, and you won't forget. Thanks, Mixerman

HOW TO SCAN: OPEN, AIM & TAP

Open the camera on your phone   Aim it at the Flowcode   Tap the banner that appears

Free Mixerman Content

Get Mixerman MINDSET cards sent to your inbox every week, including potent tips. "The exclusive things go to those who join my list." Open the camera on your phone and point it at the QR Code.

Visit me at mixermanpublishes.com

ATTENTION: This is an Amazon Print On Demand product. In the unusual event that this copy does not print properly, or if you find the binding is falling apart, or if there are any other issues, please contact Amazon for a replacement. Tell them that your book did not print properly. If that doesn't work (it will), email me: mixerman@mixermanpublishes.com

About **MIXERMAN**

Mixerman has been awarded multiple Gold and Platinum awards for his work as a mixer, recordist, and producer. He's made records with The Pharcyde, Ben Harper, Tone Loc, Spearhead, Amy Grant, Lifehouse, Barenaked Ladies, Hillary Duff, Foreigner, and Australian phenom Pete Murray, just to name a few.

Mixerman gained notoriety as an author from his first work, *The Daily Adventures of Mixerman*, a satire of a Major Label recording session from the early aughts that delighted and surprised well over 150,000 readers. In 2008, Hal Leonard picked up his Adventures, and since 2010 he has written a number of books on the recording arts, including his most popular work to date, *"Zen & the Art of MIXING 2021."*

Be sure to check out Mixerman eBooks and audiobooks on the marketplace of your choice.

Mixerman books available in Trade Paperback

Musician's Survival Guide to a Killer Record
The Daily Adventures of Mixerman
Zen & the Art of MIXING 2021
Zen & the Art of Producing 2021 (Coming in July 2021!)
Zen and the Art of Recording

Contact, inquiries, permissions: mixerman@mixermanpublishes.com

Made in the USA
Coppell, TX
12 November 2022

86239373R00184